Family Therapy Beyond Postmodernism

D1452095

Postmodernist ideas are widely used in family therapy. However, it is argued that these ideas have their limits in meeting the richness and complexity of human experience and therapy practice. *Family Therapy Beyond Postmodernism* examines postmodernism and its expressions in family therapy, raising questions about

- reality and realness
- the subjective process of truth
- the experience of self.

Alongside identifying the difficulties in any sole reliance on narrative and constructionist ideas, this book advocates the value of selected psychoanalytic ideas for family therapy practice, in particular

- attachment and the unconscious
- transference, projective identification and understandings of time
- psychoanalytic ideas about thinking and containment in the therapeutic relationship.

Family Therapy Beyond Postmodernism offers a sustained critical discussion of the possibilities and limits of contemporary family therapy knowledge, and develops a place for psychoanalytic ideas in systemic thinking and practice. It will be of great interest to family therapists, psychotherapists and other mental health professionals.

Carmel Flaskas is a Senior Lecturer in the School of Social Work at the University of New South Wales, where she convenes the masters programs in couple and family therapy.

Family Therapy Beyond Postmodernism

Practice Challenges Theory

Carmel Flaskas

BR Brunner-Routledge
Taylor & Francis Group

HOVE AND NEW YORK

First published 2002 by Brunner-Routledge
27 Church Road, Hove, East Sussex, BN3 2FA

Simultaneously published in the USA and Canada
by Taylor & Francis Inc.
29 West 35th Street, New York, NY 10001

Brunner-Routledge is an imprint of the Taylor & Francis Group

Cover design by Sandra Heath
Typeset in Times by Mayhew Typesetting, Rhayader, Powys
Printed and bound in Great Britain by TJ International Ltd,
Padstow, Cornwall

British Library Cataloguing in Publication Data
A catalogue record for this book is available from the British Library

Library of Congress Cataloging-in-Publication Data
Flaskas, Carmel.
    Family therapy beyond potsmodernism : practice challenges theory /
Carmel Flaskas.
        p. cm.
    Includes bibliographical references and index.
    ISBN 0-415-18299-9 – ISBN 0-415-18300-6 (pbk.)
    1. Family psychotherapy. 2. Postmodernism–Psychological aspects. I. Title.

RC488.5 .F536 2002
616.89'156–dc21

                                                                      2002025444

ISBN 0-415-18299-9 (hbk)
ISBN 0-415-18300-6 (pbk)

For Chriss, my mother, and in memory of Harold, my father

Contents

Acknowledgements

Chapter 5 and Chapter 6 of this book are edited versions of previously published articles. Chapter 5 'Truth as a process' appeared as 'Reclaiming the idea of truth: Some thoughts on theory in response to practice' in the *Journal of Family Therapy* (1997) 19, 1–20. Chapter 6 'The narrative self and the limits of language' appeared as 'Limits and possibilities of the narrative self' in the *Australian and New Zealand Journal of Family Therapy* (1999) 20, 20–7. One of the case studies – 'First Piece' – used in Chapter 9 was originally discussed as part of an article entitled 'Engagement and the therapeutic relationship in systemic therapy' which appeared in the *Journal of Family Therapy* (1997) 19, 263–82. The copyright for the *Journal of Family Therapy* is held by the Association for Family Therapy and Systemic Practice; the copyright for the *Australian and New Zealand Journal of Family Therapy* is held by the journal itself. I am grateful for permission to include this material.

In thinking about the process of developing this book, I would like to thank first my family therapy colleagues over the years, for all the work talk and hallway chats, the conference discussions, the sharing of work that has gone well and that has not gone well, and for their passion and humour about family therapy and the project of knowledge for family therapy. I am of course including in this group people I have supervised and taught. However, because practice always holds the greatest challenge, I would also like specifically to acknowledge the people I have worked with in therapy.

Could I also thank friends and colleagues who work psychoanalytically, though not necessarily in family therapy, and who in many ways have become a second reference group for me despite the differences in context and approach? Here I will thank Coll Osman, and members of a long-time reading group in contemporary psychoanalytic theory – Risé Becker, Ofelia Brozky, Gill Burrell, Mary Cameron, Louise Gyler and Jan Williams.

A number of people have been generous enough to read different parts of this book from its first proposal, and I would like to thank them for their time and comments and encouragement. They are Damian Grace, Kerrie James, Sarah Jones, Peg Le Vine, Coll Osman, Amaryll Perlesz, David Pocock, Graeme Smith, Bebe Speed and Michael Wearing.

I also want to acknowledge the importance of the support of my colleagues in the School of Social Work at the University of New South Wales (UNSW). Like many social work schools, we are a federation of different research and practice interests, yet it is very much the home base of my research and teaching. I will also record my appreciation of a fellowship awarded to me by the Humanities Research Program of the Faculty of Arts and Social Sciences at UNSW, which allowed a period of uninterrupted writing and thinking time at a critical stage in the book's development.

On a more personal note, I think it is only right that I should thank fellow members of my local bridge club (otherwise known as Gill Burrell, Nick Burrell and Anthea Lowe), for thousands and thousands of games of bridge, increasingly appallingly played across the last decade or two – that, plus the many bottles of red wine, would have to count for something in this whole process! And finally, I will thank my partner Anthea Lowe for all her encouragement, which is simply beyond any adequate acknowledgement.

Chapter 1

Connections in postmodern times: An introduction

I want to write about the complexities of postmodernist ideas in systemic family therapy. I came to this theory project via practice concerns, and it was practice which was at the same time continuing to interest me in some ideas from psychoanalysis and the kind of space that may be created for them in the current systemic context. This book has come to be an exploration of the postmodern turn in systemic family therapy which intersects with particular psychoanalytic ideas as a way of extending systemic thinking. Though this last sentence is succinct enough, it does not really give much sense of the connectedness of the topic, and so I will use the first part of the introduction to lay things out more carefully, before moving to a discussion of some embedded commitments of the project, then outlining the structure and chapters of the book.

The project of the book

The postmodern turn is both the context and the focus of my enquiry. Postmodernism came belatedly to the systemic field, yet its influence has been dramatic. Some postmodernist ideas initially slipped in the back door in the early 1980s, via second order cybernetics and theories of constructivism drawn from biology (Dell 1985; Efran and Lukens 1985; Keeney and Sprenkle 1982). These ideas were framed in a modernist way – with familiar exhortations that they should become a foundational base for systemic therapy, continuing with systems metaphors drawn from cybernetics and biology. Nonetheless, they introduced the postmodern opposition to the idea of a knowable external reality and moved, through the emphasis on circularity, to contextual and relational understandings. They also debunked the modernist fantasy that the observer is separate from the observed by insisting that the therapist is always part of the therapist-family system, and therefore not able to assume the position of 'acting on' or 'intervening in' the family system.

However, it was not until the very early 1990s that the explicit interest in postmodernism emerged, and the whole set of postmodern oppositions came to be laid on the table. The rejection of the modernist assumption of objective reality was held alongside the rejection of a singular and external truth, the rejection of the desire for certainty, and any related modernist description of the therapist as observer-expert (Doherty 1991; O'Hara and Anderson 1991; Parry 1991; Sluzki 1992). Taking on board this postmodern critique led to different theory and practice ideas – so we have since seen the flourishing of the narrative metaphor in systemic therapy, the elaboration of collaborative descriptions of the therapist position and the therapeutic process, and the use of social constructionism as a way of understanding the social world and our experience of it. Thus, over the past 15 years, in quite a decisive way, systemic therapy has stepped away from cybernetics and biology toward sociology and social psychology, and to a lesser extent, toward philosophy and literary theory.

There is no question that the postmodern turn has been creative of new theory and practices and liberating with respect to the censorships of the earlier systems metaphors. At the same time, I have experienced an uneasiness about the implications of any full immersion in the constructionist/narrative metaphors which have accompanied the postmodernist turn. The unease arises in practice, and the concerns flow around the questions of what it might mean to suspend any interest in external reality; or in the process of truth; or indeed to find ourselves relying on understandings that largely confine human experience to constructions and language. These kinds of concerns are beginning to surface in the literature (Flaskas 1995, 1997b; Frosh 1995, 1997; Held 1995; Lannamann 1998b; Larner 1994; Pilgrim 2000; Pocock 1995), and I think their timing reflects a sufficient period of development of narrative and constructionist ideas in family therapy to allow a second stage of thinking about the implications of the postmodern turn.

This book, then, is primarily an exploration of this space of knowledge in systemic therapy. It examines the way in which systemic therapy has embraced postmodernism, the influence of narrative and constructionist metaphors, and it maps both the possibilities and the limits of these ideas for therapy. While it is certainly the case that the project has a critical edge, I would deliberately shy off describing it as a critique. 'Critique' connotes a judgment made from outside, assuming (and ensuring) a distancing of the author from that which is critiqued. I do not especially want this position of distance, and at any rate I identify too closely with the systemic tradition to make it possible. I hope that this close identification will turn out to be a strength, for it allows an 'internal' discussion that assumes the power of alliance rather than the power of opposition. In assuming the power of alliance, I hope to be able to argue for a position of conditionality with respect to the use of postmodernist ideas in therapy, yet retain a passion for using their potentialities.

But if the main frame of the book is an exploration of postmodernism in systemic therapy, it has a secondary support in its intersection with particular psychoanalytic ideas. Of course, historically systemic family therapy has had an oppositional relationship to psychoanalysis, and in the first decades of its development a dichotomy was created between the self and the system, and between individual and family therapy. At a practice level, this dichotomy was perhaps always something of a challenge to sustain, and it showed itself in its most rigorous form at the level of theory and formal professional discourse. However, the recent theory developments have opened the door to reconsidering the territory of self and relationships. For while cybernetic and biological metaphors dominated the earlier knowledge of systemic therapy, the current relational and contextual focus collapses the earlier dichotomies.

The central issue now is not so much whether you have one person or six people as clients in the room with you, or whether you are choosing, in an either/or fashion, to explore individual experience or the family 'system'. Rather, it is how you are thinking about who is in the room with you, the relational ideas which inform both the position you speak from as a therapist, and how you might be exploring family relationships and human experience. With this emphasis, the dichotomy of self and system simply disappears in relational understandings that move far more directly into the territory of intersubjectivity. Intersubjectivity is about relationships between, and the way in which the experience and construction of personhood and self takes place in (and is sustained by) the context of relationships. Subjectivity is the way in which we come to experience our 'selves' in that relational context. It is all part of a territory which is irredeemably social.

Oddly enough, the systemic opposition to psychoanalysis has tended to persist, and every so often psychoanalysis is wheeled out as the outdated modernist frame against which the new post-modernist ideas of (usually) narrative therapies are posed (Pocock 1997). It is odd because, as you would expect, the effects of postmodernist ideas have been felt within psychoanalysis as well, and indeed the interest in narrative and postmodernist ideas within sections of the psychoanalytic world began before the equivalent move in the systemic field (Barratt 1993; Finlay 1989; Morris 1993; Schafer 1983, 1992, 1997; Spence 1982). Beginning in the early 1980s, this interest has continued, though it is true enough that it remains a tendency within psychoanalysis rather than a dominant theory frame. Perhaps more importantly, a reflex opposition to psychoanalytic ideas is odd because it ignores the extent to which intersubjectivity is a shared space of psychoanalysis and systemic thinking. Long before postmodernist ideas made themselves felt, psychoanalytic thinking addressed the relational context of the intrapsychic world, and many ideas – of attachment, psychic representation, transference and projective identification, to name but a few – are at heart radically relational.

But though the reflex opposition continues, there have also been strong signs of a renewal of interest in psychoanalysis, and this is in large part a response to the opportunities provided by the postmodern shift with its clearer emphasis on intersubjectivity and its greater permission for the inclusion of other knowledges. In the English-speaking context of family therapy, the renewal has been most evident in Britain and Australia, and indeed the leading journals in these countries have each recently published special issues on psychoanalytic thinking and its relevance for systemic family therapy.[1] This kind of formal recognition comes in the wake of a number of publications which link psychoanalysis and sys-temic therapy (Flaskas 1993, 1994; Frosh 1995; Gibney 1991, 1996; Larner 2000; Maloney and Maloney 1996; Pocock 1995, 1997; Quadrio 1986a, 1986b; Smith, Osman and Goding, 1990). As David Pocock (1997) notes, it also reflects a reclaiming of local knowledges – the work which over many years has crossed the systemic/analytic boundary, regardless of fashion.[2] From Britain, John Byng-Hall's work on family scripts and on attachment would be an outstanding example of this kind of local knowledge (Byng-Hall 1986, 1988, 1995a, 1995b, 1999).

I am inclined to think that the trend to re-embrace psycho-analytic thinking, though very noticeable in Australia, is stronger in Britain. At a sociological level, this may not be surprising, for the development of British family therapy has been more inter-twined with the analytic world (Daniel 1998). It may even be that the gap between the earlier theory censorship versus the continuing practice influence of analytic ideas was greatest in Britain. In a 1997 survey in which British family therapists were asked to nominate the three approaches which most influenced their practice, psychodynamic approaches were second only to Milan-systemic in the frequency of nomination (Bor, Mallandain and Vetere 1998).

However the North American situation has been rather different. Historically, psychoanalytic approaches there have either been pursued quite separately in object relations family therapy (Scharff and Scharff 1991; Slipp 1984, 1988) rather than the systemic arena, or alternatively, versions of specific analytic ideas have become embedded in particular models of family therapy. The intergenera-tional practice models of Murray Bowen (1978) and Ivan Boszormenyi-Nagy (Boszormenyi-Nagy and Krasner 1986; Boszor-menyi-Nagy and Spark 1973) spring to mind here, while Mike Nichols (1987) has offered an integrative project of the self and system. The current 'postmodernist' renewal showing itself in Britain and Australia, though, is not yet as clear in North America, and the closest equivalent has come via the feminist interest in psychoanalysis being brought into systemic therapy. Virginia Goldner (1985, 1991; Goldner et al. 1990) and Deborah Luepnitz (1988, 1997) have made major contributions in this respect, and both these writers are informed by a strong postmodernist awareness.

But this is an introduction, so let me resist any further discussion here of sociological differences in the development of family therapy and simply pull together at this point the connectedness of the topic and its location. My exploration of the current space of knowledge in systemic therapy and the narrative and construc-tionist metaphors is part of a broader emerging literature which is appreciative of, yet conditional about, the postmodern turn in therapy. The intersection with psychoanalytic thinking is at the junction of the common interest in intersubjectivity, which has in itself come to be possible in the shift to postmodernist ideas. I will

be making strictly strategic choices in examining particular psychoanalytic concepts, and my choice will be guided by the dilemmas
which emerge in the discussion of the limits of postmodernist ideas.
In this sense, I am not attempting any grand integration of psychoanalysis, but rather looking toward particular psychoanalytic
ideas that may speak to some current concerns in the theory and
practice of systemic therapy. This layer of my project has its wider
location in the renewal of interest in psychoanalytic ideas that has
accompanied the shift to a postmodernist awareness.

It will probably come as no great surprise now for me to say that
the structure of the book reflects this movement from an exploration of the possibilities and limits of postmodernist ideas to a
discussion of particular psychoanalytic ideas. But though we could
move on at this point to a preview of the chapter structure and
how the discussion will unfold, it is important to pause, for there
are two themes which are embedded as commitments of the
project. Though not so much part of its content, they shape its
form, and will show themselves in the way in which I tackle the
discussion. The two themes, which are related, are first a core
interest in experience, and second, a conditional approach to
knowledge in therapy which looks for description and metaphor
rather than foundational theory frameworks.

Embedded commitments: experience and conditional knowledge

So let me begin to make these commitments visible, for when I say
that this is a book about theory fuelled by practice, I am necessarily bringing in a background perspective on the relationship of
practice and knowledge in therapy. This perspective has a broader
context in the nature of knowledge in practice disciplines, and it is
also a response to the specificity of the activity of therapy and
human experience which is its subject.

One of the great pleasures of thinking in practice disciplines is
exactly the central dynamic of practice and knowledge, in all its
richness and messiness. Of course there are moments when we
yearn to box it up neatly and somehow try to act as if practice can
prove or illustrate theory, as if theory has an exalted and privileged
position outside the practice it attempts to describe and inform.
Yet though we might keep these fantasies for periods of time, or
for particular purposes (like learning or teaching), they fortunately

have the tendency to break down in the everyday complexities of therapy. For unlike theorising in 'pure' academic disciplines, the knowledge of practice disciplines is in constant if complicated interplay with practice. There are, of course, many ways in which practice may be thought about. However, in theorising therapy practice, one is always holding the experience of the realities of practice alongside the theory ideas. Practice gives the momentum for theorising, theory in turn influences practice, coming full circle to challenge the theory ideas. None of this happens in any neat or unilateral fashion. But if we can allow this messiness, there may be a creative reflexiveness that meets the demands of doing therapy in a more adequate way.

In a rather lunatic moment in the middle of a class one day, I found myself trying to say something about the methodological similarity of theory research and empirical research. Without pushing the similarity too far, one can think of empirical research and the way in which data is brought into tension and interplay with hypotheses and research questions, which in turn provide a response to the questions raised by the data. When one works with ideas in theory research, something of the same thing happens. One set of ideas is always brought into play with another, and questions and ideas are generated in a responsive spiral. In both empirical and theory research, it may well be that the tension and the play *between* the different sets holds the greatest potential for creativity in the development of knowledge.

The beauty of knowledge in practice disciplines is that there is ready-made tension and a constancy of play between practice and the ideas that one is trying to generate around practice. Practice is always both provoking and challenging theory ideas, and the challenge goes from the sublime to the ridiculous and everywhere in between. I get inspired by ideas of radical constructionism and the primacy of meaning in experience, then walk into a room with a family where domestic violence is a daily event, and the mother's terror seems something more than a meaning or construction. Or sessions in which any ideas about systemic hypothesising or collaborative practice disappear as I mainly try to work out how on earth we might all get through the session before the 6-year-old tries jumping out of the second floor window to the hospital swimming pool below. Or, as was the practice fashion of the time, finding myself overplaying the tentativeness of an idea I was offering the family, only to have a kind and hopeful 9-year-old boy look me straight in the eye and say: 'you should just say what the idea is – you never know, it might be a good one'. This is a moment in which I feel touched by his directness, and also realise that I have left him holding the authenticity of the experience of the therapy.

We come then to the theme of experience – the lived experience of clients and the experience of ourselves as therapists. When I was toying with a sentence in the first paragraph of this section (where it says that the subject of therapy is human experience), it suddenly seemed a rather absurd thing to be writing, and I wondered if I should follow it up with 'and the ocean has a lot of water'! I find that even the word 'practice' begins to feel reified in this discussion about the relationship of theory and practice in knowledge for therapy, for it begins to sound like a thing in which one's own subjectivity as a therapist becomes lost, as does any sense of the real connectedness we have with families and clients we work with. But now I have said the ocean has a lot of water, I may as well continue. Therapy is a human activity – indeed, at times, alarmingly personal – and the stuff of therapy is the lived experience that clients bring, regardless of the framework of therapy we find ourselves working in. To take this back to the relationship of theory and practice in therapy, experience is located at the heart of this relationship, for 'practice' stands as a shorthand word for 'the experience of the practice of therapy' and therapy as an activity directly engages with human experience.

The commitment to experience embedded in this book, then, reflects a particular perspective about therapy itself as well as a perspective on the theory/practice relationship in therapy knowledge. This commitment becomes linked to a position on conditionality about knowledge, for in privileging experience in this way, the power of knowledge is necessarily decentred. In therapy, knowledge becomes something which is more or less useful in describing, reflecting on, informing, or generating practice. It can only 'hold' as long as it relates in a meaningful way to experience. And because we are talking about the complexity of social and emotional experience, and indeed the complexity of the very construction of therapy as a particular cultural and social practice, the idea of a foundational knowledge providing a base for practice rapidly loses its appeal.

The postmodern critique has itself been a major force in dismantling the desire for foundational knowledge, and this critique is by no means confined to the knowledge of practice disciplines. Modernism as a project of knowledge was built around the desire for discovering the world, which bit by bit through the description of observation could come to be represented in knowledge. In this project knowledge attempts to produce a mirror image of the nature of the world, aiming for greater and greater accuracy in its description and reflection. The desire to search for knowledge which, in the accuracy of its reflection, may then serve as a foundational base is thus part of the modernist dynamic. Richard Rorty, in his seminal critique of the historic role of philosophy and epistemology in embodying this dynamic, writes of 'a desire for constraint – a desire to find "foundations" to which one might cling, frameworks beyond which one must not stray, objects which impose themselves, representations which cannot be gainsaid' (Rorty 1980: 315).

Postmodernism profoundly challenges the modernist push for foundational knowledge. The modernist idea of knowledge coming to show a singular truth about the world is replaced with an idea of a multiplicity of knowledges that bear limited, specific and contextual relationships to the part of the world with which knowledge is trying to engage. Thus, there come to be very different notions about knowledge in the move beyond modernism. All show the departure from foundationalism, yet having said this, there is no 'one' postmodernist epistemology or theory of knowledge. For this is, of course, the internal contradiction which both drives and sustains the postmodernist dynamic: how can one move against the desire for '"foundations" to which one might cling' without creating a desire for postmodernism itself to serve as a foundation to which we might cling? It is a complex dynamic which is necessarily contradictory.

This dynamic means we cannot seek refuge in any singular form of proper postmodernist knowledge. And so we are left with notions of knowledge which, though they may never truly be anointed 'postmodernist', nonetheless show a harmony with the postmodernist critique by their very departure from foundationalism. At a pragmatic level in family therapy, there has been an expression of this in the re-emergence of a tolerance for eclecticism and its allowance for diversity of theory (Doherty 1991). The knowledge-as-lens image (Hoffman 1990) has also been circulated as a way of thinking about knowledge as providing particular kinds of lenses which may be used at different points for different purposes and with different effects. This image has gone alongside the move from the 'either/or' approach to knowledge to the 'both/ and' position, and this distinction has become almost commonplace in the current systemic discourse.

In all these notions, foundational knowledge is undermined, and there is a move beyond modernism. So instead of the idea of knowledge coming to claim a truthful representation of the world, we have knowledge standing in an 'as-if' relationship to the part of the world it is trying to describe. Knowledge becomes something like metaphor. It also becomes forever contextual and in relationship to the world with which it is attempting to engage. It is necessarily specific and always partial. And here we are again to some extent unwittingly beginning to reify knowledge. For knowledge does not exist by itself – it is created and embedded in a set of relationships, and it is enmeshed with the subject who wants to know. In more postmodernist language, it is embedded in a network of subjectivities and power relationships. It is peculiar that within two sentences I find myself using (postmodernist) language which, despite the content of the point I am making, continues to dehumanise the context of knowledge. If we were in therapy, we might start wondering about this pattern and replication!

Now of course this would be a fine point to launch into a fuller discussion of power and knowledge and patterns, but I have to admit it would be premature, so let me return to the focus of this part of the introduction. If in the shift beyond modernism, knowledge becomes something like metaphor, always partial and specific and relational, then it also becomes always conditional. The metaphor idea has a nice pragmatism and starts to have a strong echo with the kind of discussion about ideas of knowledge that meet the theory-practice relationship of practice disciplines. A metaphor can never exist in a vacuum, it only has life in relationship to what it is attempting to describe, but then once you use the metaphor, it gives a shape to the way you are thinking. It remains though 'just' a metaphor, conditional on its usefulness. As Paul Rosenblatt (1994) lays out so well in his discussion of core metaphors in family systems theory, any metaphor both highlights and obscures. Thus, the shape the metaphor gives to what we are trying to think about in the same moment offers a particular way of thinking about it and excludes other ways of thinking.

We come back again in this part of the introduction to my own commitment in this book to conditional knowledge, a commitment which is informed both by the struggle to think about the place and role of knowledge in therapy as a practice discipline and ideas about knowledge which have emerged in the critique of modernism. I will be approaching knowledge as something like metaphor, and the form of my own discussion will show the absence of an alliance with foundational aims for knowledge. In all this, experience becomes privileged, for the conditionality of knowledge for therapy rests on the understandings we are trying to have both of our own experience as therapists, of the experience clients bring to therapy, and indeed of the experience many of us have had ourselves as clients in therapy (not to mention in life). This is not to say, of course, that experience itself is any straightforward thing which we can capture in a neat way, but all this will be discussed along the way, and it is enough here to say that experience will stand as a core interest throughout the book and as the central reference point for the conditionality of knowledge.

Plan and chapters

It is time now for me to give a preview of the book's chapters and the structure and flow of the discussion. The first layer of the book has five chapters which explore the potentials and limits of postmodernist ideas in therapy. Chapter 2, The Shape of Postmodernism, maps the general shape of postmodernism and the extent to which it may be thought of as a social condition, a framework for theorising, an epistemology and a form of politics. That postmodernism is shaped as an oppositional domain to modernism is a main theme throughout this exploration, and this oppositionality leads to a number of paradoxes including the tendency to decentre the subject and subjective experience.

Chapter 3, Social Constructionist Ideas and the Narrative Metaphor, locates the popularity of narrative and social constructionist theory in systemic therapy, for these ideas have come to be the most influential expressions of postmodernism in our field. I am particularly interested in exploring the specific versions of social constructionist ideas that have become influential and some of the differences and congruences in the way in which the metaphor of narrative has been used. Taken together, Chapters 2 and 3 lay the groundwork for the next three chapters which each highlight some of the difficulties in the current use of postmodernist ideas.

Chapter 4, The Question of Reality and Realness, focuses on reality. Within systemic therapy, there is a growing concern about the extent to which postmodernist ideas may negate the possibility of independent realities existing separate to our consciousness of them. They may also negate the power of independent realities in the construction of meaning and the experience of subjectivity and personhood. This becomes very important in the territory of therapy, where we are involved in people's experiences of realness in their own lives. In this way, the context of therapy demands a more recursive and complex theorising of reality than one which stays within an oppositional positioning of independent *or* constructed realities.

Chapter 5, Truth as a Process, takes up these themes again, but in this chapter the exploration is specifically of the idea of truth and the process of the experience of claiming truth. I will be arguing that in the momentum to distance systemic discourse from modernist ideas of certain and universal truth, 'truth' has become subsumed in the concept of languaged meaning, so the opportunity to consider truth as an emotional and social process becomes lost. Meaning as a concept has its limits in therapy, partly because the space for external reality in shaping meaning can easily become lost and partly because the process of coming to claim knowledge/ 'truth' about one's own personhood and subjectivity is too easily obscured. In this chapter's exploration, another layer is added to the theme of the centrality of language in the postmodernist discourse, and this then bridges to the next chapter.

Chapter 6, The Narrative Self and the Limits of Language, looks at the idea of self in postmodern narrative discourse and argues that the notions of the autonomous self and relational self may be seen as different levels of description of the self, rather than competing (modernist and postmodernist) descriptions. Language is central in the narrative and social constructionist theory used in systemic therapy, and an idea of self bounded by the confines of language seems to have some major limits in the context of therapy.

Chapters 4–6 in combination move through practice concerns to the theory limits of postmodernist ideas in the context of therapy. Chapter 7, Postmodernist Limits and Intersecting Psychoanalytic Ideas, integrates the discussion of these chapters, and re-examines the limits in the family therapy context in light of the earlier discussion of the general shape of postmodernism. It is this critique which becomes the springboard for an exploration of particular ideas from psychoanalysis that can be seen as an example of a framework offering alternate possibilities in theorising subjectivity and intersubjectivity. I also take this opportunity to outline more fully my own orientation to using psychoanalytic ideas.

The scene is then set for the next three chapters which discuss particular psychoanalytic ideas and their relevance for systemic therapy. In general, the search is for psychoanalytic ideas that attempt to meet and describe relational processes, that do not negate the lived experience of self, that allow for a process of subjective truth, and that give descriptions of subjectivity and intersubjectivity in a way that allows for experience outside language. And so Chapter 8, Attachment and the Unconscious, explores the process of attachment and relational understandings of the unconscious and their usefulness in naming and describing some aspects of practice experience. Chapter 9, Transference, Projective Identification and Time, explores transference, countertransference and projective identification as particular kinds of descriptions of intersubjective processes in therapy. These psychoanalytic ideas offer one way of understanding the living past in present time, so the chapter moves to a broader discussion of time and the extent to which past and future time becomes expressed in the immediacy of stories and patterns in the present time of therapy.

Chapter 10, Further Thoughts on the Therapeutic Relationship, brings forward some of the themes from Chapter 9 and again intersects psychoanalytic thinking with more specific discussions from systemic therapy. There is further exploration of understanding and empathy in family therapy, and the family therapy discussion of the position of 'not-knowing' is held alongside some of Wilfred Bion's ideas on not-knowing and the conditions of thinking. An argument is made that we hold the space of not-knowing alongside the space of reflection, and this can help us in times of therapeutic impasse.

The last section, Concluding comments, integrates the work of Chapters 8–10, reflecting back on the way in which psychoanalytic ideas have been used, and presents a synthesis of this part of the work of the book with the project on postmodernism in family therapy.

I have just given a signpost summary of the content of the book. Yet there remains one last thing to be done, for you may well be wondering how or where you will see the practice concerns which I have said are the motivating force, so let me note that from Chapter 4 through to Chapter 6, and from Chapter 8 through to

Chapter 10, each chapter takes the form of beginning with practice, moving to theory and then circling back to practice. I hope it will prove a way of holding the practice-theory relationship in the foreground of what is essentially a discussion about theory ideas. As well, the circular move from and then back to practice more faithfully reflects the process of enquiry of the book, and practice is used to challenge, prompt and reflect on theory.

For these reasons, I do not plan to use 'case studies' or 'case illustrations' in the time-honoured way. Case studies are very useful in a teaching context, and case illustrations fit an idea of theory building where theory is foundational to practice. Their methodology is essentially about showing how theory can work, but this methodology is not a good match for my project, which is neither didactic nor makes any attempt to build a model for practice. Instead, though it is looser and far less neat, I will use pieces of practice that represent fragments of work with clients, moments in therapy, and partial descriptions of my experience as the therapist. In the process of writing the book, I have simply allowed myself to begin each chapter with fragments of practice that came to mind while I was struggling with the topics at hand. I have tried not to be too artificial in tidying up the practice reflections at the end of each chapter to 'match' the theory discussion. The theory themes of the chapter are wound in and out of the practice reflections, rather than being carefully battened down. This could prove somewhat frustrating at times. Again, I am hoping that what is lost in neatness will be more than made up for by an openness of discussion that more accurately reflects the interplay of theory and practice.

It goes without saying, of course, that in all this I am only able to give my own descriptions of other people's stories and of my own story as a therapist, and this is nothing more or less than a process of therapist reflection. To say this means we cannot be too grandiose about the status of the practice reflections; on the other hand, practice reflection is the stuff we have to work with as therapists in theory for therapy, and in this way it is precious and to be used.

However, 'using' practice always feels problematic. Though I will not be making up cases, I will be calling on the standard ways of safeguarding confidentiality – changing identifying details, running some common experiences together, and fictionalising some details, while trying to keep the integrity of the core of the therapy experience I am trying to describe. The ethics of confidentiality are only one part of the difficulty, for I think there is some breaching of the therapeutic relationship that happens when we choose as therapists to use our relationship with clients in discussions with colleagues. It is clear enough that I am not being black and white about this, given I intend to use practice, yet there remains something uncomfortable about it, and it may well be that that discomfort should stay because it cannot be written away.

For what it is worth, I will simply say that the practice reflections in this book are only ever a small part of the story of the therapy, that other people's (my clients') stories are filtered through my own impressions and limits, and some of what I say will be wrong. I know that the last sentence is strictly speaking out of place in a book introduction, and in many ways I am saying it more to the people I have worked with as clients than to the people who are likely to be reading this book. For all that, I think I will still allow the sentence to sit here at the end of this first chapter and move now to the work of the book.

Notes

1 See the special issue on 'Psychoanalysis and systemic approaches' in the *Journal of Family Therapy* (1997) (19)3, and the special issue of the *Australian and New Zealand Journal of Family Therapy* (1998) (19)2.
2 Having just used for the first time the first name as well as the surname of an author I am referencing, I would like to explain the convention I will adopt throughout this book. Mindful of the arguments that the use of only surnames tends to depersonalise authorship and make gender invisible, I have decided to give the first name of authors when I first reference their work in the text of each chapter. I will not give first names in references which are cited in brackets only, and generally will give first names once only in each chapter (very occasionally I will vary this for stylistic reasons).

Chapter 2

The shape of postmodernism

As I am about to embark on a tiered exploration of postmodernism and its appearance in systemic therapy, let me begin in this chapter with a baseline discussion. Mapping postmodernism is complicated, for one can engage with it on many levels. Is postmodernism a social condition, a framework for theorising, an epistemology or a form of politics? From different angles it may be claimed to be all these things, and in this chapter I am interested in tracing the outline of postmodernism via these different layers, and then considering the specific issue of the postmodern subject and therapeutic commitment. The cohering identification which becomes apparent through this exploration is the extent to which postmodernism may be thought of as an oppositional domain. This commentary then lays the groundwork for a consideration of the particular ways in which family therapy has engaged with the postmodern.

Postmodernism as a social condition

Postmodernism is a complex phenomenon, situated in the Western cultural and intellectual environment of the late twentieth century and having many different layers of meanings and uses. Yet in its translation within family therapy, understandings of postmodernism have tended to become homogenised. There are no doubt a number of reasons for this, not least being the process of translation that occurs when a practice discipline responds to and takes in broader intellectual ideas. Whatever the reasons, though, it is fair to say that the assumption that we all knew what we were talking about when we said 'postmodernist' came to be made very quickly in family therapy and on the basis of remarkably little initial excavation of its different layers and broader contexts.

One can point to only a very small handful of articles and texts in family therapy which attempt to situate postmodernism and postmodernist thought in any detail, and these contributions have come mainly from North America (see, for example, Anderson 1997; Parry 1991; Parry and Doan 1994). By contrast, the great majority of the writings using postmodernist ideas in North America, Britain, and Australia and New Zealand have tended to rely very heavily on the assumption of prior understandings, or alternatively they have given highly selective and often severely annotated versions of what postmodernism 'means' for therapy.

Understandably, this situation has led to a good deal of variation in what in fact we do mean when we claim that our ideas are postmodernist, and one can be forgiven for wondering at times what kind of territory we have landed in: that it is fashionable in family therapy there can be no doubt; that it might represent a philosophy or even a world view flies about as well; that it becomes a foundation for different kinds of theory and practice is certainly part of the picture; and that it can maybe act as a linchpin for a progressive politics seems to be around as well. Concerns have begun to be expressed about the extent to which postmodernism may have become a new kind of unquestioned – and unquestionable – orthodoxy in family therapy (Amundson 2001; Doan 1998).[1] This is surely a worry, but it is perhaps more of a worry if we are not even too sure quite what the postmodernist landscape looks like.

Attempts to map the postmodern in family therapy have generally framed it within a progressive narrative, with postmodernism being painted as something like an historical advance, part of the flowering of the 'better' and 'new' replacing the 'old' and supposedly 'worse'. I would love to go off on a tangent and note that in family therapy we have always been rather vulnerable to heralding the new and vanquishing the old, but of course this would be a distraction which I should resist till much later in the book. Instead, I will simply note here that as soon as you look outside family therapy to the broader intellectual milieu of postmodernism you find, as you would expect, far more complex accounts. These accounts draw distinctions about postmodernism across time (particularly, the postmodernism of the 1960s and 1970s, and the postmodernism of the 1980s and beyond); across countries and continents (particularly the flavour of postmodernism in Europe versus North America, and the pivotal role of

French intellectuals in postmodernist theorising); and across its expression in the diversity of the fields of the creative arts, the humanities, cultural studies and the social sciences.

To think of postmodernism as, at one level, simply a social and historical condition, is to situate it in a neutral way without the positive valence of a progressive narrative. Accounts both from within and outside family therapy reference the relationship between the major social changes in the latter part of the twentieth century and the move beyond modernism. Retrospectively, modernism has come to be understood as a dominant metaphor for knowledge and the arts which emerged from, and fitted with, the social conditions of the second half of the twentieth century.

As examples of these accounts, we could look at the description given by Steven Best and Douglas Kellner (1991), writing from their position in philosophy and their interest in critical theory. Their immediate identification of postmodernism is as a response to 'a variety of economic, political and social transformations' (Best and Kellner 1991: 2). Andreas Huyussen (1986), a German studies scholar, addresses the interface of modernism, postmodernism and mass culture, and makes a strong argument for differentiating the postmodernism of the 1960s and 1970s, which he characterises as the swansong of modernism, from the post 1980s period. He places the earlier forms of postmodernism as a transitional historical moment, a moment in which the modernist images of order and factory and the machine gave way to the cultural crisis of late capitalism and its major technological and political shifts. Kenneth Gergen (1991), from the perspective of social psychology, begins his text on identity and self by locating his own shift to social constructionist theory via postmodernism and its location in the technological developments of the late twentieth century.

Of the very large number of maps of postmodernism available in the literature, I pull out these three simply because they span the fields of the humanities, cultural studies and the social sciences, and because they each faithfully exemplify the first identification of postmodernism as a social and historical condition. The literature within family therapy that attempts a 'lie of the land' discussion of postmodernism, also unfailingly gives some version of the social context of postmodernism. There is no need, then, for me to labour the point that postmodernism has emerged in a specific historical, cultural and economic context, for this is really quite uncontroversial.

Rather, let me move to noting that once we take in the specificity of the social context, it is possible to see ourselves more clearly as being in a relationship with postmodernism. For though it is true that we 'live in a postmodern world' (O'Hara and Anderson 1991), there is nothing automatic about the position we might take about this. It is possible to construct a progressive narrative and implicitly or explicitly frame postmodernism as a historical leap forward. Or we could align ourselves with the kind of critique developed by David Harvey (1990), who remorselessly pins its shape to the economic and cultural transformations of late capitalism, and in the process demystifies any magic of postmodernism as an adequate description of contemporary experience.[2] Or we could go down the path of Best and Kellner, neither glorifying postmodernism or damning it but instead looking for its meanings, its shape and its possibilities in the development of theory. Let me conclude this discussion of postmodernism as a condition by underlining that we have some freedom about the way in which we might choose to relate to it, even if we are at the same time part of the social environment that produced it.

Postmodernism as a framework for theorising and an epistemology

Thus far, I have been addressing postmodernism as an expression of a particular historical and social context and in its breadth as a cultural metaphor, as well as a metaphor for knowledge. Having viewed it from this broad angle, I would like to narrow the focus to postmodernism as a metaphor for knowledge, and more specifically, its parameters as a framework for theorising and as an epistemology. Some of this discussion was begun in the first chapter. It can be a frustrating discussion, for although postmodernism does provide parameters for theorising, it does not provide in and of itself any coherent framework. Best and Kellner express this dilemma when they note:

> . . . there is no unified postmodern theory, or even a coherent set of positions. Rather, one is struck by the diversities between theories often lumped together as 'postmodern' and the plurality – often conflictual – of postmodern positions. One is also struck by the inadequate and undertheorized notion of the

'postmodern' in the theories which adopt, or are identified in, such terms (Best and Kellner 1991: 2).

The core issue to be grasped here is that postmodern theorising is defined by what it is not, rather than by its own set of unifying features. In many ways it is a shame that we are not able to routinely insert a hyphen to indicate visually that the minimum definition of postmodernism is that it is 'post-modern'. The defining feature of the parameters of postmodern theorising, then, is that it moves beyond the parameters of the modernist project for knowledge. If there is an essence to be found, it is this – postmodernism is an oppositional frame to modernism, and its parameters are the parameters of critique.

Given this core oppositionality, something clearly needs to be said about modernism, and let me confine myself to five fairly short sentences. Modernism as a project of knowledge relies on an image of a split between the object which is to be known, and the subject who wants to know. Within this frame, what we desire to know is thus thought of as possessing an 'external' reality and being a 'thing' in and of itself. The modernist aim, then, is objective knowledge which comes to represent and reflect that external reality. Though certainty may never be attained, it may be approached incrementally as we build up a picture of the world through the processes of knowledge. Truth enters as a concept at this point, and shadows externality, objectivity and certainty.

I know it is hard to bear the familiarity of even this quick rendition of modernism, because it is the most frequently spelled-out aspect of postmodernism and so has become something of a mantra. Given that the content is familiar, I would prefer to emphasise the form of the engagement in the development of postmodernist ideas. What is postmodernism? Not this (not modernism). And the 'not this' is what comes to be spelled out as the unifying feature of postmodernism as a framework for theorising. Of course, there is then a second question in this sequence. What is postmodernism? Not this (not modernism) . . . then what?

Postmodernist knowledges (and here I think we have to start using the plural) address the further question 'then what?'. In this way, the oppositional parameters of the postmodern framework become a springboard for the elaboration of a myriad of theories, which are indeed diverse and often conflictual. To pull out of the hat some theories that have become influential in family therapy discourse: social constructionist theory, narrative theory, Foucault's ideas on power, Derrida's work on deconstruction. Are all these postmodernist? There is an easy answer to this question – yes, they all share the postmodern critique of modernist commitments and theorise within those oppositional parameters. Do they form a coherent set of ideas, or are these theories even in harmony with each other? By contrast, this is a complex and very different kind of question. It is not a question that I intend to tackle here, although I will be tackling part of it in the next chapter. But for the moment, I will leave the discussion of postmodernism as a framework for theorising defined by oppositional parameters and move to the closely related layer of postmodernism as an epistemology.

The kind of frame postmodernism provides for how we might theorise about knowledge itself was exactly the layer addressed in the first chapter, for my own project is embedded within a postmodernist epistemology, and hence the need for me to own it at the outset. There is something ironic about the position in which I find myself at this point. Could I admit to longing to adopt a style of studied naiveté and take the modernist refuge of acting like there is some complete split between what I am talking about and what I am doing? Or should I take comfort from Barnaby Barratt's words in his work on postmodernism and psychoanalysis: 'talking is never metaphysically or politically innocent. Nor can a metadiscourse – talking about talking – achieve such innocence' (Barratt 1993: 16)? Perhaps I could add for the sheer fun of it here: and theorising about theorising is never metaphysically or politically innocent, and discussing epistemology when you are embedded in an epistemology cannot be either!

To recall the ideas about knowledge, we can note that in the same way that postmodernism as a framework for theorising is defined by oppositionality, a postmodernist epistemology is also shaped in opposition to the modernist epistemology. The modernist search for foundational knowledge which may come to mirror the externality of the objective world is countered by the postmodernist commitment to non-foundational knowledges. The modernist idea of aiming for universal knowledge is replaced with a commitment to a multiplicity of knowledges, which each bear partial and very particular contextual relationships to what we are trying to know. We can say that there is no longer any grand theory or totalising framework to be had.

In revisiting these postmodernist ideas on epistemology which were previously spelled out, we are now in a position to take stock of them from a somewhat different angle. For in the same way that the layers of postmodernism as a framework for theorising and as an epistemology share the oppositionality to modernism (which is, of course, the historical path of the emergence of postmodernism), these layers also show the preference for the specific and the partial. Indeed, the anti-foundationalism which characterises a postmodernist epistemology is expressed at a different level by the very lack of coherence of the theories that come under the umbrella of postmodernism. The elements of the piecemeal, the diverse and even the conflictual that show in the exploration of postmodernist theorising are thrown into relief when paralleled with the commitments of a postmodern epistemology.

Finally, in bringing together the layers of postmodern epistemology and postmodernism as a framework for theorising, we can note one further parallel effect of the shared anti-foundationalism. I have argued before that one cannot reach for, or claim to have, *the* postmodern epistemology and that instead we are only left with approaches to knowledge which are harmonious with *a* postmodern epistemology. Similarly, one cannot really ever make claims to *the* postmodern theory position, only to theory and theory ideas that may be described as postmodernist through their harmony with its oppositional parameters. In short, an epistemology that opposes totalising frameworks cannot itself produce a totalising theory framework.

Postmodernism and politics

There is one further layer to be addressed, and that is the question of the politics of the postmodern. It is a thorny issue, and I am addressing it directly because of the tendency in family therapy to link postmodern explorations with a commitment to a progressive politics. Examining the specifics of this link in contemporary family therapy theory, and indeed developing some ideas about the politics of postmodernism with respect to reality, truth and the self, is all part of the work of the next few chapters. Right now, I simply want to open the door and sketch some general themes, and the questions to be posed are these: to what extent and in what way is postmodernism a form of politics? What have been some of the main areas of ambivalence about the idea of a postmodernist politics?

Given the discussion so far in this chapter, it will come as no great surprise to note that postmodernism represents a very powerful politics of critique. The history of its emergence as an oppositional form to modernism as the entrenched paradigm of the humanities and the social sciences, places its development as a form of resistance and protest. In the humanities, one could perhaps argue that it has now gained dominance as the primary theory discourse, but I do not think that the same could be argued in the domain of the social sciences. In terms of the politics of knowledge, it exists in the social sciences as the dominant 'other' in the discourse of critique, though some disciplines in particular contexts (perhaps particularly psychology in the English-speaking environment) hold fast to the modernist paradigm. If I were to be foolhardy enough to venture a comment about the form of postmodernist politics that is the most coherent (and of course, I am risking ridicule putting 'coherent' and 'postmodernist' in the same sentence), then I would point to its strength as an oppositional politics of knowledge.[3]

There is an implicit recognition of the capacity of postmodernism as a progressive politics of knowledge in much of the family therapy discussion. However, more explicitly, postmodernist themes have been drawn out as a context for a broader level of progressive politics. These themes are by no means special to the family therapy discussion, and I know I will not be doing them justice by naming them in a bald way. If you could bear with me doing just this, though, then I will point to the way in which the postmodernist opposition to a singular reality and any aims of certainty and truth have been translated into a politics that values multiplicity and diversity and allows room for tentativeness and uncertainty. As well, the postmodernist emphasis on the specific and the contextual has informed a politics of bringing the social to the foreground in our understandings of the personal, the individual and the 'private'.

I have absolutely no interest in detracting from the ethics embedded in this translation of postmodernist ideas to a contemporary progressive politics, and I am myself part of this political milieu. Yet I think it is important to make the distinction between the extent to which postmodernist themes 'fit' with particular political commitments, and the extent to which postmodernism is itself the 'base' for a progressive politics. We could note that postmodernism would be hard-pressed to provide the foundation for a politics, given it is so profoundly anti-foundationalist, but this is essentially a charge of lack of purity, which I find it hard to be too passionate about. Beyond the issue of purity, though, are a number of other reservations that have come to be expressed about the implications of any exclusive reliance on postmodernism as a form of progressive politics. Again, for the sake of the discussion right now, I will restrict myself to simply naming these concerns, for the explorations that are more finely tuned to family therapy are planned for later.

The most common sticking point has been the issue of relativism, and this question has been canvassed in family therapy discussions and well beyond. The core argument goes like this: if within the postmodernist frame we are left with multiple realities and diverse knowledges, what basis is there for choosing or privileging one over the other? Are we left with 'anything goes'? There are wider questions about what this might mean for our relationship to knowledge and for the question of political choices. Indeed, the question of whether it is possible for a commitment to social justice to hold within postmodernist parameters has been frequently raised (see, for example, Montero 1998; Brown, Pujol and Curt 1998). In a professional discipline like family therapy, the issue of relativism strikes at the very heart of practice. It is very useful to have the space to think about multiple realities when you are in the room with a family with multiple realities. Yet how do you as a therapist relate to those multiple realities? Would an over-zealous commitment to the validity of each reality lead to a sliding-away from very important issues of power and abuse in family relationships?

While there has been quite a lot of discussion about the issue of relativism in family therapy, there has been far less discussion of the related issue of the extent to which postmodernism leads to fragmentation at the levels of theory, politics and practice. There has been heated debate about this in the wider intellectual environment. The most famous is perhaps the historical attack by critical philosopher Jurgen Habermas (1981) on the politics of postmodernist philosopher Michel Foucault, whom he called a young conservative. This attack is aligned with an extended discussion of the relationship of critique and power in postmodernist discourse (see, for example, Kelly 1994). In the contemporary discussions, there is a momentum to move beyond the fragmentation created in postmodernist discourse toward a position which Christopher Falzon (1998) terms social dialogue.

Whether the politics of postmodernist discourse engenders fragmentation and/or can be used to promote social dialogue remains a contested territory. That we have seen very little engagement in family therapy with this debate around fragmentation is, I suspect, a sign of the extent to which our own discourse about postmodernism has tended to be homogenised, and aspects which are more incompatible with therapy have thus been screened out in its presentation. This is perhaps why one is so struck by the critique given by Stephen Frosh (1995) in an article published in the (British) *Journal of Family Therapy*, where he questions the very compatibility of postmodernism and psychotherapy. He argues the case that contemporary postmodernist theorising shows a momentum toward fragmentation and the celebration of irrationality and indeed dissolves the desire for 'holding' meaning that is intrinsic to the process of therapy. When I first read this article, it resonated loudly with the wider discussions of postmodernism and fragmentation, yet Frosh's critique appears to be almost on another planet compared to the received version of postmodernism in the family therapy literature.

The last area I will flag here is the ambivalence towards postmodernism that has emerged from feminist theory and politics. Again, we find a contested territory, and in various ways the concerns raised about relativism and fragmentation show themselves again in the context of the interests of feminist theory and practice. As Lynn Hoffman (1990) notes in her discussion in family therapy, gender as an essentialist category does not sit easily with the postmodernist emphases in social constructionist theory, and she argues for a plurality of lenses in allowing for differential engagement with both the theory and politics of gender and postmodernist influences. A number of feminist theorists have queried the fit of postmodernism and feminism (see for example, Bordo 1990; Lovibond 1993), and if one is looking to postmodernism to provide any clear programmatic for reform politics, one is bound to be disappointed. There is nothing black and white in this debate, as many feminist writers have developed their ideas using postmodernism, and indeed some would argue that postmodernism allows an engagement with some of the problematic aspects of feminist constructions (see for example, Fraser and Nicholson 1993; McNay 1992).

In terms of feminist interests, then, we may be left with a series of convergences and divergences. It may well be in the end that this is the best that can be said of the broader relationship of post-modernism and a progressive politics. For alongside the political commitments to diversity and plurality that accompany post-modernist discourse, are the shadow political difficulties of relativism and fragmentation. The dynamic of diversity/plurality and relativism/fragmentation is thus more a site of political debate, rather than any easy home of progressive politics. By comparison, the politics of postmodernism as epistemological critique look relatively straightforward, exactly because critique is a more circumscribed (and one could argue, limited) commitment.

The postmodern subject and therapeutic commitments

Though I have been trying to hold the exploration in this chapter to the general shape of postmodernism, there is one particular issue that is central to the intersection of postmodernist ideas and psychotherapy and has a strong bearing on the discussions to come. What kind of image of the subject and subjectivity is addressed by and created through postmodernist discourse itself, and how does the postmodern subject fit with the commitments of psychotherapy?

The conceptualisations of the subject, of subjectivities and of the processes of intersubjectivity are primarily situated within post-modernist theorising and discourse. In this sense, they are postmodernist terms that accompany the major concerns of postmodernist analyses, and so let me note these alignments first. The concept of the 'subject' refers to the social creation of person-hood. Though this idea often moves through the same waters as discussions of the self or the individual (self), it would be wrong to simply equate the idea of subject with self or the individual. Dominant understandings of self, and indeed the very idea of the individual self, are themselves particular examples of the construc-tion of the subject which are historically and contextually specific, and to use the term 'subject' is to flag the social location of personhood and the way in which it is created.

The concept of subjectivity refers to the way in which the person comes to be known and understood by others, that in turn affects the way in which we come to think about and understand our 'selves' in that relational context. If you like, subjectivity is the social category of personhood, and it is a multiple social process with each person coming to have many different and often fragmented subjectivities. The relation between different subjectivities, and the way in which powerful subjectivities may come to be a totalising description of the person, is a complex process. The concept of intersubjectivity refers to this complex relational field in which the subject and specific subjectivities come to be created and shaped, and as I noted in the last chapter, it is all in a territory that is irredeemably social.

From the discussion so far in this chapter, we can begin to guess the general concerns that arise when we hold postmodernist understandings of the subject and subjectivities alongside the commitments of the activity of therapy. The postmodernist parameters of the contextual, the specific and the partial can on one level transfer to the concerns of psychotherapy – they forge an emphasis on the social and relational field of individual experience and indeed draw attention to very particular individualising practices. Yet the momentum toward fragmentation does not sit easily with the activity and aims of therapy, and in the process of privileging fragmented and relativised descriptions of the subject and subjectivities, the subject becomes decentred. Along with this, the interest in the experience of self becomes decentred, which is of course a major problem, as this stands at the heart of the practice of psychotherapy.

The critique developed by Frosh (1995) effectively takes up this point when he underlines the celebration of irrationality and the splintering of meaning, which is so much part of contemporary postmodernist discourse, and holds this against the therapeutic attempt to make and hold meaning. We could well ask what kind of subjectivity would be created in a therapy which truly took on board the postmodernist emphases of fragmented subjectivities and the 'decentred' subject. Exactly how collaborative and client-sensitive would such a therapy be? Barbara Held asks a similar question when she queries the postmodernist idealisation of fragmentation, decentring, relativising, partialising and incoherence, and their applications to the field of psychotherapy. She answers quite bluntly: 'in my opinion, this is certainly no ideal of mental health – itself a seemingly global, modern construct – to which any serious practicing clinician, *modern or postmodern*, would in all good conscience subscribe' (Held 1995: 19, emphasis in original).

Held asks this question in the early part of her critical exploration of the postmodernist theorising of reality and its adequacy for psychotherapy. Her central points of reference are the narrative therapies that have emerged in the field of family therapy, and she directly addresses a number of tensions around the therapeutic focus on individuality and the postmodernist visions of the subject and subjectivities. Again, she sees the harmony of the postmodernist attention to practices of individualisation with the interests of the narrative therapies, yet she notes the incompatibility of their commitment to the individual and individual experience with the fragmented and decentred postmodern subject. She also notes the anti-humanist flavour of some of the politics that have emerged in postmodernism and how uneasily these sit with the traditional humanist commitments of psychotherapy, which if anything have tended to be reasserted rather than challenged in the radical critiques of the mystifying and pathologising aspects of some psychotherapeutic practices.

If we turn to discussions that centre on postmodernism and psychoanalysis, we see something of the same concerns being expressed. Anthony Elliott (1995) talks about the dismantling of the human subject in postmodernist discourse and the analyses within social and political theory of the 'death of the subject'. In his discussion of the relationship of the psychic subject and contemporary cultural forms and of psychoanalysis and postmodernity, he points to emerging psychoanalytic theory that holds the possibility of conceptualising the intrapsychic in the social conditions of postmodernity. Kimberlyn Leary (1994) has less interest in this kind of possibility in her critique of postmodern 'solutions' to psychoanalytic 'problems'. In particular, she queries the confusion of postmodernist description and idealisation. Like Held, she is not enamoured with the possibility of making a therapeutic ideal out of the postmodernist description of the contemporary subjective experience of fragmentation.

This final section has canvassed the question of the compatibility of postmodern visions of the subject and subjectivity with the commitments of the activity of psychotherapy. Let me leave the general controversy at this point and simply signal it for the more specific explorations that are to come.

Conclusion

My interest in this chapter has been to set out the broad parameters of postmodernism as a social condition, a framework for theory and an epistemology, and as a form of politics. In the course of this commentary, one theme holds strongly through the different examinations: that theme is the oppositional structuring of post-modernism in relation to modernism. The historical conditions of the emergence of postmodernism place it as a 'counter' discourse situated in social and cultural change. Its momentum as a frame-work for theory and as an epistemology is embedded within the oppositionality to modernist premises. The move from founda-tionalism to anti-foundationalism, from grand theory to specific and partial theories, from the universal to the particular and local, from singular truth to multiplicity and diversity – all these moves mirror the postmodernist challenge to modernity. The postmoder-nist visioning of the subject and subjectivity reflects these emphases, and the question of its compatibility with the activity of psychotherapy immediately arises.

Postmodernism stands very clearly as a politics of epistemolo-gical critique and yet more ambivalently as a source of progressive politics. This is not to say that its commitments may not fit with a progressive politics, but there is no easy one-to-one relationship here. Political convergences and divergences require a more com-plicated map which may well follow the contours of the post-modernist dynamic of diversity/plurality and the shadow of relativism/fragmentation.

In her discussion of the complexity of the relationship of feminism and postmodernism, Linda Nicholson concludes: 'In sum, I am suggesting that we think of postmodernism as linked in both continuous and reactive ways to modernism and evaluate it in light of the political needs of our time' (Nicholson 1992: 91). It will be interesting to see whether something of the same thing may be said as we examine the particularities of the influence of post-modernism with the interests of family therapy, but all this is by way of summary, and I am happy for this chapter's discussion to sit as background now, and turn my attention very directly to the appearance of postmodernism in family therapy theory and practice.

Notes

1 Similar concerns are raised in a number of the contributions to a special feature in the *Australian and New Zealand Journal of Family Therapy* (2000) (21)3 entitled 'Dialogues of diversity in therapy: a virtual

symposium'. See in particular the contributions by Doan (2000) and Stagoll (2000).

2 Harvey's critique of the relationship of postmodernism to the conditions of late capitalism is echoed by Eagleton (1996) and Jameson (1993), while Tester (1993) offers an example of another kind of debunking of the transformation of postmodernism.

3 For examples of two different discussions of the postmodernist politics of oppositional epistemology, see Rosenau (1992) and Yeatman (1994).

Chapter 3

Social constructionist ideas and the narrative metaphor

If postmodernism is a domain in opposition to modernism, then what can be said of the way in which family therapy has come to engage with it, and what has it meant about the theory and practices that have been generated in its train? I spoke in the last chapter of the pattern in approaching postmodernist theorising. What is postmodernism? Not this (not modernism) . . . then what? The discourse in psychotherapy in general and in family therapy in particular has followed this sequence, fine-tuned to our own interests. What does postmodernism look like in the theory and practice of therapy? Not this – not 'modernist' therapy and all its assumptions. Then what? The 'not modernist' part of the sequence is essentially critique and marks the point of departure. It involves an identification and elaboration of the way in which modernist premises show themselves both in historical and contemporary theory and practice. Yet though elaborating this oppositionality continues to be a focus in family therapy, the creativity of the postmodernist position lies more in the response to the second question. For to begin to answer 'then what?' is to begin to meet the challenge of the postmodern critique and its emphases on context, specificity, and relationship. In psychotherapy, these emphases land us very squarely in the province of subjectivity and intersubjectivity, and in attempting to theorise subjectivity and intersubjectivity, family therapy has in the main turned to narrative and social constructionist theory.

It is thus via narrative and social constructionist ideas that family therapy has come to 'know' postmodernism, which is not to say that the postmodernist critique was not showing itself in family therapy before we embraced narrative and social constructionism. In line with the foundational ideas of Gregory Bateson (1980), the much heralded shift from first order to second order therapies in the early 1980s should be identified as the first move beyond modernist framings. As Karl Tomm (1998) argues in a recent commentary, the first order perspective that informed the earlier structural and strategic models was based on the theoretical position of seeing families as 'observed systems'. We could understand this perspective as being firmly attached to the modernist idea of splitting subject from object, and the idea of subject free objective knowledge. Tomm notes that the second order perspective is marked by the shift from the idea of the family as an observed system to the idea of therapy as being an *observing* system. The influence of observing is recursive, and the therapist becomes an integral part of the intersubjective field that is the therapist-and-family system. Again, postmodernist emphases are easily recognised in this move.

Tomm (1998) also notes that this second order perspective informs the Milan systemic therapy of Luigi Boscolo and Gianfranco Cecchin, the collaborative language systems therapy as developed by Harlene Anderson and Harry Goolishian, the solution focused therapies that are associated with Steve DeShazer and Insoo Berg, and the version of narrative therapy that has emerged in the work of Michael White and David Epston. All these second order therapies are characterised by the shift to a central interest in meaning, and this shift to meaning is underlined by Rudi Dallos and Amy Urry in their analysis of the development of theory in family therapy (Dallos and Urry 1999). Indeed, at the level of practice, the most striking change in Milan therapy was the change from the focus of the structural and strategic therapies on patterns of behaviour to the rigorous focus on patterns of meaning. The intersubjective construction of meaning, the relationship of meaning and language, and the extent to which meaning comes to construct both behaviour and observation were thus all held strongly as implicit themes in the Milan systemic therapy of the early 1980s. These themes were then to become explicit in the move to social constructionist and narrative ideas.

It is at this point that the main exploration of this chapter begins. Social constructionist and narrative ideas have had a pivotal importance in the expression of postmodernist ideas, and the particular kind of theorising they offer has come to hold centre stage in the way in which contemporary family therapy theorises the space of intersubjectivity. Let me turn to a closer examination of social constructionism, its context and emphases, and in particular the influence of Kenneth Gergen's work in the dominant version within family therapy. I will then explore the metaphor of narrative and its overlap with social constructionist ideas, before examining the different theory and practice ideas of Harlene Anderson and Michael White. The term 'narrative therapy' collapses the diversity of the way in which the narrative metaphor has been used in family therapy, and the final section gives a rough map of the complexity and localness of its practice influences.

Social constructionism: context and emphases

Social constructionism as a set of ideas has been a cornerstone of modern sociology. Since the publication in 1966 of the seminal book by Peter Berger and Thomas Luckman *The social construction of reality* (Berger and Luckman 1966), there has been a major elaboration of theory that draws the connections between social process, the social world, and our experience and understanding of social realities. The move to social constructionism was a departure from the paradigm of structural functionalism that dominated sociology in the 1950s and 1960s and faithfully reflected modernist premises. The very nature of sociology as a discipline is that it becomes an interface for the other social sciences, most notably in its close relationship to anthropology as a discipline and to the field of social psychology. The development of social constructionist ideas was, as Lynn Hoffman notes (1990), primarily an American 'product', and she singles out the work of social psychologist George Kelly (1983) and his development of personal construct theory, the work of anthropologist Clifford Geertz (1973 and 1983) on culture and knowledge, and the work of Kenneth Gergen (1991, 1994), again from social psychology.

Family therapy came to take up social constructionist ideas more than 20 years after the beginning of their development in sociology, and this happened in a rather peculiar way. Until the mid-1980s, the theory terrain of family therapy was still marked out by systems metaphors drawn from biology and cybernetics via the work of Bateson (1972, 1980). Following Bateson's argument for the need to think of patterns of circular causality rather than linear causality in understanding living systems, family therapy became interested in the constructivist theories of the Chilean biologists

Humberto Maturana and Francisco Varela. In particular, Maturana's work on the perceptual apparatus of the frog's eye led to his conclusions that what a frog 'sees' is determined by the extent to which the image is able to be matched and discriminated by its internal structure, hence the idea that seeing is 'structure-determined' with images becoming shaped by a process in which the organism finds a fit between its perceptual structure and the environment of observation. This metaphor was then translated within family therapy as a way of theorising the relationship of 'fit' in human systems.

The influential North American magazine, *The Family Therapy Networker*, devoted a special feature in 1985 to constructivism, and the articles in this feature showed primary reference to these biological theories of constructivism (see for example Efran and Lukens 1985; Simon 1985). Six years later, it ran another special feature, again on constructivism, but this time the focus was on postmodernism, and the primary references to constructivism were to sociology and social psychology (see for example Doherty 1991; O'Hara and Anderson 1991). In this short time frame, then, we saw an unannounced shift from biology to sociology and social psychology for core metaphors in family therapy theory. For a period, there was some confusion about the way in which 'constructivism' was used in family therapy literature, with an oscillation between biological and sociological ideas and little demarcation between the two. Yet in an illuminating article published in *Family Process* in 1990, Hoffman delineated the (biological) theories of constructivism from the 'new' (sociological) theories of social constructionism, and this article came to be an important early marker of the popularity of social constructionist ideas in family therapy.

The comments I have been making so far are more about the context of social constructionist ideas and their appearance in family therapy, and so let me move now to explore the content of social constructionist ideas as they have influenced family therapy. Social constructionism makes a decisive break with the modernist framing of an objective and external social world that we can come to know in a direct way, unmediated by the social process of knowledge. The alternate theorising offered by social constructionism is of a social world which comes to be known via our interactions with it, and thus what counts as both everyday knowledge and more formal knowledge of the social world is constructed in a socially interactive environment through language and communication. As Hoffman notes, social construction theory 'holds that our beliefs about the world are social inventions' (Hoffman 1990: 2), and it 'sees the development of knowledge as a social phenomenon and holds that perception can only evolve within a cradle of communication' (Hoffman 1990: 3).

What has been said so far can stand as a fairly uncontroversial initial description of social constructionist ideas. Yet as you expect in a set of ideas spanning more than thirty years, social constructionism itself is not a single theoretical entity, and indeed its different emphases have been a source of considerable theoretical and political contention. The description so far stresses the social construction of our knowledge about the social world, and the central role communication and language play in the process of our interaction with, and construction of, social realities. The short quotes from Hoffman's description reflect this emphasis on social constructionism being a theory that primarily addresses how we come to know the social world. Yet a second emphasis running in some social constructionist theory goes well beyond this interest in how we come to *know* the social world, through to a central interest in the nature of the social world itself as constructed reality.

The dual emphases of social constructionism as being both a theory about the process of knowing the social world as well as being a theory about the nature of the social world itself is reflected very strongly in the descriptions given by Harry Goolishian and Harlene Anderson in the family therapy literature. Their 1988 article laid out the major theoretical premises of their collaborative language systems approach, and these were developed in their later joint work (for example, Anderson and Goolishian 1992), and subsequently by Harlene Anderson (for example, 1997) in her own work following Harry Goolishian's death. In the 1998b paper, they drew their intersection with social constructionist ideas in this way: 'Human systems are language-generating and, simultaneously, meaning-generating systems. Communication and discourse define social organization. . . . Meaning and understanding are socially and intersubjectively constructed' (Anderson and Goolishian, 1988: 372). This core intersection was developed in a 1992 paper:

> Our current position leans heavily on the view that human action takes place in a reality of understanding that is created

> through social construction and dialogue. . . . From this position, people live, and understand their living, through socially constructed narrative realities that give meaning and organization to their experience. It is a world of human language and discourse (Anderson and Goolishian 1992: 26).

It was developed and extended again in Anderson's 1997 book, and she writes:

> . . . ideas, truths, or self-identities . . . are products of human relationships. That is, everything is authored, or more precisely, multiauthored, in a community of persons and relationships. The meanings of language, that is, the meanings we attribute to the things, the events, and the people in our lives, and to ourselves, are arrived at by the language people use – through social dialogue, interchange, and interaction that we socially construct (Anderson 1997: 41).

I present these quotes to give a first-hand flavour of the double layering of emphases in social constructionist ideas, to draw some difference between the theory social constructionism offers of the process of social knowledge and meaning-making and its theorising on the nature of the social world itself. One sees in the quotes from the work of Anderson and Goolishian a strong commitment to both emphases, as they move between outlining how we come to understand and give meaning to our social experience, through to outlining the social world itself being defined as 'a world of human language and discourse' where 'everything is authored, or more precisely, multiauthored'. Hoffman's description of social constructionism, on the other hand, largely confines itself to addressing the layer of social constructionism as a theory of social knowledge (Flaskas 1995). In both layers, of course, the place of language and meaning is central.

Having given this initial overview of the context of the appearance of social constructionist ideas in family therapy and delineated two emphases of the way in which its theory may be used, I will move to a more detailed consideration of the received version in family therapy and in particular to an identification of the influence of Kenneth Gergen's work.

Kenneth Gergen's influence and the issue of continuity

The above delineation of the two emphases of social construction-ism may seem a little laboured, yet I want to make the difference clear for a number of reasons. The first reason is simple enough: thus far in the family therapy literature there has been little distinction made between the two and often they are simply run together, which in turn can confuse how we might position our-selves in relation to the use of social constructionist ideas. More-over, the contentions within sociology and social theory have in the main centred not so much around the layer of social con-structionist ideas that theorises the *process* of social knowledge, but more around the layer of social constructionist ideas that theorises the *nature* of the social world itself. Politically, there are issues about social power and the extent to which we may want to allow the social world to have some existence outside our lan-guaging of it (Flaskas 1995; Lannamann 1998b). These political issues are necessarily of interest to psychotherapy, and they become of direct clinical relevance when we move to the level of the individual's relation to the social world and how we might choose to think about the individual's languaging and construction of the social world. Is it possible, for example, that we have social and emotional realities outside our languaged constructions of them?

But before I foreshadow some of the concerns of the next chapters, let me rein the discussion back in and simply reiterate that social constructionist ideas that privilege languaged constructions as defining the nature of social realities have been more contentious than social constructionist ideas that privilege languaged construc-tions in the process of coming to know the social world and its realities. To bring this back again to the way in which family therapy has engaged with social constructionism, it is important to identify that the version of social constructionist ideas offered by Anderson and Goolishian has become the received version in the family therapy literature, not the least because their descriptions give the most thorough and sustained attention to social constructionist ideas. Thus, their version has become the 'base' version of social constructionist theories used in family therapy, and it is centrally referenced in family therapy discussions of social constructionism.

It has come to feel like a detective hunt to ask the question: well, exactly what kind of version of social constructionism has held most sway in the family therapy discussion, and where does it come from? Having located the importance of the work of Anderson and Goolishian, we can take another step and look at the shaping of their version of social constructionism. When we do this, we run directly into the work of Gergen, the North American social psychologist whom Anderson describes as being considered by many to be the 'leading proponent' of social constructionism (Anderson 1997: 41). Increasingly throughout the 1990s his work came to be the major 'outside' theory reference point for social constructionist ideas in the family therapy literature.

Gergen published two influential books in the early 1990s – *The saturated self: dilemmas of identity in contemporary life* in 1991, and *Realities and relationships: soundings in social construction* in 1994 (Gergen 1991, 1994). These have been heavily referenced in family therapy. In addition, he has been very interested in the rich intersections of social constructionist ideas and therapy, and indeed he co-edited a collection entitled *Therapy as social construction* (McNamee and Gergen 1992). This collection was dedicated to the memory of Harry Goolishian and featured chapters by well-known family and narrative therapists. A more recent example of family therapy's relationship to his work would be his invited response (Gergen 1998) in the journal *Family Process* to a discussion of the problem of materiality in social constructionism (Lannamann 1998b). All this is to say that the interest in Gergen's work by family therapy has been a reciprocal relationship.

Now the point of this detection work is simply to identify that when we talk about social constructionist ideas in family therapy, we are in the main talking about Gergen's work in its application to family therapy. Moreover, when we take Gergen's ideas back to the wider milieu of theorising about social process and the social world, two aspects may be drawn out. The first is the primacy Gergen gives to language in his theory of social construction, and he does this particularly in his later work which theorises the self and social life through the metaphor of narrative (see Gergen 1994, especially Part III). The second aspect of his work on social constructionism is its wide-ranging terrain. His work theorises social constructionism as a process by which we come to know the world, but it is also a process by which the social world and the world of 'self' is constructed through language and always in the generative context of relationship (see Gergen 1991, 1994).

Gergen has also recently been emphasising a strand that has been in his thinking for some time, and that is the idea of social constructionism as a dynamic lens of critique; here, the aim of social constructionism is drawn almost as an alternate form of deconstruction (see Gergen 1994 Part I, and 1998). This strand of his ideas is only just beginning to appear in the family therapy literature, and it is showing initially in Anderson's discussions of social constructionism (see Anderson 1999), though Dallos and Urry also draw attention to its role as a 'meta-theory' (Dallos and Urry 1999). However, though this last emphasis is not as yet a strong theme, family therapy's use of social constructionist ideas otherwise quite faithfully reflects Gergen's privileging of language and his theorising of the construction of the social world and self through the world of relationship and language.

We are at the point in the discussion where we can move to narrative ideas and the influence of the narrative metaphor. Having considered the context of the appearance of social constructionism ideas in family therapy and the particularity of the emphases that family therapy has embraced, let me make a concluding comment about the general question of difference versus continuity in this theory's development. Lannamann (1998b) notes that the notion that understanding arises out of social process has been a strong theme in family therapy for decades, and in this sense it has been an easy 'home' for social constructionist ideas. Dallos and Urry make a strong argument that despite the 'dramatic shift' (Dallos and Urry 1999) that is represented by social constructionism as a 'third order' frame, one can appreciate both the difference it brings, as well as the connecting themes it holds with first and second order theorising.

I would like to echo these comments and note that the difference of social constructionism is the extent to which it demands and prioritises that we theorise social process and social context as a primary frame of reference. Moreover, it offers a particular way of doing this, and family therapy has engaged with particular emphases and layers of social constructionist ideas in its version. The centrality of relationship is highlighted in the process of construction, and language is privileged as the medium of construction. Yet though the demand for attention to social context and the privileging of language may mark the difference of the contribution of social constructionism, the momentum to theorise context and relationship shows itself as a core theme in family therapy theory, even though the theorising has taken very different forms in different periods. The strength of this continuity may indeed go some way toward explaining the ease with which social constructionist ideas have found a home in recent family therapy theory.

The overlap of narrative and social constructionist ideas

Narrative ideas in family therapy have often gone hand-in-hand with social constructionism, and at different points in the struggle to structure this chapter, I have been querying my own decision to discuss them sequentially rather than together. Indeed, precisely because narrative often accompanies social constructionist ideas and vice versa, you can easily find yourself coming to have some conglomerate category in your head like 'narrative/constructionist' without getting into hot water at either a practice or theory level. Just above, I have given a discussion of Gergen's work, his centring of language and his ideas of the construction of the social world and the self always occurring in relationship and through language. Already we have moved into the overlap of the territories of social constructionism and narrative, and in the development of Gergen's theory, narrative ideas are the spine for elaborating the process of construction in language.[1]

The relationship of narrative and social constructionism is thus one of overlap, and for a rough sketch we could draw the overlap of social constructionism with narrative as being bigger than the overlap of narrative with social constructionism. Narrative is a broader field of theory – it spreads, with varying degrees of influence, through literary theory, cultural studies, philosophy, sociology, social psychology and anthropology. It spans the humanities and social sciences, whereas the location of social constructionism is more restricted to the social sciences. As well, social constructionism is primarily (though not solely) a theory from the North American milieu, whereas narrative theory has been generated more broadly across the English-speaking and European intellectual environments. I could say 'social constructionism embraces the narrative metaphor', and this would be more or less correct, and in fact quite accurate with specific reference to Gergen's work. However, if I were to say 'narrative theory embraces social constructionism', this would be far more misleading as a statement about the relationship between the two bodies of ideas.

As we know from couple therapy, an uneven embrace suggests possible complexities! And though in the interests of easy identification we have come to speak of narrative 'therapy' (in the singular) in the family therapy field, this should really stand as a shorthand for a number of theory and practice ideas that have emerged within the influence of postmodernism and that use the idea of narrative as a guiding metaphor for the therapeutic process. In providing some map of the different ways in which narrative ideas have been used in family therapy and of the different alignments of narrative and social constructionist ideas that have been brought to bear in their application to therapy, I am also making a plea that we begin to move from the singular narrative 'therapy' to the plural narrative 'therapies'. Using the plural would be one way of signalling some of the differences in the use of 'narrative' in our own field, and indeed it could also help to signal that these versions sit alongside other versions in social psychology and psychoanalysis.

I have already noted that many of the ideas of Milan therapy provided a good transition point for the shift to narrative ideas, for Milan therapy laid the groundwork by focusing on patterns of meaning rather than patterns of behaviour and insisting on contextual and relational understandings. That the Milan lens for contextual analysis was initially largely confined to the traditional family system became one source of critique of the early model (MacKinnon and Miller 1987), and indeed the rather purist rigour of systemic hypothesising led to a second set of concerns about the extent to which the individual's emotional experience of relationships could come to be marginalised in the practice of the model (Flaskas 1989; Flaskas and Perlesz 1996; Luepnitz 1988). Of course, the social constructionist lens allows the movement of the contextual field well and truly beyond the confines of the 'family'. The narrative metaphor gives a particular theorisation of patterns and processes of meaning-making, and the idea of the process of 'storying' and 'restorying' one's life in the context of social, familial and interpersonal relationships allows both a broader contextual space, while retaining the link to the individual's experience. In this sense, constructionist and narrative ideas have an intersection both with what was seen to be 'new' about Milan ideas and what also came to be seen as its limitations.

The British family therapy scene stands out for the extent to which a broad use of constructionist and narrative ideas has grown with and elaborated a more critical 'post-Milan' frame of theory for systemic therapy. One sees this integration in the discussion Elsa Jones (1993) gives of the place for constructionist ideas in broadening contextual understandings; in the way in which Dallos and Urry (1999) and Dallos and Draper (2000) locate the social constructionist influence; in the congruence of John Byng-Hall's integration of the narrative metaphor in his work on family scripts (Byng-Hall 1995b); and in the melding of the metaphor of narrative with a range of systemic understandings in the edited collection produced by the Tavistock systems group, appropriately entitled *Multiple voices: narrative in systemic family psychotherapy* (Papadopoulos and Byng-Hall, 1997). All these are examples of the eclecticism that has characterised the British use of postmodernist ideas and the way in which narrative and social constructionist ideas have been used broadly in harmony with Milan systemic ideas, which is the approach most frequently nominated by British family therapists as influencing their work (Bor, Mallandain and Vetere 1998).

It is not surprising then, that when you list the important 'names' in the development of narrative therapy, there is a noticeable absence of British family therapists. To develop and claim a newness in approach requires a focus on how the narrative approach differs from what came before, whereas in Britain the tendency has been to use the ideas in harmony with what came before. To begin, then, to locate influential sources in the narrative field, let me note that the most influential and thoroughgoing approaches have been developed by Harlene Anderson, building on her earlier work with Harry Goolishian, and the body of ideas developed by Michael White. Harlene Anderson is from the United States, while Michael White is Australian. I will consider these quite different examples of the use of the narrative metaphor, before continuing to sketch the broader map of the diversity of narrative practice influences in family therapy.

The different ideas of Harlene Anderson and Michael White

In beginning with Anderson's work, let me be clear that she herself does not call her approach 'narrative therapy', and instead it is increasingly being identified as 'collaborative language systems therapy'. Anderson specifically names her primary theory influences as 'various postmodern philosophies, including social construction and contemporary hermeneutic premises' (Anderson 1999: 8). Her use of the narrative metaphor, which is strongly embedded in her recent book (Anderson 1997), has social constructionism as its main linkage point and narrative is located as a constructionist process, echoing Gergen's positioning of narrative in his theory. Narrative is the way in which 'everything is authored, or more precisely, multiauthored, in a community of persons and relationships' (Anderson 1997: 41), and it is through language as an intrinsically social process that we come to construct and understand ourselves, our emotional and interpersonal lives, and our social identities.

Anderson maintains the continuity of her earlier work with Goolishian in which 'problems' were theorised as constructions in language – therapy as a languaged activity was thus framed as a 'problem dis-solving system' (Anderson and Goolishian 1988). In terms of the process of therapy, then, they built the metaphor of therapy-as-conversation, and developed the idea that the therapist needs to take a not-knowing position in order to engage in a more meaningful way with clients, their language and experience (Anderson and Goolishian 1992). In this frame, the process of therapy becomes one of collaborative conversation in which new narratives and meanings may emerge. For Anderson, these practices have also been embedded in an ethical and political position that emphasises respectful and client-centred practices, and nurtures the space for different voices and stories-not-yet-told (Anderson 1997). The practice flavour of this approach is collaborative, empathic and reflective, the pace is gentle and more client-led, and though the theory premises are postmodernist, the practices themselves seem to have much in common with the humanist psychotherapies.[2]

On the other hand, Michael White's work is most commonly referred to as 'narrative therapy', and in his approach it is narrative which is the organising theory. White's first use of narrative was as a literary metaphor – indeed, his joint book with David Epston *Narrative means to therapeutic ends* (White and Epston 1990) was titled in its first publication *Literary means to therapeutic ends* (White and Epston 1989). In his work then, narrative does not enter via social constructionist theory, and indeed his use of narrative is independent of social constructionism. At the same time, White's work still gives very deliberate attention to context, but rather than drawing on social constructionism, he draws instead on some of the ideas of the French poststructuralist philosopher Michel Foucault as a way of theorising power and knowledge and the relationship of social context to individual experience.

The foundation for the way in which White uses Foucault's ideas is laid out in the first part of *Narrative means to therapeutic ends* (White and Epston 1990), in subsequent papers (for example, White 1991), and in his most recent book *Narratives of therapists' lives* (White 1997). Foucault's ideas are used in a highly selective way, and there are very particular themes that White applies to individual experience. He takes up Foucault's idea of the intimate relationship of power and knowledge and the extent to which power comes to be exercised through knowledge.[3] Foucault's work on power and knowledge is almost materialist in the importance it places on the effects (and the power) of everyday social practices (Flaskas and Humphreys 1993) and the extent to which these day-to-day practices create the possibility of specific ways of thinking about and languaging experience. Dominant discourses are created which then censor and marginalise alternate and subjugated discourses and understandings. Unlike social constructionism, which privileges the way in which social realities are formed by languaged construction, Foucault argues that it is the power of everyday social practices that creates the possibility of languaged construction. In a recursive way, these dominant discourses then in turn shape everyday social practices, but in this recursive spiral it is social practice that is initially privileged rather than languaged construction. Thus as a theory of social context and relationship, Foucault's understanding of discourse and the relationship of language to social practices stands in very strong contrast to social constructionism.

Though Foucault himself did not use these ideas in relation to individual experience, White's project has been to graft them to the metaphor of narrative with a focus on lived experience.[4] Using the central metaphor of narrative, he draws the way in which our own dominant stories are shaped by familial, interpersonal, cultural and social relationships, and the way in which dominant stories can come to restrain us from exploring and knowing other stories about ourselves and our experience. Therapy thus becomes a process of deconstructing dominant stories and reconstructing alternate narratives which free up the possibility of difference and change. In therapy, this is tackled through the externalisation of the problem, through the exploration of 'unique outcomes' (or exceptions to dominant stories), and through the encouragement and nurturing of alternate stories.

In terms of practice emphases, the therapeutic style in Michael White's therapy is more purposefully interventive, and the therapist takes quite an active role in sequencing the deconstructing and restorying movement in the therapy. In this sense, one could say that the therapist position is more directive, not in terms of outcome as such, but in terms of the framing of the therapeutic movement and the discourse of change. The power issues involved in this style are mediated by an ethical commitment to practices of transparency in the process of the therapy.

Thus there are marked differences between Anderson's use of the metaphor of narrative in her collaborative language systems therapy and White's narrative therapy. The therapeutic pace and style and the therapist's position in directing the therapeutic movement are all elements of practice which 'look' quite different in each framework. In terms of theory, it is Anderson's use of social constructionist ideas that organises her use of the narrative metaphor, whereas White uses narrative as the main organising theory, bringing in Foucault's ideas to theorise social context rather than the quite different ideas from social constructionism.

Noting the diversity of practice influences

Anderson's collaborative language systems therapy and White's narrative therapy stand as examples of approaches that are strongly influenced by postmodernism and use the narrative metaphor but which nonetheless have quite different theory and practice flavours. Anderson's work is firmly part of the North American tradition, though it shows the enrichment of colleagial exchanges with Tom Anderson and the Norwegian group.[5] Michael White is Australian, and there are strong practice crossovers and collaboration with the ideas of David Epston from New Zealand. Beyond this, the Australian and New Zealand environment for narrative includes work from Michael White's colleagues from the Dulwich Centre and the New Zealand 'Just Therapy' group. Michael White's approach has become very influential in the North

American narrative developments, and the versions of narrative therapy of some North American therapists such as Jill Freedman and Gene Combs (1996) follow his approach closely.

There is, though, another broader layer to be added to this map of the influence of the narrative metaphor. For though Harlene Anderson and Michael White have been building and elaborating particular approaches to theory and practice, a number of other writers and therapists have been more selectively exploring possibilities within the frame of postmodernist, constructionist and narrative ideas. Here we should certainly include the work of Lynn Hoffman (1990, 1993, 1998) and others such as Karl Tomm (1993, 1998), Alan Parry and Robert Doan (1994), Carlos Sluzki (1992), Kathy Weingarten (1998), and Jeffrey Zimmerman and Victoria Dickerson (1994). All these North American writers align themselves with postmodernist possibilities in therapy, and in different combinations, their work shows the influences of social constructionism and the narrative metaphor.

Hoffman, for example, developed ideas in parallel with Anderson and Goolishian around collaborative practice and therapy as a process of conversation, and she also draws heavily on social constructionist theory. Hoffman herself has moved away from any search for one practice model or foundational approach in guiding her work, and she has made a recent plea for allowing diversity in theory and practice ideas (Hoffman 1998). Many of the other writers also combine the narrative metaphor with social constructionist ideas, and many integrate particular ideas from White's work. The practice flavour of some of the discussions has far more in common with the style of White's narrative therapy (see for example, Parry and Doan 1994). Others have a practice flavour that resonates more strongly with Anderson's approach, yet still uses some of White's ideas (see, for example, Weingarten 1998).

In the varying uses made of White's ideas, I think it is the practice of externalisation that has had the most far-reaching influence. However, oddly enough, though White's use of Foucault is routinely noted in discussions of his work, there has been scarcely any recognition of the major differences between Foucault's theorising of social context and relationships and the ideas of social constructionism. Apart from a flagging of this difference in two recent footnotes (Anderson 1999; Flaskas 1999), one would have to go back to an article by Vincent Fish in 1993 that critiques White's use of Foucault (Fish 1993). Fish's description of Foucault locates him quite clearly as something other than a social constructionist theorist. In many ways, it is hard to understand why there has been such a slippage here; for though it has not been part of White's own project to locate the intersections he makes with postmodernism in contrast to other intersections, in the secondary descriptions of his work, one would usually expect this kind of clarification.

I am inclined to wonder again about the particular sociological contexts in the development of family therapy knowledge. The strength of the influence of social constructionism in North America has perhaps meant that any other postmodernist theorising of social context has tended to be seen as 'like' rather than different – a kind of cultural dilution effect, where major differences are not sufficiently discriminated. This may also be part of the general homogenising profile noted earlier with respect to family therapy's use of postmodernism. In North America, too, there seems to have been a more seamless popularity of narrative and social constructionist expressions of postmodernism. I say this as an outsider, and no doubt it misrepresents 'on the ground' family therapy, yet I think it is an accurate enough representation of ideas in the formal venue of major journal publications.

And as an outsider, one also notes the paradox of the extent to which what is posed as a 'critical other' position about theory and practice has come to be lodged so firmly with very little 'internal' critical discussion. In the major North American journals there is a near-absence of critique of social constructionist and narrative ideas from a position that is sympathetic to postmodernism – Lannaman's discussion stands out as an exception here (1998b). And Salvador Minuchin, a long-time leading figure in family therapy through his development of the structural model, seems almost single-handedly to have been left with the task of raising political and practice challenges (Minuchin 1991, 1998, 1999). He has done this from a position which has not been particularly sympathetic to postmodernism, and in many ways it has been all too easy to cast his critique as an 'external' modernist inspired attack.[6]

This situation stands in contrast to the British one. There the more low-key use of ideas of narrative and social constructionism may explain why there are no 'leading edge' advocates, and conversely it may explain why there seems to have been greater space for discussion of the benefits and difficulties of postmodernist ideas. *The Journal of Family Therapy*, for example, has published a number of articles across the past ten years that critically tackle aspects of postmodernism without falling into a polarised modernist-postmodernist debate (see for example Flaskas 1997b; Frosh 1995; Launer 1996; Pocock 1995; Speed 1991). My own home base is Australia, which in many ways is a kind of cross between all these situations. For in Australia there has been an environment of creativity around White's narrative therapy, and in terms of written discussions this has largely centred around the Dulwich Centre and its publications. The focus of the Dulwich Centre's project has been on generating narrative ideas rather than internal critique. Meanwhile other family therapy venues and literature have taken up postmodernist, constructionist and narrative ideas in their broader forms.

To some extent, the question of the specificity of the location of knowledge is really a secondary issue here, yet I have become more intrigued by it as I have tried to find my way around the complexity of the way in which family therapy has used construc-tionist and narrative ideas. In the process I have also become more aware of my own Australian vantage point on family therapy theory and the kind of outsider/insider status this gives me, perhaps particularly with respect to the North American literature and its importance. Though it is entirely obvious, I also want to say that my discussion of family therapy knowledge here is limited to its English-speaking environment, and I cannot even really conjecture what else might be said if I had a wider familiarity with European and South American traditions of family therapy. Of course, I could usefully repeat a version of this sentence in every chapter of this book, but instead I will restrict myself to saying it just here, as a clear acknowledgement of some of the limits of my own exploration.

Conclusion

This chapter has explored social constructionist ideas and the narrative metaphor as the major forms of expression of post-modernist ideas in family therapy. In mapping the influence of social constructionism, I was interested in drawing a distinction between its emphasis on how we come to construct our knowledge about the social world and the emphasis on the way in which the social world is itself created (and limited) by the process of construction. Both these emphases have been current in the family therapy discussions, which have been informed particularly by Harlene Anderson's work and in turn by her popularisation of Kenneth Gergen's theory of social constructionism.

In turning to the use of the narrative metaphor, the map became more complicated. I have tried to avoid using the unqualified singular term 'narrative therapy', because it collapses the different layers of the use of narrative ideas and also some of the important distinctions. Harlene Anderson's use of narrative in her collaborative language systems approach was considered alongside Michael White's narrative therapy. These two approaches were drawn as having quite different theory and practice flavours, and whereas Anderson centrally uses social constructionism, White has turned to Foucault's ideas, which offer a very different theorising of the relationship between social practice and language and discourse. Viewing the broader layer of the influence of narrative ideas threw up a range of ways in which postmodernist, narrative and social constructionist ideas have been framed.

Along the way I have signalled more critical and conditional discussions in the literature, but I have deliberately held back from discussing the content of these discussions in any detail. This is because I am now about to move on to an examination of some of the dilemmas and limits of constructionist and narrative ideas, and so it is more sensible to incorporate these discussions as we go. This next part of my project is organised, chapter by chapter, by themes that have been raised in my practice. These themes have been the questions of reality, of truth, and of understandings of self. Because my own momentum here comes from practice, I will not be using the form of the purely theoretical discussion that has characterised these last two chapters. I will move to a different kind of exploration, one which uses practice as a beginning point for theory challenge, as well as a point of return and reflection.

Notes

1 This is particularly the case in Gergen's work in the book *Realities and relationships: soundings in social construction* (1994).
2 In a recent article, Anderson (2001) has herself drawn out the significant similarities as well as the points of difference between her collaborative approach and the ideas and practices of Carl Rogers.

3 Foucault wrote across a thirty-year period, until his death in 1984. It is in the second period of his work (in the 1970s) that he developed his power/knowledge studies. This is the main period White draws on. Gordon's collection (1980) gives a good sense of Foucault's thinking during this period, and Foucault's two major works during this time were *Discipline and punish* (1979) and the first volume of *The history of sexuality* (1981). The third period of his studies shifted to an interest in governmentality of the self. See Flaskas and Humphreys (1993) for a fuller location.

4 There has been an interesting if peripheral debate about White's use of Foucault. There is no question that White believes his application of Foucault's work to individual experience to be quite harmonious with Foucault's project. However, this assumption has been challenged by both Vincent Fish (1993) and Deborah Luepnitz (1992), and there is a counter-response to Fish's critique by Fred Redekop (1995). I agree with Fish and Luepnitz on this point, and in this sense I think White's use of Foucault is somewhat maverick. Whether this affects the usefulness of White's ideas is another issue, though it does raise questions about mystification in the use of 'outside' theory.

5 Tom Anderson is perhaps best known for his work on the use of the reflecting team (Anderson 1987, 1990, 1995), and his themes of language and relationship (see Anderson 1992) resonate with some of the themes in Harlene Anderson's work.

6 See the recent debate in the *Journal of Marital and Family Therapy*, sparked by Minuchin's critical essay (1998), responded to by Anderson (1999), Combs and Freedman (1998), Sluzki (1998) and Tomm (1998), with a final reply by Minuchin (1999).

Chapter 4

The question of reality and realness

This is the first of three chapters to explore difficulties in the use of constructionist and narrative ideas in family therapy. Here I will be focusing on the question of reality and realness in therapy, while the next chapter examines the idea of truth particularly with respect to the individual's own experience of truth, and Chapter 6 turns to the narrative self and its potentials and limits as a set of ideas. The topics of reality, truth and self are closely related. Questions of reality and realness are bound up in ideas of truth, and to highlight the experience of reality and the process of claiming truth is to raise understandings of the nature of self. Themes come to be repeated and layered across the three chapters and core dilemmas of narrative and constructionist ideas are thrown into relief as the exploration progresses. This then lays the groundwork for an integration of these themes in Chapter 7.

In tackling the question of reality in this chapter, I will begin with some short descriptions of practice experience as an introduction to what is essentially a discussion of theory and ideas. The theory discussion will move from the problem of abandoning any idea of reality separate to our languaged constructions, to issues of the power of realness, and then to the task in therapy of becoming involved with realness. The final part of the theory discussion will consider the complexities of trying to theorise reality and the need to hold on to recursiveness rather than oppositionality in thinking about the nature of social reality. The pieces of practice experience are then used as a return point of reflection.

Some practice experience

Let me begin, then, with some pieces of practice.

First Piece

I see a family where the eldest child and only boy had been referred for verbally explosive fights with his mother. He is 13, and has two sisters 11 and eight. Though the boy is described by his mother as always being 'a bit of a firecracker', the fights have been much worse over the past year, coinciding with his beginning high school and his parents' separation. His mother understands the fights as being caused by her son's anger with her, as she believes that he blames her for the separation, and he consciously tries to punish and humiliate her. The mother had experienced her relationship with her husband as being emotionally abusive, and she says: 'he thinks he can just stand in for his father now'.

I am talking with the family about this, exploring the idea that the boy wants to humiliate his mother and that he blames her for the separation. The mother becomes exasperated, and turns directly to me to protest: 'it's not just an idea you know, it's what actually happens'.

Second Piece

I meet with a mother and her son who has just turned three. It is four days since the father committed suicide by shooting himself in the shed in the back yard of the family home. He had had a chronic physical illness and had never attempted suicide before. His wife returned home from work having collected the little boy from child care and walked through the garage to the shed to find the horror of her dead husband and his body. She is beside herself with grief and shock, and in the session she tells and retells the story of coming home and going toward the shed. Each time the story stops at the door of the shed, and she says: 'at least my son didn't see'. It is very hard to understand how the boy did not see, though entirely easy to understand why this would be an unbearable thought for the mother. Meanwhile, when we go to collect the boy who is waiting to join us, he is in the corner of the room quietly playing the game 'bang bang you're dead through the head'.

The woman wants just one session at the time but then rings me nearly three years later when the boy is finishing his kindergarten year at primary school. There is a nebulous kind of referral from the teacher, and she wants to come with her son for some help. She is uncertain about whether they should see me – she wonders whether seeing a man might be better for her son, but then again I had seen them both at the time. That I had seen them at the time seems in itself to be the greater source of ambivalence, but she decides that we should go ahead.

Third Piece

A 10-year-old girl is referred for behaviour problems at school, walking out of classes and 'disappearing'. She lives with her (paternal) grandmother and her 12-year-old sister on a public housing estate. Her mother died of a heroin overdose when the girl was six, and her father is in jail. The grandmother has looked after both girls on and off since they were babies and full-time since their mother died. I am told it is hard for the grandmother to get out because she has 'chest problems', but the local neighbourhood centre organises the transport for the first appointment. I go to get the family from the waiting room. The grandmother looks dreadfully unwell. I hear myself think: 'I hope she doesn't die on the way down the hall.' Throughout the session, I alternately hold-off and allow-in the thought that the grandmother will die. This thought is accompanied by a terrible feeling of catastrophe.

I can think of a great many practice situations which could be used to begin a theory discussion of reality and realness. These three families, among others, came to mind when I started to tackle the questions in this chapter and stayed in my mind as a rough reference point while the work proceeded. The quick introductions I have just given are simply fragments of the stories of the therapies and I am not attempting to do justice to them in this chapter. However, I would like these families, and my experience as a therapist in relation to them, to stay somewhere in the background as the chapter proceeds. I will be returning to them again later for further reflection after the theory discussion.

Reality, realness and power

As discussed in Chapter 2, much of the critical discussion around constructionist and postmodernist views of reality has centred on the difficulty of relativism. The concern has been that when you let go of a commitment to external reality and create a space for multiple (and supposedly equally valid) versions of reality, you also take away the capacity to make judgments between competing versions. There has been quite a lot of to-ing and fro-ing in this debate, which is certainly familiar to family therapy, and there is a lot at stake here. Personally I am inclined to think that in any committed human endeavour one would be hard-pushed to rely on constructionist ideas without an accompanying independent ethical position and preferably some ideas about power! But though the question of relativism is an important discussion, it is not the one which I am choosing to address here. My concern is not so much how you can identify and justify your choice of the 'right' reality. Rather, I have been bothered by other problems that emerge in any exclusive idea of a reality bounded and limited by our consciousness and constructions. In abandoning a core interest in the idea of an external reality, do we risk minimising the power of the human experience of reality and realness, and what might this mean for the process of therapy?

Let me say some things about the idea of an external reality. In the last chapter, I explored the layer of social constructionist ideas which moves beyond theorising the process of how we come to know the social world to theorising the limits and nature of the social world itself. In this layer of ideas, the interest in any external reality fades, and it is replaced by the interest in the process of the 'making' of reality through social construction in language. Following this through in terms of human experience, we live in socially constructed realities and these define the nature of the social world.

When I talk here of the idea of external reality, I am talking about an idea of a reality existing separately to our constructions and consciousness of it. As Daniel Levine notes in his discussion of socially constructed realities and psychoanalytic group processes, a concern with reality is a concern with the existence of a sphere outside the individual's subjective being. He writes:

> What makes something real, then, is this quality of being external. Put another way, what is real exists independently of our (individual) subjective attitude toward it. . . . To be external, and thus to endure independently of, also places reality outside the control of the subject (Levine 1999: 82).

Thus, this quality of externality does not have as its boundary a line between the individual and the social world. So it is not that what I am (my body, my thoughts, my self) is the internal reality and that the world 'out there' is the external reality. Rather, it is the extent to which a reality exists separate to my consciousness of it which gives it the quality of externality.

Now to think of the physical non-living world as being an external reality does not require too much of a leap. The table I am writing on, the computer I am using, the fan that is whirring in the background – all exist separately to my thoughts about them. I do not bring forth their reality, though I may use them all in particular ways. However, it begins to become more complex when we think of our bodies and their materiality. Let me try another 'and the ocean has a lot of water' sentence and say that the body exists only in the physical world and under particular conditions, that it is also a social body, and that it is always in relation to our psychological and emotional selves. Thinking about the materiality of the body, its relation to (and yet its independence from) our consciousness raises in a more difficult way the boundary of constructed and material reality.

Still more difficult again is the sphere of emotional and psychological reality and the intimate experience of relationships, and yet this is the land of the activity of therapy. In a paradoxical way, it is tempting to breathe a sigh of relief that at last we have reached a territory uncluttered by physicality and the material, where descriptions of socially constructed realities may best hold. Though this is the territory where social constructionism probably has the most to offer, it is at the same time the place where I become most worried about letting go of the idea of a reality separate to our languaged constructions and the realness of the social world.

I think it is quite possible, and indeed a part of ordinary human experience, to find ourselves unable to have languaged constructions of important realities that exist separate to our consciousness of them. We can often then come to know these things, but in the times of not knowing, these realities still exist independently of our knowledge of them. For example, I come to know that some of my family (including myself) find depression hard to meet and name, and we tend to take various tracks around it, and this affects how we relate. There are very good reasons for this situation, including migration on both sides of the family and a lot of dead babies on one side. When I come to 'know' this aspect of myself and my family in language, I feel as if I have always in some ways known it, or at least known the shape of its reality which has been painful.

Of course, the knowing is a process of construction, and the construction shapes how I relate to the reality and what I do with it and how I feel about it, and different people in my family would construct it in very different ways. The construction of it will change over time, and indeed, even at the one point in time, what it is we might say or not say about it would be a source of contention. Yet for all this – whether it is known, how it is known, how it is named, who thinks what, and the ripple effects – there still exists something in this landscape that has a realness separate to the consciousness of it, and indeed it has a realness before and after the languaging of it.

While writing this, I have been wondering whether part of the difficulty of claiming a commitment to an idea of external reality is that it sounds like you think that there are social and emotional realities outside the world of people. Of course, in postmodernist times and long before, this is a tautology. It has muddled in it, I think, the idea of 'external' as being 'external' to people, rather than the idea of it signalling an existence separate to our consciousness and languaged constructions. Perhaps the use of 'independent' rather than 'external' reality might make this clearer. One way or the other, though, I have been wanting simply to lay out here the idea of an external/independent reality and to move to the problems of abandoning the interest in this level of reality.

Of all the particular points of critique of postmodernist ideas in family therapy, the concern with the possibility of minimising or even negating realness has been the most consistent theme (see for example Held 1995; Lannamann 1998b; Larner 1994; Minuchin 1991; Pocock 1995; Speed 1991). John Lannamann addresses the issue of materiality, arguing that there are limits to the indeterminacy of meaning and that these limits are strongly in play in therapeutic settings. He highlights the responsive materiality of the body and develops the idea of relational embodiment as a way of meeting the interface of material and social realities (Lannamann 1998b). Lannamann's critique is located firmly within a commitment to the project of social constructionism.

Salvador Minuchin, on the other hand, makes an 'outsider' challenge to constructionist and postmodernist thinking and has argued passionately against the dangers of embracing constructionist and postmodernist ideas (Minuchin 1991). He particularly takes issue with the idea that we 'co-construct narratives' and the ability of this idea to meet the powerful social realities of poverty, oppressive regimes, and multi-layered institutional effects. In following through the experience of a woman (Marian) and her family caught up in an increasingly disastrous chain of events with the child welfare system, he notes the totalising effects on her reality, and comments:

> . . . a constructivist therapist who sees many people like Marian might have to restory the entire sociopolitical system as well. For Marian, and anyone who tries to work with her, this reality is not a construct; it is a stubbornly concrete world (Minuchin 1991: 50).

Bebe Speed, David Pocock and Glenn Larner also query the constructionist and postmodern understandings of reality in family therapy. Though tackling the concern in different ways, these writers all attempt to hold an appreciation of postmodernist ideas of realities alongside a demand for another kind of accounting of the real. Speed (1991) advocates a co-constructionist view of reality, Pocock (1995) writes of bridging modern and postmodern positions, while Larner (1994) uses some of Derrida's thinking to argue for a both/and 'paramodern' position in family therapy.

It is maybe not surprising that it has been this issue of reality and realness that has pressed most heavily in the critiques, for it raises important questions about politics and the implications for therapy. I do not share Minuchin's general stance of opposition to postmodernism, yet I cannot help responding to his words about a 'stubbornly concrete world'. Many of the families I have worked with in therapy have been living in chronic poverty; many have been on the receiving end of systemic racism across generations; many have histories of very real tragedy; and many have had destructive experiences with health, welfare and justice systems as well as seriously abusive experiences within family relationships. I have to say that I have often been struck more forcefully by the concrete realities of social existence than the limitless possibilities of construction in language. The latter idea can even come to have a rather bizarre quality, and yet at the same time the work in therapy is to try to find some leeway for change.

There is perhaps even an argument that in the most oppressive social and familial environments, the power of mediating those realities through language is itself dismantled. The repetition of colonial attacks on the languages of the colonised was scarcely accidental, but effectively attacking the language of protest does not take away the injustice. In abusive relationships within families, the silencing of a child from naming (or even having any words for) her abuse does not 'dis-solve' the problem. Indeed, some forms of abuse are forged very directly on the body, with constructions in language scarcely anywhere to be seen. It is hard to escape that we are in the territory of the relationships of power and both Lannamann (1998b) and Larner (1995) address this very directly, as does the feminist literature in family therapy which emerged so strongly in the 1980s (see for example Goldner 1985; Hare-Mustin 1986; Imber-Black 1986; MacKinnon and Miller 1987; Perelberg and Miller 1990; Taggart 1985).

None of this discussion takes away from the value of the ideas of the process of the social construction of knowledge or from the idea that social and emotional realities are always contextual and relational. However, social constructionism becomes problematic if we include the idea that language and social construction define the limits of the social world, and move away from an interest in an external or independent reality and the realness of this experience. Let me move at this point more directly to the process of therapy, and an exploration of the task in therapy of bearing witness to and becoming involved with realness.

Becoming involved with realness

Amaryll Perlesz, in a discussion of the complexity of bearing witness as a therapist to the experience of trauma, uses the idea of 'bearing witness' in both the senses of *giving and listening* to testimony' (emphasis in original, Perlesz 1999: 18). She quotes Dori Laub (1992), a psychoanalyst who has worked on a project of interviewing survivors of the Holocaust for video testimony archives, and who is herself a child survivor. Laub notes that the interviewer is at the same time both a witness to the person giving the testimony and that the witness also witnesses herself in the process of witnessing. I am interested in this part of the chapter in the idea of bearing witness to the power of realness in people's lives and becoming involved with realness, and in making links with the theory of narrative and constructed realities.

As noted previously, Stephen Frosh (1995) challenges the possibility of a postmodern psychotherapy, drawing attention to the emphases in postmodernist thinking that decentre the subject and any enduring meaningfulness in language. He argues that what is often called postmodern psychotherapy could more accurately be characterised as psychotherapy which shows a postmodern aware-ness of the complexity of truth and that the claiming of a post-modern status in an unproblematic way may be reneging on what we know and do as therapists in the context of therapy. He says: 'What we know is that it is generally helpful to make the best sense we can of our experience and to try to imagine alternatives' (Frosh 1995: 189), and 'we have to keep trying to help people live *as if meaning can survive*' (my emphasis, Frosh 1995: 190). Whereas Lannamann draws attention to the problems of the indeterminacy of meaning in constructionist ideas, Frosh draws attention to the problem of the fracturing of meaning in some postmodernist theory and the extent to which this flies in the face of psycho-therapy and its aims.

In another paper, Frosh (1997) gives a moving example of a supervision group of young psychologists working with a family following the murder of the children's father. He speaks of the way in which the mother's devastation may be cast in narrative terms, as may the children's experience of the loss of their father and of the mother they used to have. There is no great argument with the usefulness of the narrative frame, yet Frosh notes that what is omitted in this description is the experience of the therapist and the team, the pain of trying to connect and stay in touch with the realness of the family's experience, and the task of a respectful and mainly silent witnessing. He writes of this:

> . . . to the extent that narrative operates here, it is as a carrier of something else, not as an end in itself. It allows the family to feel in contact with – contacted by, one might say – the therapeutic team. In particular, it flags up the continuing attempt to maintain meaning, to understand. My claim is that the success of this piece of work depends not on the therapists' ability to generate new stories, but on their capacity to stay with the family's experience of the real . . . (Frosh 1997: 97).

Virginia Goldner, Gillian Walker and their colleagues at the Ackerman Institute in New York give descriptions of their work with heterosexual couples where the man is violent that evoke some similar themes (Goldner et al. 1990; Goldner 1998; Walker and Goldner 1995). Through this long-term project, they have come to argue the need for using multiple theory and practice perspectives, and their descriptions of their clinical work underline again and again their orientation to reaching for, and staying with, the experience of realness. They use as a central practice description the idea of bearing witness, not to stories as such, but to the speaking of the realness of experience for both the woman and the man (see for example Goldner 1998). Another North American contribution to understandings of witnessing has come from Kathy Weingarten (2000) in a recent article based on an address she gave in South Africa. She gives a moving discussion of the complexities of witnessing, using her own experience of illness and weaving through the task of witnessing political realities and their multiple traumas. She considers the dynamic of voice and silences in naming trauma and the differences in the witnessing position itself in terms of the witnesses' awareness/unawareness and empowerment/ disempowerment.

The quality of bearing witness to, and engaging with, realness and trauma is also at the heart of the description that Perlesz (1999) gives of working with families where one member has suffered traumatic brain injury (TBI). She discusses the difficulties of bearing witness and the frequency of the 'crises of witnessing'. Drawing some parallels between post-Holocaust experience and surviving the trauma of TBI, she considers the range and possibilities of human experience in meeting trauma. A contrast is made between Viktor Frankl's capacity for optimism in the bleakness of the concentration camp and Primo Levi's ongoing pessimism. This contrast is not made with a view to valorising optimism, but rather with a view to drawing the integrity of these different responses as part of the range of human responses to trauma.

Working from both clinical experience and empirical study with families with TBI, Perlesz notes that far from being an oppositional polarity, both hope and despair frequently co-exist, and continue to co-exist across time as the family comes to live with, and recover from, trauma. She writes of her work with a woman whose husband suffered TBI through a motor bike accident. Over time, many things changed for both the woman, her husband and in their relationship, and it is a moving story of personal growth and great resilience as the woman re-stories the trauma and its effects on her life and her relationships. This growth, however, did not shift her embedded clinical depression, and Perlesz notes that this is not unusual. The depression in itself bears testimony to the realness of the tragedy and the loss and can sit right alongside the reality of resilience and the capacity to find and create transcending meaning. The therapeutic task of bearing witness to trauma, then, often demands an involvement with the co-existing realness of hope and despair.

But what am I saying here about the theory of socially constructed and narrative realities? I will begin by noting that tragedy, trauma, abuse, mortality and the finiteness of our bodies have been circling as themes in the work I have just quoted from, and indeed in the pieces of practice which bookend this chapter. It seems that these kinds of situations stretch the limits of social constructionist and narrative descriptions, or at least make the weaknesses more visible. Constructionist descriptions begin to sound rather two-dimensional – perhaps serving as a polemic or strategic intervention in the theory of reality, rather than meeting the complexity of human experience. A critique, if you like, which has one eye all the time on countering another set of theory ideas rather than fully attending to understandings of the territory in question.

In trying to think about 'reality' in all the above therapy contexts, it is hard not to become more interested in the relationship between material and constructed realities and the experience of reality, rather than a debate between external *or* constructed reality. Narratives sometime do not just construct realities, they can also act to fragment realities. A narrative of resilience and hope that acts to censor a co-existing experience of despair does not just construct reality, it fragments that reality. And at times languaged construction dismantles reality. Listening to men who are violent in intimate relationships or who have routinely sexually abused children, and what they say about this, raises the power that their languaged constructions have to obliterate the consciousness of reality and not just construct it.

For me to say what I have just said requires allowing for the idea of an independent reality, and I have been arguing that we need to do this in order to bear witness to the realness of experience, and to become involved as therapists with realness in the process of therapy. At this point, though, I will move to the wider discussion of the complexity of theorising reality.

Theorising reality and its recursiveness

That family therapy has gravitated to Kenneth Gergen's version of social constructionism may turn out to be a very peculiar thing. I noted in the last chapter that he articulates constructionist ideas as a dynamic lens of critique and that this framing is clearly represented in the family therapy literature. In reading both *The saturated self* (1991) and *Realities and relationships* (1994) (Gergen 1991, 1994), one is struck by the strongly polemic tone, and it is easy to appreciate the powerfulness of Gergen's ideas as an intervention into dominant modernist knowledges of reality and the self. In the powerfulness of the critique, Gergen constructs his theory of socially constructed realities, as Barbara Held notes, at the extreme end of anti-realism (Held 1995).

Held also notes some of Gergen's comments on the implications of his ideas for the process of therapy, and in addition to the search for new solutions and richer narratives, he hopes for a 'thorough *relativizing* of experience' and a 'freeing from experience which comes from acceptance of unbounded relativity of meaning' (emphasis in original, Gergen and Kaye 1992: 183, quoted in Held 1995: 237). Gergen collaborates with therapists in his work but that he is not primarily a therapist himself may show in the enthusiasm of these comments. As a therapist, I find myself wondering who these clients might be that they would be freed by an acceptance of unbounded relativity of meaning. My mind becomes immediately peopled with clients I have seen struggling with conditions that attack the ability to hold on to the reality of their own experience, and I am thinking here especially of the disconnecting effects of abuse. However, at a broader sociological level, we could note once again that the social conditions of postmodernity have bred presentations of fragmentation, disconnection and alienation. Louis Sass (1992) comments on this symptomology of postmodernity, which in a paradoxical way is not necessarily met very well by postmodern ideas that breathe the same air.

Thankfully, the family therapists who have been interested in Gergen's ideas have not embraced these programmatic aims of therapy, and indeed Harlene Anderson's (1997) description of her own work shows conversely the sensitive attunement of client-focused practices. Held (1995) also notes that a number of family therapists who use Gergen's ideas present a more tentative anti-realist position than Gergen himself and that there is often an oscillation that shows itself in the narrative therapies between realism and anti-realism.

The question I am raising as to whether we locate Gergen's ideas primarily as a powerful theory critique or as a set of ideas finely tuned for use as theory for therapy, is in some ways a tangent – and in some ways not. It is not a tangent if we value the integrity of a set of ideas bound as critique, and if we appreciate in its own right, the project of a political intervention into dominant knowledges. Within the terms of this project, it is easier to have an unambivalent admiration for Gergen's development of social constructionist ideas. However, 'using' ideas for therapy contextualises knowledge in a very specific way. Whether we like it or not, we cannot stay in the waters of critique in the process of therapy, which requires a real involvement in experience and at the same time an ongoing tentativeness about ideas – this stands in contrast to other contexts of knowledge. An acknowledgement of the difference in context of knowledges should perhaps modify my own critique of Gergen's version of social constructionism, yet I still find myself wishing that family therapy had taken on ideas which allow more space for thinking about the relationship *between* constructed and independent reality.

Lannamann's discussion (1998b) wrestles with bringing a dialectic into the relationship of materiality and social construction. Gergen's commentary (1998) on Lannamann's paper is entitled 'The place of material in a constructed world', reasserting the primacy of constructed reality. Lannaman's rejoinder (1998a) is entitled 'The place of the constructed in a materially responsive world', holding out for the separate space of recursiveness and a different emphasis. The debate goes on within social constructionism and has been going on for some time. John Shotter is an important social constructionist theorist, and he very directly locates constructed reality in a dialectical relationship to the world. In laying out this relationship, he diagramatically relates ways of talking and the 'background' or 'world' and writes of 'this dialectical emphasis of *both* our making of, *and* being made by, our own social realities' (emphasis in original, Shotter 1993: 34).

Yet of course there are other postmodernist ideas outside social constructionism that give different possibilities for theorising the recursiveness of reality. In the last chapter, some differences between Michel Foucault's ideas and social constructionism were discussed, and power relations are in the foreground of his exploration which is the first. Another is his map of the recursiveness of everyday social practices and languaged discourse, and the strong emphasis he gives to social practices and the extent to which they *generate the conditions of possibility* for specific discourses. I also noted that Foucault's ideas have tended to become homogenised with social constructionism in family therapy discussions and that this reading perhaps relates to the North American context of the narrative and constructionist influence.

In the last chapter, the differences between Michel Foucault's ideas and social constructionist theory were discussed. That power relations are in the foreground of Foucault's ideas is one point of distinction. This commitment shows especially in the kind of questions White uses in tracking the conditions and the history of the 'old' (problem-saturated) narrative. It also shows in his insistent interest in the effects of institutional realities and practices. In some of the secondary renditions of White's work, though, this aspect of his therapy is downplayed, and it is the ideas relating to the encouragement of new narratives which are given centre stage.

The versions of White's ideas which privilege eliciting new narratives and de-emphasise the interest in the context of the 'old' story are the same versions where we find the merger with social constructionist theory. So we hit at this point the same difficulties with the unbounded possibilities of meaning. In addition, the practice of externalisation deliberately fans an opposition between 'new' and 'old' stories. I think there are some wider issues about externalisation as a technique and the extent to which it uses a frame of separation rather than a frame of integration with respect to experience (see Flaskas 2000). More specifically here, one can see the way in which a quite directive pursuit of a preferred new story may leave out, or split, co-existing realities of experience that do not fit neatly in a singular and preferred narrative form. Perlesz (1999) draws out, for example, the problem of the assumption of the oppositionality of hope and despair in the structure of some of White's externalisations.

But all this is to say that there are other possibilities for theorising the recursiveness of reality, that different emphases within social constructionism may give more leeway for exploring the dialectics of reality, and that Foucault's ideas also give more leeway. I had originally intended to wrap up my discussion at this point by referring to the realist-antirealist continuum so frequently used as a way of categorising theory about reality, and by aligning some of my arguments with a critical realist position.[1] Yet as the exploration of reality and realness has unfolded, this kind of conclusion is no longer so appealing. In a multiple-choice exam, when presented with a limited range of possible positions, I would probably tick the critical realist box, but reluctantly, because this identification is located somewhere between the oppositional poles of realism and anti-realism and there may be something quite impoverishing about staying within this polarity.[2]

The oppositionality of this discourse can fling us to ideas about social constructions defining the nature of the social world or back again to some reified notions of unattached objective social reality: a kind of ping-pong between objectless subjects and subjectless objects. Either way, we eclipse the space for an exploration of the recursive relationships of independent and constructed realities and the experience of realness which is so important in the context of therapy. I notice I have been adding in 'and the experience of realness' to the idea of the dialectics of independent and constructed realities, because otherwise there remains a dyadic quality which in itself may be a reflection of the impoverishment of the oppositional formulation.

It is time to draw a line under this part of the chapter, and having resisted the urge to tidy my own conclusions into a neat category, I will have to be content to make a general plea for holding the context of therapy and our involvement in the realness of human experience in our minds when we approach theorisations of reality. I have been arguing against negating the space for the reality of an independent social world outside our consciousness and constructions and for ideas that allow an interest in the relationship of independent and constructed realities and the experience of realness. To do this would mean moving outside a dyadic oppositional discourse and insisting on an interest in the recursive relationships of reality.

However, it is time now to suspend this discussion of theory, and return to practice.

Practice reflections

First Piece

There seems very little room for change in the fights between the 13-year-old boy and his mother, and the mother's belief that the boy is 'standing in for his father' and punishing and humiliating her is powerfully constructing in their relationship. The talking-around which is going on in the session is, of course, an

attempt to see if the idea can be loosened. The mother protests to me: 'it's not just an idea, you know, it's what actually
happens'. It is a moment that disconcerts, yet something is
being laid on the table again, only this time the mother says it
very directly to me, and we are involved in a conversation in
which something real is being struggled with. It seems that I
have cut across her experience in the way I have been talking:
that when she is fighting with the boy, she is 'actually' in the
same spot she was in when her husband was contemptuous of
her. I think that I have not really engaged sufficiently in the
reality of this for her or indeed in the reality of the spot the
boy is in when the fights get nasty, and he comes to experience
standing in for his father.

The question is not about whether the mother's belief about
the boy's position is correct; conversely, the process is not at
this moment about re-languaging an unhelpful idea and unhook-
ing it from their relationship. The mother rightly protests that I
need to involve myself in what actually happens. I need to take a
deep breath, look at her, and try to say something back about
what she has just said to me.

Second Piece

What are the emotional conditions for knowing, in language, a
terrible reality and a terrible loss? When I see the mother and
son four days after the father has committed suicide, it is
beyond the mother's human capacity to know that her son has
witnessed his father's bloody and destroyed body, and he is
(like her) having to make some sense of the terrible thing that
has happened. 'Bang bang you're dead through the head', played
out in front of the mother and another (me) is not a bad start,
yet this very graphic languaging goes alongside a 'not-being-
able-to-know'.

Nearly three years later, his teacher finds him a 'lovable boy'
who daydreams a bit in the kindergarten class and finds it hard
when he does not have her attention. His mother rings me,
uncertain whether I am the right person to see. I am not a man
(father?) and that I saw them at the time is complicated. It is
true that I have a crystal clear image in my mind of both the
mother and the son on that occasion, I know that the son knew
and that it was impossible for this to be known, and I have even
formed an image of the father, though more in his death in the

shed than in his life. Understandably, the mother both wants to see me and does not want to see me, but she takes a chance on it and the two of them end up coming in.

We go around various everyday things, how it has been for them, what it is like now. The anniversary of the father's death comes, and for the first time the mother takes her son to the grave and they put flowers on it (the last two anniversaries she has done this on her own). She hears a song on the radio on her way to work in which an adult son sings about his father who has died. She cries when she hears it, and it becomes a special song that her son comes to know as well.

There are various ways as a therapist in which I can language this process and my witnessing of it. It could certainly be described as a process for both the mother and the son of making, and coming to allow, meaning. But these are far from being unhinged constructions or preferred stories, and the difficulty is to create meanings as close to their reality as is humanly possible to bear. In the fabric of the attachment between them, the son can only know at a point that his mother can know, and she can only know when she thinks they can both survive. The holding environment of the therapy is important in this, and it is one step at a time.

Third Piece

The 10-year-old who 'disappears' from school, her stoical 12-year-old sister who tries to do the right thing and set an example, and the grandmother who physically struggles with every breath. I am appalled by the unmistakable reality of the grandmother's ill health, the catastrophe that her death would be for the girls who have already lived through their mother's death, and their father's coming and going in and out of jail. There is a minefield around any talk of the grandmother's health, and yet I know I am not the only one in the room who fears impending catastrophe. The presenting problem now seems scarcely symbolic, as the girl acts out disappearing in a concrete way several times a week at school. She brings them all in, and we sit there all knowing the fear, but finding it hard to know how to start naming it in any safe way.

There is the reality of the grandmother's health and her mortality, her experience of her own life, and the limits of her capacities now to mother her son's daughters. That she has been, and still is, a lifeline for the girls is clear. That she too may die and leave them is becoming a very painful possibility – one which is hard to know, yet increasingly cannot not be known. We embark on the work.

Of all the things that I might say about the therapeutic process with this family, in the context of this chapter I will simply note again the complexities of the realities which need to be faced. The notion of constructing transcending narratives misses out on the realness of the fear, pain and love, the actuality of them all facing a death, and for the girls, another irreversible loss. Yet the work is about human connections and emotional meanings, how something very difficult may come to be experienced, and how the girls may indeed live to 'tell the tale'.

Conclusion

This chapter has begun the work of a critical exploration of social constructionist and narrative ideas in the context of their use in family therapy. Practice formed the bookends of a discussion of theory. An argument was made for the importance of keeping some space for the existence of realities independent of our consciousness of them and for an adequate recognition of the power of the experience of realness. Attention was also paid to the very specific nature of the activity of therapy, to the task which faces us as therapists of becoming involved in, and bearing witness to, realness. This task makes particular demands on the theorising of reality and through this exploration I have been making a plea for moving beyond oppositional formulations of external versus constructed realities. Essentially, I am arguing for theorising the recursiveness of reality, and the interweaving relationships of independent and constructed realities in the experience of realness.

The question of reality and realness is central to the chapters that follow, and many of the explorations begun in this chapter are picked up again and elaborated from the different angles of truth and the nature of self.

Notes

1 See Andrew Collier's discussion (1998) of critical realism as a position in the constructionist/postmodernist debates.
2 Maritza Montero (1998) gives a very interesting discussion of the limits of monism and dualism in structuring critical exploration.

Chapter 5

Truth as a process

Whereas the last chapter began the critical exploration of post-modernist ideas in family therapy by focusing on questions of reality and realness, this chapter takes a different route and approaches the limits of postmodernism through an exploration of truth as a concept, as it relates to therapeutic concerns. The questions of truth and reality are intimately related, for within a modernist paradigm, 'truth' stands at the pinnacle of universal claims about the nature of reality. Moreover, at the level of individual experience, the idea of truth is usually accompanied by notes of certainty, closure and at times moralism. If the idea of independent realities has been jeopardised in the contemporary discourse of family therapy, then any commitment to the idea of truth has been well and truly banished.

Let me be clear from the start that I have no interest here in reviving the modernist notion of truth as objective, certain and universal. However, it seems to me to be crucial in therapy to hold some understanding of truth as an emotional and social process that enables a person to claim knowledge ('truth') about her or his experience. This chapter, then, is a plea for embracing the idea of truth as a process, rather than completely rejecting any notion of truth. The passion for reclaiming truth comes primarily from practice, and so it is practice that challenges theory. In the process of the exploration, new light is thrown on the complexities of postmodernism as a metaphor for therapy, and themes from Chapter 4 reappear as part of this discussion.

I will begin again by presenting some pieces of practice, stepping on to theory and an exploration of the relationship of systemic therapy and postmodernist ideas to the idea of truth. This will be done in three parts: the first part will map the paradox of modernist therapies with respect to the splitting of subject and object; the second part gives a potted history of modernist and postmodernist times in systemic therapy and the chequered career of truth; and the third part gives a critique of the concept of meaning that has come to subsume the idea of truth in contemporary systemic discourse. This critique leads to considering truth as an emotional and social process, and so the chapter returns to practice.

Some practice experience

First Piece

I see a young woman in individual therapy. She initially contacts me distressed about a 14-year-old girl with whom she is in love. The relationship with the girl seems very confused and full of pain for the young woman. Indeed she seems to be clouded in confusion about everything, and I feel like we are swimming in a very murky sea. Six months into the therapy, she brings me a letter in which she details scenes of sexual abuse of her sister by her father, and which she and her mother routinely witnessed. It seems like the tip of the iceberg. Later in the session I say: 'This is so abusive'. She looks directly at me, bewildered, and says: 'but how do you know?', which I find very moving.

Second Piece

I see a mother and daughter. They are referred to me by the child welfare department after the mother had contacted them, believing her daughter was being sexually abused by her father on access visits. The daughter is three, and after interviewing her, the protection workers see no evidence of abuse and think it may be a crisis that has been produced in the context of an access dispute. The child is unable to disclose verbally to anyone other than her mother, and in therapy I witness an enormous anxiety that comes in like a tidal wave around themes connected with her father. It is another 12 months before the access is completely stopped by the Family Court on the grounds of possible sexual abuse. Two years later, when the child is six, her father turns up outside her ballet class, and she sees him from the door. She says to me about this: 'I saw him, I couldn't think, I didn't know anything, I couldn't think, I didn't know, I couldn't think'.

Third Piece

I see a man who knows he was sexually abused by his father from when he was about three, probably until he was ten. Or at least, he knew what happened with his father, but he did not know it was abuse, he did not really think about it. Even now, he sometimes does not really recognise the word 'abuse' in relation to himself. He feels confused all the time, anxious, his thoughts can race, and sometimes it feels a bit crazy. Does his boss really fancy him, or is he just imagining it? Is his wife really in love with another man, or is he making a mountain out of a molehill? Again and again, he is immersed in the same dilemma – what is really going on? Is he imagining it? How bad is it? How will he know the truth? He is a very good thinker and forces himself to reason it through, but neither outcome of reason offers much consolation. No, nothing sinister is going on, he has just imagined it – and so he must be crazy. Yes, something is going on, he has not imagined it – and so his worst fear has come true.

It is perhaps not surprising that the people whose situations I have chosen to tell you about have all experienced early abuse, because early invasive abuse (physical, emotional, sexual) can crash through the capacity to know your own experience and claim some truth about it. Other traumatic experiences can have a similar effect. And indeed, even if you have been lucky enough not to be abused or severely traumatised, it can still be quite a struggle to come to a knowledge about your experience that allows for growth and that allows you to claim some sense of truth about your own emotional and social world. The ramifications of this struggle and how people engage with it, are often seen in couple and family relationships and in the difficulties presented in therapy.

This chapter is not about the specific situations of these people, nor their therapies, nor the experience of abuse and trauma. However, it is about the questions that confront me very directly as a therapist in these kinds of practice situations: how can I think about and understand the process of a person being able to claim a truth about her or his experience and what ideas about truth might be helpful in this therapeutic endeavour?

The paradox of modernist therapies

I would like to take a step back now to theory and explore the relationship of systemic therapy to the idea of truth. Most of the current discussions about postmodernist ideas in systemic therapy imply that before the postmodernist influence, systemic therapy fully embraced modernism and by implication, the modernist version of truth (see for example Doherty 1991; O'Hara and Anderson 1991; Parry 1991). I am not at all convinced of this and will begin by discussing the modernist version of truth and the paradox of trying to fit the activity of therapy into a modernist frame, before moving on to consider the peculiarities of the relationship of systemic therapy to the modernist idea of truth.

Within the modernist frame, truth takes up a specific position with respect to reality, knowledge and certainty. As has been discussed before, modernism is fully embedded in the premise that it is possible to split the subject who wants to know from the object (or that which we desire to know). Indeed, the project of modernism continuously replicates a subject-object split in all its practices. In the modernist desire to build knowledge about objective reality, truth has the privileged position of representing the most certain claims that may be made about the nature of the world, and those who can most legitimately claim to be the holders of truth are those who are most involved in producing 'objective' knowledge. Here we are in the domain of the expert and the specialist.

Though at a sociological level who gets to proclaim truth is always a contested field, power has been weighted heavily in favour of modernist credentials. This contest has major effects on individuals' lives, and indeed on their ability to claim truth about their own experience. Modernism has had very little to offer on the experience of claiming truth in relation to experience, and the territory of the intimate experience of truth has largely been confined to religious and spiritual discourse. Yet the intimate experience of claiming truth about one's own experience is very much a part of the therapeutic process.

In this way, far from modernism providing any easy fit as a metaphor for the field of therapy, it has always been quite problematic. For though it may be quite nice as a fantasy for the therapist to subscribe to the idea of objective knowledge and the tidy split of subject/object, and to bask as an expert in some space (or at least hope) of certainty, the activity of therapy itself has always made these categories very hard to sustain. Therapy is centrally about human experience. In the territory of understanding human experience, we are at one and the same time both the subject searching for understanding *and* the object to be understood. Thus, the foundational splitting of subject/object, as well as the external position of the observer, the framing of objective knowledge and the idea of certain truth, rapidly falls apart as any viable metaphor for the activity of therapy.

This may seem a dry and obscure point when phrased in the abstract, but in human experience and in the practice of therapy it comes very much to life. The sterility of trying to impose a modernist split of subject and object in the process of therapy is beautifully illustrated by Ronald Fraser. Fraser, a social historian by profession, describes his own experience of trying to piece together some truths of his life in his own analysis. He documents this dialogue with his analyst:

> 'I've always thought that history served one purpose at least. By discovering the major factors of change one could learn from them. The same ought to be true of an individual's history.'
> 'Yes . . . You want to be the subject of your history instead of the object you felt yourself to be', he (the analyst) replies warmly.
> 'The subject, yes – but also the object. It's the synthesis of the two, isn't it?'
> 'The author of your childhood then, the historian of your past' (Fraser 1984: 187).[1]

That we are able to be both authors *and* historians of our own experience (and use the freedom of moving between the two) lies at the heart of therapeutic possibility, and the process of understanding human experience is a synthesis of our experience of ourselves as both subject and object in relation to the world. It is interesting to see how different therapies have shown the tension of trying to exist within a modernist frame, despite the contradictions for both theory and practice. For example, Allan Parry identifies earlier Freudian psychoanalysis as the quintessential modernist project in the field of therapy (Parry 1991). This is correct at one level, yet at the same time Freudian psychoanalysis has a long history of difficulty in establishing its modernist credentials, and the debate around the legitimacy of its knowledge has centred exactly on the enmeshment of subject/object in the process of therapy.[2] The behavioural therapies stand as another example of the effects of this tension. Emerging directly from the disciplinary context of English-speaking psychology, the behavioural therapies show the pursuit of a pure modernist empiricism, where human experience needed to be reduced solely to observable behaviour in order to provide a legitimate focus for (modernist) 'scientific' knowledge.

But let me draw the discussion back to systemic family therapy and truth. I have been wanting to lay the groundwork for the argument that it is too simplistic to assume that before the influence of postmodernist ideas, systemic therapy fitted in any neat way into the modernist frame, even though it emerged in modernist times and reflected modernist assumptions. The tensions of describing the process of therapy in modernist terms and adhering to modernist ideas in the practice of therapy, showed in a number of ways in systemic therapy. We could begin a very long list: an ambivalence about 'scientific knowledge' (seen in the paucity of empirical research); a preference for 'how-to-do' knowledge; a use of 'outside' knowledges in fragmentary and often ideological ways; an intense pragmatism in practice . . . this list could go on, but the item I want to spotlight names the ambivalent relationship of systemic therapy to the modernist idea of truth. So let me pick up at this point and discuss directly the peculiarities of this relationship. This involves some history, which will necessarily be brief.

Truth in modernist and postmodernist times in systemic therapy

The frameworks that emerged in modernist times in systemic therapy have major differences, at the level of both theory and practice. It becomes impossible to make a sweeping generalisation about the relationship of (modernist) systemic therapy to (modernist) truth. For this reason, there is no shortcut to considering some representative models, and I will comment on the models of structural, strategic and Milan therapies with respect to their relationship to the idea of truth.

Perhaps the only systemic therapy model with a vaguely straightforward relationship to the modernist idea of truth has been structural family therapy. This is probably not surprising, for though structural therapy emerged in the 1960s, it was very much grounded in structural functionalism, the ruling 1950s American sociological paradigm. Production of expert 'truths' about families were enshrined in unproblematic diagnostic categories such as hierarchies, boundaries, enmeshed and disengaged relationships and the functions of family sub-systems. Yet the experience of people living within the dynamics that the structural categories attempted to define – and their 'truth' about that experience – was addressed only insofar as those truths acted to aid or hinder the goals of structural change. The tension, then, shown in the structural model was on the one hand a strong commitment to the knowledge and truths produced by the therapist but an indifference to the families' knowledge and truths. At the same time, this indifference was significantly tempered by a pragmatism about how those truths impacted on the therapy.

The paradox of this indifference-yet-pragmatism in relation to families' truths remains a practice theme throughout the first order therapies. Indeed the shift in the early strategic therapies with respect to truth was not a difference in how the therapist positioned herself/himself vis-à-vis the families' truths but rather a removal of the strictures on the therapist of diagnostic 'truths'. This gave the therapist a much greater flexibility, for there was no need to align with any diagnostic 'truth' unless that 'truth' was constructed specifically to induce a particular (behavioural) change. In this sense, the early strategic therapies extended the position of indifference-yet-pragmatism to the knowledge and truths of the therapist. This is not to say, of course, that there was any abandoning the position of the therapist's expertise. In terms of ethics, charges of opportunism dogged the earlier strategic therapies. I would argue that these charges related very directly to the tricky position of the therapist bearing no commitment to 'truth', yet introducing new meanings as if they were true and relying very directly on the families' desire for 'better' truths to sell a particular therapeutic intervention (Flaskas 1992).

The early 1980s saw the beginning of the influence of the Milan model. As a second order therapy, it reflected commitments to Bateson's later ideas. These commitments were shown in two ways. The first was a stringent adherence to circular causality as an explanatory frame for understanding human relationships (and relatedness). The second was a conceptualisation of the therapist-family system as the venue for therapeutic change: no longer could the therapist be seen as 'outside' the field of therapeutic change, although a belief was nonetheless maintained that in some way the therapist could remain 'meta' or neutral in the process of therapy. The other major shift, already discussed, was the centring of meaning in the way in which problems were understood and in therapeutic intervention and therapeutic change. This centring of meaning was very different from the behavioural focus of the earlier strategic therapies.

These points of difference brought a shift in the relationship to truth. With circular causality, the indifference to truth – both therapist truth and client truth – became a theory commitment not just a pragmatic issue of enabling therapeutic flexibility (though in practice, it was that as well). The opposition to any linear ideas of cause-and-effect began to more directly challenge fundamental modernist premises, and indeed Bateson's theory of circular causality was part of the movement away from traditional modernist understandings within the field of biology. The conceptualisation of the therapist-family system brought with it more finely tuned interactional techniques (for example, circular questioning) aimed at the production of different meanings. The privileging of meaning in the Milan model in one way gave a way of engaging very centrally (and not just pragmatically) with clients' truths, but in another way negated the idea of truth altogether by treating it simply as one-meaning-among-many-meanings.

Now I am well aware that this trip through the structural, early strategic and Milan models and their relationship to truth has been rushed and schematic. But hopefully, enough has been said to draw out the points that are central to the thesis of this part of the chapter. Though systemic therapy was conceived and developed within modernist times, it is simplistic to assume that it therefore bears an unambivalent relationship to the modernist equation of external reality, objective knowledge, certainty and truth. Indeed, the very activity of therapy flies in the face of the fundamental modernist assumption of the split between subject and object, which underlies the modernist equation. Like other therapies, systemic therapy historically shows the strains of existing within modernism. The peculiarities of its relationship to the modernist idea of truth may be seen in this context.

When we begin to look at some representative models of systemic therapy, it seems that the idea of truth does indeed have a chequered past. Structural therapy adopted a modernist idea of truth with respect to the therapist's truth, yet took an indifferent-yet-pragmatic position with respect to the clients' experience of truth. Strategic therapy kept a similar position to clients' truths, but pragmatically relieved the therapist of the necessity to look for truths. Milan therapy entered this field adding a theoretical and philosophical commitment to this lack of interest in truth. At the same time, though, by centring the idea of meaning, it promoted an explicit focus on clients' truth, but this truth was reduced and relegated to the category of meaning.

The move to postmodernist times and social constructionist and narrative ideas has further immersed us in the territory of meaning, and it has further removed us from a commitment to truth, modernist or otherwise. For following the idea that our beliefs are social constructions that emerge through relationship and that we live through socially constructed realities that give meaning to our experience, therapy is drawn as an activity that attempts to change the meanings or 'narrative realities' that have shaped our perception and experience of the emotional and social world. Life becomes a story of our experience, and that experience may be re-storied to allow different possibilities, both in terms of how we experience ourselves and how we experience ourselves in relation to others. This in turn creates different possibilities in our significant relationships.

Far more than in Milan therapy, there is an intense interest in individuals' understanding of their own experience in the stories and narratives they have come to have about themselves and their lives, and truths-as-narratives are centre stage. Indeed, some of the criticisms of the narrative therapies have been the extent to which meaning becomes the province of individual stories, with the family somehow being left conceptually, and in practice, as a conglomeration of individual stories (echoing a much earlier conception of the family as the sum of individual psyches). Salvador Minuchin has challenged this aspect of narrative therapies head-on in asking the question, 'where is the family in narrative family therapy?' (1998). The tension of holding individual experience and yet creating the theory and practice space for working with relationship and relationship patterns is scarcely new to family therapy, and indeed each framework has wrestled with it in different ways. It is interesting to note the pendulum swing between the critique of Milan therapy as decentring individual experience and the critique of the narrative therapies as privileging individual experience at the expense of here-and-now relational processes.

Despite this pendulum swing, for the purposes of my discussion here, I am more interested in the commonality of the way in which meaning has come to occupy the place of truth through the Milan and narrative therapies. Regardless of the question of the individualising focus, meaning as constructed meanings and narrative meanings is in the foreground of the narrative therapies, paralleling very closely the extent to which meaning is in the foreground of Milan therapy.

The limits of meaning: losing subject and object

There has been no question throughout this book that social constructionist ideas and the narrative metaphor give an appealing and often very useful description of therapy. However, it is a description that begins to take some dents in practice when clients bring experiences in their lives which have not simply been 'narrative realities' or 'constructed realities' but oppressive and abusive realities that have carried a destructive force separate to the meanings and narratives attached to them. We find ourselves back again with the questions raised in Chapter 4 about independent realities, but now there is the opportunity to specifically examine the dominance of 'meaning' as an alternate theory construction.

Of course meanings can change, and some stories are much better to live with than others.[3] And at the risk of repeating arguments already made, let us note again that meanings and stories and social constructions are not free-floating and limitless, and they are created and exist in a very particular environment of specific events, actions and people. Moreover, generally people do not take on new meanings or re-story their experience simply on the basis of the freeing potential of the new story for their interpersonal lives. This may be an okay enough description for the agenda of therapists, but it is not a very good description of clients' experience of 're-storying', or indeed of therapists' experience of coming to have more helpful meanings about their own lives.

The prospect of a rather appalling gap between what therapists might say about the process of therapy and what clients (and indeed ourselves as clients) might say about the experience of therapy is of course scarcely confined to the narrative therapies. My point here though is to draw attention to the lived experience of therapy versus the programmatic theory descriptions. If we leave aside programmatic descriptions, it may be easier to recognise the desire that most of us have to hold meanings against 'the facts' of our experience in all its specificity, to see how new meanings 'measure up' as better descriptions of that experience, and to form an attachment to meanings which 'speak to' something very important about our experience.

To bring this discussion back to the concept of meaning as it is currently being framed in systemic therapy, meaning as a concept is insufficiently attached to an idea of reality that allows for the existence of an independent world, separate to the meanings we come to have of it. This point is raised by Edwin Harari, who reflects on the fit between the metaphor of narrative and the experience of holocaust survivors:

> The narrative approaches . . . have provided bridges between subjective experiences and the social and historical contexts in which subjectivity is constructed. However, the Holocaust survivor is not just telling a story. He/she is also a witness, someone who is giving testimony. For the survivor, there is not a plurality of readings or multiple perspectives of equivalent validity from which the story may be told. The survivors fear that if the *empirical links between life experience and its narration* are modified in any way their story will be lost (my emphasis, Harari 1995: 13).

However, if meaning as a concept is insufficiently attached to an idea of (independent) reality, it is also insufficiently attached to the process of a person measuring meanings against her/his specific experience, privileging and cherishing meanings that speak to the heart of that experience. Of course, it is very hard for people to privilege and cherish meanings that speak to the heart of an abusive experience which still feels unbearably toxic. Two of the clients I have written about have been in exactly this spot. In this position, the problem then is not so much to come to have a different story, rather to come to have a story that can actually begin to 'hold' because it has some congruence with both the events that occurred and the reality of the person's subjective experience of those events.

In theory terms, we could summarise these points by saying that meaning as a concept is insufficiently attached to either the object of experience or the subject who is trying to understand her/his experience. We may be out of the modernist problem of a complete splitting of subject and object, but somehow we are now in a territory where neither object nor subject has any reliable space, nor indeed any recursive space in-between. Meanings (narrative and constructed) can too easily become free-floating ideas, any ideas, as long as they are more helpful. As a concept, then, the current framing of meaning misses out both the realness of experience and the process of a person coming to claim knowledge/ truth about their experience.

The last three sections have covered quite a lot of ground. I have argued that the idea of 'modernist' therapy has always been paradoxical, for the splitting of subject and object inherent in modernism makes us hard-pressed to describe an activity centrally about human experience in which therapists and clients are at one and the same time both subject and object. More specifically, a pure form of modernist truth is hard to find even in the first order systemic therapies. In the second order therapies, Milan and the narrative therapies centre meaning, albeit in different ways, and it is meaning that has taken over the space of (modernist) truth. I have been arguing that there are some problems in relying solely on the concept of meaning in the activity of therapy, for meaning lacks a commitment to the object of experience in all its specificity and reality, and it also lacks commitment to the subject of the person and her or his struggle to make sense of the reality of their experience in the world. Whereas modernism posed a problem of splitting subject and object, we can find ourselves losing subject and object in a too rigorous adherence to the postmodernist metaphor.

So what might all this mean about the idea of truth? For all its historical shortcomings and the bad press it has received in its modernist form, an idea of truth may still be worth salvaging. As a concept, truth has some advantages that are lacking in the idea of meaning currently being used in postmodernist systemic discourse. With truth, there is at least a subject and an object and the space in-between. A person struggles to find and know some truths. Those truths are about her or his experience in the world. Experience is not the province of either (just) subjectivity or (just) objectivity – it is indeed, repeating Fraser's words, a synthesis of the two (Fraser 1984). To speak of a person's 'search for meaning' with respect to experience is fine as a description a lot of the time in therapy, but for as long as 'meaning' is not understood as being grounded in a reality of experience, and to the extent that the process of the individual's attachment to meaning is not encompassed, it can also fail as an adequate description for therapy.

To begin to think of truth as an emotional and social process, is to begin to think of the necessary conditions for a person being able to claim a sense of truth about her/his own experience, the barriers that make this difficult, the relationship between truth and the sense of self, and the effect of truths on both the sense of self and other people. Truth may no longer be objective, certain and universal, but it may be claimed as a process which is experiential, conditional and multi-levelled. And so to return to practice and the beginning of this chapter . . .

Practice reflections

First Piece

As her therapist, I find myself asking what would need to happen for the young woman in love with the 14-year-old girl to be able to make sense of her feelings, to survive the pain, and to steer some course through the potential for abuse of the girl in this relationship? How much of the woman's experience of sexual abuse in her family needs to be known and thought about, and connected with feelings more specific, more painful and probably far more dangerous than bewilderment? In what ways may she be able to come to a knowledge for herself of her own experience, a knowledge which does not negate the reality of the past but which also allows some freedom from it? And what truths can she both find and allow that remain faithful to her knowledge of the world and her sense of self?

Second Piece

The 6-year-old child says of the experience of suddenly seeing her father who sexually abused her when she was very little: 'I saw him, I couldn't think, I didn't know, I couldn't think, I didn't know'. She says it with surprise, and in the telling of the story there is also a sense of some revelation. I am reminded of the waves of wordless anxiety I had witnessed when she was three, and I am moved by her ability now to recount the meeting with him, to wrap some words around her experience, and indeed to tell a story in which she is able to keep a sense of herself and her own world at the centre. But I think she is doing more than telling a story – I think she is claiming some truth.

Third Piece

In many ways, it is not hard to understand the terrifying dilemma of the man who lurches between fearing the worst and believing he is crazy. But it is very hard to find a platform of safety from which he can make some sense of it all. I can keep a memory of this person being sexually abused for many years as a child, but although he is able to hold the memory of the events, he is unable to hold the associations of abuse. I could beat him around the head with the reality of it (and it is interesting how often I feel like doing just that), but this is clearly a useless (if not abusive) course, and instead we track around the day-to-day confusions while he tries to find some space for something other than (another's) abuse or (his) craziness. It is slow work, a long way from any magical reframes or alternate stories, and it is sustained by a hope we both share that it may be possible for him to come to know something and not be terrified of it. It may be that if he could hold an attachment to some knowledge/truth that matched reality and his experience, there would be some relief from the ricocheting between abuse and craziness.

Conclusion

Beginning and ending with practice, this chapter has extended the discussion of the limits of postmodernism by exploring the idea of truth. The traditional position of truth within the modernist frame was juxtaposed with the paradox of the modernist metaphor for the activity of therapy, and the complexity of the relationship of the earlier systemic therapies to truth was drawn in this context. In considering the postmodernist shift, I have argued that it is the concept of meaning that currently assumes the position of the idea of truth in systemic discourse. However, meaning has its limits, for at the moment this concept is insufficiently attached to either an idea of reality or to an understanding of a person's relationship to knowledge about her or his own experience. If you like, neither object nor subject has any reliable place in the attempt to understand experience. An argument was made that the modernist metaphor that splits subject and object has been replaced by the postmodernist metaphor that loses subject and object, and both metaphors are limited in understanding human experience and describing the activity of therapy.

In struggling to understand human experience and therapeutic change, the idea of truth potentially has more to offer. If we abandon the modernist notion of truth as objective, certain and universal, and we try to think of truth as experiential, conditional and multi-levelled, it becomes possible to begin to think about the process of a person being able to claim knowledge/truth about her or his experience in the world. In short, my argument has been that we may need to reclaim the idea of truth as an emotional and social process, and that to do this is one way of recentring human experience.

This chapter's exploration of truth flowed from the previous consideration of the question of reality and realness. In turn, the question of truth and the experience of truth begs an attention to how we think of 'self'. A critical discussion of the narrative self is the subject of the next chapter, which adds the final tier to this examination of problematic themes in postmodernist ideas in therapy.

Notes

1 John Shotter (1993) gives an interesting discussion of Fraser's description of his own therapy and gives a longer quotation of this dialogue, p. 127.
2 The essays in Wollheim (1974) and Wollheim and Hopkins (1982) give a good flavour of the history of this debate.
3 See Pocock (1995) for a discussion of possible therapeutic criteria for 'better' stories that bridge modernist and postmodernist understandings.

Chapter 6

The narrative self and the limits of language

The last two chapters have explored concerns with reality and truth in the use of postmodernist ideas. This chapter takes as its focus the idea of self, how it has been reconceptualised in postmodernist narrative thinking and some of the questions that may be raised about this.

Though the concept of self has been heavily trawled in psychoanalysis, psychology and psychiatry, historically there has been a vacuum in systemic therapy. Indeed, it has only been in the move to social constructionist and narrative ideas that we have seen the start of an interest in theory of self, and the beginning literature so far is not all of a piece. A number of writers have addressed the specific theme of the self of the therapist (Hardham 1996; Hildebrand and Speed 1995; Paterson 1996). There has also been an interest in the idea of culture, personhood and the self (Krause 1995), and in the construction of the gendered self (Hart 1996). In developing his version of narrative therapy, Michael White (1991, 1993, 1997) has been writing of practices of the self and the centrality of lived experience, while Harlene Anderson (1997) writes of the 'narrative self' in her development of postmodern ideas and collaborative language systems therapy. Robert Rosenbaum and John Dyckman (1995) have argued very strongly for a fluid and relational concept of self as consistent with constructionist and contextualist thinking, and Mona DeKovan Fishbane (2001) explores relational narratives of the self within the broader shifts to relational perspectives.

In considering the ideas of self that flow from social constructionist theory and the metaphor of narrative, I would like to map the postmodern narrative self, with its ideas of self as relational, always fluid, and existing in narrative form. These ideas open a number of doors in terms of both theory and practice, and yet at the same time it could be problematic to rely exclusively on them. The chapter moves once more from practice to theory and back again. In doing so, I will be arguing that we may need to allow for the dialectic of self as both relational and autonomous, that there are very real boundaries on the fluidity of self, and that narrative may perhaps more usefully be thought of as one form of knowing the self, rather than the total way of 'being' self.

The discussion, then, will explore the possibilities and the limits of narrative and social constructionism with respect to the self. As a development of the discussions in the last two chapters, core themes are now resonating strongly. The same limits with respect to reality and truth show themselves again in the theory around self. The inherent paradox of the oppositional positioning of postmodernism shows itself in the particularity of ideas on self, and the limits of life defined by language emerge very clearly.

Some practice experience

But let me begin with some practice. I am choosing to write of a boy and his family who came to mind when I was trying to think about the implications of the narrative self.

I receive a referral of a 13-year-old boy in his first year at a working class boys high school. He is being picked on – the referrer said that he was being called a 'sissy', but it was clear enough that this was a euphemism for 'fucking poofter'. He is the youngest in a family of four children, something of an afterthought, the next sister is 20, then another sister 22, then a brother 25.

He comes to the first session with his mother and father, and I go to get them from the waiting room. He is sitting between his parents, very much belonging to them. His parents are in their mid-50s, but somehow look older, and they both give the impression of being tired and kind and unassuming and ground down.

The boy looks almost incongruously alive and beautiful. It is winter, and he is wearing a black coat and black jeans, and a long woollen scarf that is a deep and vivid blue. He looks pretty fabulous, but let me just say that his choice of aesthetics is not what you would call common in his particular peer group.

There have been, and still are, a number of tragedies in his family. His brother has been institutionalised from the age of three: he had been born with a serious disability and was institutionalised when the mother had what she called 'a nervous breakdown' in the year after the next child was born. The pain and guilt the parents (and especially the mother) felt about his institutionalisation are still very present. His older sister, 22, is doing well in her last year at university. His younger sister, 20, is sometimes living at home and sometimes not. She has had problems since she was 18 and has spent short periods hospitalised in a psychiatric unit. The father had been diagnosed three years before as having a potentially fatal illness, but is now symptom-free.

Of course, there are many things I could write about my experience of work with this family. But I am giving this small description here at the beginning of this chapter, because the boy's struggle to develop and claim a sense of himself was striking, and in this particular struggle, gender and sexuality were in the foreground. The terrain he faced in coming to develop and know his sexual and gendered 'self' was complex, both within his family and in the wider social context.

I would like this boy and his family to sit somewhere in the background of what will now be a theory discussion, and I will come back to them again later as a point of reflection.

The narrative self

To give a flavour of the emerging ideas on the narrative self, I will begin with three quotes:

> to appreciate the possibility (of a new reality of self), two preliminary steps are useful: first to bid final adieu to the concrete entity of self, and then to trace the reconstruction of self as relationship . . . (Gergen 1991: 140).

> the self is not an accrual of experience but an ongoing, ever-changing manifestation of potentiality . . . (Rosenbaum and Dyckman 1995: 28).

> (postmodernism) invites a shift from a modernist logical understanding (verifiable reality) of self to a narrative social understanding (constructed reality) of self . . . the self becomes a narrative self . . . (Anderson 1997: 212).

This section lays out the thinking reflected in these quotes. The theorising of the narrative self has followed the usual sequence of beginning a postmodernist investigation by identifying and rejecting the modernist view. And so, I will follow this sequence here too, and unfold the ideas of the narrative self by marking first the point of departure from modernist ideas of self.

Within modernist discourse, the self was theorised as an essential self and an interior self, capable of being thought about as a separate form. If our ideas become limited to this modernist conception which sees self as a thing to be discovered, then it can very easily become a thing which we can either have too much of, or too little of: 'she's full of herself', 'he doesn't have a very strong self'. Rosenbaum and Dyckman (1995) argue that it is the thinking of self as a 'thing' that informs what they call the 'deficit hypothesis' of psychotherapies which aim to build and strengthen the self.

Alongside this modernist understanding of self as a concrete entity is the idea of the self as the property of the individual – herself, myself, himself. The self is a core self, capable of being described in terms of fixed qualities. We can see this operating in everyday discourse: 'he's always been a very jealous type, even as a little boy', 'she's a prickly type, but really very generous deep down'. We also see it operating very powerfully in the formal elaboration of the knowledges of psychology, psychiatry and particularly the earlier forms of psychoanalysis. One need only think of the detail of personality tests and the categorisation of personality 'types', the construction and enumeration of the psychiatric categories of abnormality, and the Freudian topographic model of self as id-ego-superego: although specifying the self in different ways, all these knowledges pose the self as a core self with fixed qualities.

It is this modernist picture of the self as autonomous, fixed, and existing as the internal property of the individual that becomes the oppositional pole for postmodernist framings of self which have begun to be articulated within systemic therapy. Rather than the self as autonomous, the self becomes a relational self; rather than the self being fixed, the self is a self-in-action, always fluid, always being created and re-created in relationship with others; rather than existing as the internal property of the individual, the self becomes a narrative self, storied and constructed in language with others.

I will expand this counter-view by turning to the work of Anderson, because it has been so influential in family therapy, and she gives an excellent elaboration of 'the wonderment of the postmodern narrative self' (Anderson 1997: 212). Anderson plots the move from an opposition to the modernist idea of a discoverable autonomous self, to locate the narrative self as 'always engaged in conversational becoming, constructed and reconstructed through continuous interactions, through relationships' (Anderson 1997: 216). She argues strongly against the notion of a core self, pointing to the way in which self is made up of many narratives across time and across experiences. The self becomes a story teller, and self-identity is created in the constancy of a continuing process of narrative that creates and changes the experience of self. Identity, then, is about narrative fluidity and the process of continuing stories about self, rather than being 'fixed' in terms of personality traits or attributions. Language is central in this, because narratives are constructed in language and in dialogue with others, and so '. . . self (and other) is a created concept, a created narrative, linguistically constructed and existing in dialogue and in relationship. . . . In this view, *the self is a dialogical-narrative self*' (emphasis in original; Anderson 1997: 220).

The ideas Anderson brings together here reflect a particular body and mix of postmodernist thinking. She draws on philosophical discussions of narrative (for example, Gadamer 1975; Kerby 1991; Madison 1988), on the narrative turn within psychoanalysis (for example, Schafer 1992; Spence 1982), as well as on social constructionism. However, it is social constructionism which most strongly shapes her theorisation of the narrative self, and as one would expect from my earlier discussion, one sees the very important influence of the work of Kenneth Gergen. We can remember that Gergen's work emphasises the communal structuring of the social world through language and the centrality of the relational context of *languaged* narratives in the structuring and transforming of self. The very particular knowledge milieu of Anderson's version of the narrative self becomes important later on in this chapter, when I consider the question of the role of language in narrative and in the experience of self. But I have perhaps skipped ahead of myself here, for it remains in this section to underline the usefulness – indeed, the creative potential – of the emerging ideas on the self in both systemic theory and practice.

At the level of theory, the elaboration of the relational and narrative self enriches the reworking and development of systemic ideas within the current framing of the systems metaphor. The very idea of the relational self cuts completely across the previous polarised dichotomy of the cybernetic metaphor in which the self becomes the opposite pole to the system. Rather than the self being assumed in its (modernist) non-relational form, the self becomes a radically relational concept. Moreover, rather than 'the system' assuming the static and arbitrary boundary of 'the family', the parameters of narrative and constructionist thinking allow a multi-levelled engagement with the social context of personal life. The experience of self is inextricably linked with the many sources of narrative understandings. These include the narratives we come to have of ourselves formed in the most intimate context of family relationships; the social narratives we come to have of ourselves in terms of gender, sexuality, culture and class; and the narratives we come to have of ourselves which are forged in the powerful institutional realities of the welfare and health systems, schools and workplaces, justice and prison systems.

At the level of practice, meaning becomes central in ideas about the narrative self, and it is of course meaning which has come to be the practice focus of the relational and contextual understandings of the 'new' systems metaphor. In keeping with the shifts in theory, ideas about the relational and narrative self make it possible to attend in practice to the experience of self in relationships, both in the intimacy of interpersonal relationships and in the complexity of social relationships. Thus, there is no longer an 'either/or' in the practice attention to self or system: exploring the experience of self in therapy is exploring the relational system. This practice shift allows a freedom for a more intimate and personal engagement in therapy, while the idea of the fluidity of self in the constancy of the narrative process seems to give some space for the hopefulness that underpins all therapeutic activity. Therapeutic change, then, does not need to rest on strategising behavioural shifts, but therapeutic change can align itself with the continual narrative process of the changing meanings we give to our lives and to ourselves in relation to others.

Clearly, what I have just written on the contributions of the postmodern narrative self to theory and practice is a very general sketch, and one needs to turn to the detail of the ideas of narrative therapists in order to see the way they fit theory to the 'how to' of practice (Anderson 1997; Epston and White 1989, 1992; Freedman and Combs 1996; Gilligan and Price 1993; Hoffman 1990, 1993; McNamee and Gergen 1992; Parry and Doan 1994; White 1989,

1991, 1995, 1997; Zimmerman and Dickerson 1994). However, I think enough has been written in this section to point to the emerging ideas of self as relational, fluid and existing in narrative, and to their theory and practice potential. At this stage in the chapter, I will move to exploring the limits of these ideas.

Questioning the limits of the narrative self

In the literature popularising French postmodernist thinking in the 1980s, the verbs 'to problematise' and 'to interrogate' were used with almost alarming frequency. I have often wondered whether something got lost in translation, as the words never seemed to quite fit in an English-speaking context. However, they attempted to describe a method of exploration in which a particular idea or set of ideas was placed in a problematic frame in order to spark a different kind of thinking. A to-and-fro pattern of questioning became a common feature of the methodology.

From the 1990s, the descriptions 'to problematise' and 'to interrogate' have become replaced by the increasingly generic use of 'to deconstruct'. Often, of course, 'to deconstruct' has come to mean not too much more than the rather unglamorous 'let's try to have a bit of a think about this', and I do want to try to have a think about the postmodern narrative self. The deconstructive method of taking ideas apart does not so much attract me for this task. However, I am interested in using the method of thinking around and about something by asking questions of it, and by stepping outside an acceptance of the idea by bringing other issues to bear on it – 'problematise' is a better description, if we could bear to use the word. I will use this method here, and the specific questions I want to ask closely follow the central ideas of the postmodern narrative self: must the relational self be always oppositionally positioned in relation to the autonomous self? How fluid is self? And in what sense is the self narrative?

The first question

In tackling the question of the oppositional positioning of the autonomous and the relational self, one faces nothing less than the oppositional polarity of postmodernism to modernism. The laying-out in this chapter of the idea of the narrative self is quite faithful to its development within the narrative literature, and the narrative relational self is itself defined against the autonomous self, which is seen to be a central part of the modernist framing of self. Thus, in being stuck with an essentially oppositional dualism, we are bumping into one of the central paradoxes of postmodernist theorising: for though the momentum of postmodernism is to allow multiple possibilities against the foundational limits of modernism, it is embedded itself in an oppositional dualism that leads to a dynamic of censorship of 'modernist' conceptions. Whether we like it or not, we are indeed in an oppositional domain.

This paradox becomes a limit for theorising in the field of therapy, for like all practice disciplines, we have a primary allegiance to practice experience in our relationship to theory, and we may want to retain and move between dualities in our work with clients, rather than accept the restrictions of an oppositional framing. To become more specific, one of the difficulties of completely abandoning any idea of the autonomous self is that we may be moving away from the lived experience of self. Fishbane (2001) warns against the moving away from lived experience that can happen if we negate the language of self. Indeed, in elaborating her understandings of the relational self, she stresses the importance of acknowledging 'an individual's own experience and history' as well as the individual's 'relational embeddedness' (Fishbane 2001: 276).

To acknowledge lived experience is central to therapy, and this may involve acknowledging the complexity of self in its autonomous as well as its relational dimensions. For all the consciousness we may have of changes in our 'selves' over time, and for all the hope we may have for those changes to be a continuous process, most of us hold an image of ourselves across time and place and relationships – a sense of core self, a sense of a physical and emotional being, an embodied self, an experience of the autonomous self. At the risk of sounding old-fashioned and pathologising, I would like to comment that it does not generally bode well for relationships with either our-'selves' or others, if we are not able to have this experience.

The dichotomizing and resultant censorship of the autonomous self in the narrative concept of self raises the issue of the extent to which any set of theory ideas is 'experience-near' or 'experience-distant'. In therapy, practice gives us the possibility of moving between these two different levels of theory understandings. It is interesting that in the systemic literature, there is very little discussion of the extent to which new theory ideas are 'experience-near' in meeting lived experience. Indeed, of all the systemic narrative writing, Michael White's work stands out for his attempts in his theory and practice discussions to create a space for, and commitment to, lived experience. That this gets him into hot water on the theory front has been noted by Vincent Fish (1993), who points out that White's commitment to Foucault's ideas, for all their value, does not sit comfortably with his interest in lived experience. But then, Foucault was not a therapist (and would probably roll in his grave at the very thought), whereas Michael White is. Perhaps allowing some discordancies to sit side by side in therapy may be alright as long as they are acknowledged, and as long as there are not too many grand claims made, modernist style, about the resulting knowledge concoction meeting all practice and theory needs.

To take up the space in theory to allow for movement between oppositional dualities in the interests of meeting therapy experience is not a new idea, and indeed Tom Paterson (1996) directly argues this with respect to the duality of the autonomous and relational self in his discussion of the therapeutic relationship. In considering Bateson's thinking, Paterson notes that traditionally in systemic theory there have been ideas about both the autonomous aspects of a system and the relational aspects of a system. He parallels this with the dual psychoanalytic ideas of the autonomous self and the relational self, the autonomous self describing the core of an individual's personhood that retains a stability of form across time and relationships, and the relational self describing the intersubjective nature of the sense of self and personhood. Paterson argues that the autonomous self and the relational self are different levels of description of the self, rather than different ideas about the self, and as such they are both useful in therapy practice.

With Paterson, I would make a plea for the flexibility of using different levels of description of the self in therapy theory. Rather than accepting the embedded censorship of the postmodernist metaphor, holding some idea of the autonomous self alongside the idea of the relational self may meet more fully the complexities of the lived experience of self as being both changing and unchanging. The issue of lived experience will come up again in this consideration of the limits of the narrative postmodern self, but at this point it is time to move to the second question: how fluid is self?

The second question

Again, we face a question which takes us directly to the tension of the oppositionality of the postmodernist metaphor, for the emphasis on the fluidity of the (narrative) self counters the modernist construct of the fixed self. The limits of the idea of the fixed self scarcely need noting, for the activity of therapy intrinsically holds some hope for change, and in this sense any belief in (only) the fixed self is antithetical to therapy. However, despite this, to swing to an unqualified idea of the fluidity of self risks flying in the face of the specificity and realness of personal histories, and the complexities and power of social and interpersonal contexts.

This point needs expansion. Though in the narrative metaphor the 'I' becomes a storyteller, some care is needed in adding conditions about the fluidity of self through our changing stories. To say that we do not have limitless possibilities in storying our lives is to acknowledge that we come to exist in very particular landscapes of events, people, ideas and histories. In the same way that we do not have limitless stories about our lives, we do not have limitless possibilities in our experience of our selves. In the therapeutic attempt to cultivate the capacities for different understandings of our lives and our selves, it might be important to re-emphasise that capacities go alongside limits, and both capacities and limits are forged in the realness of experience. The idea of the fluidity of self emphasises the capacities, but fluidity is boundaried and not free-floating. Following this train of thought, we can revisit the quote from Rosenbaum and Dyckman: 'the self is not an accrual of experience but an ongoing, ever-changing manifestation of potentiality' (Rosenbaum and Dyckman 1995: 28). In reading it again, we may ask the questions: why the need to force this duality? and could the self be thought of as *both* an accrual of experience *and* an ongoing ever-changing manifestation of potentiality? Surely allowing this duality gives us more leeway in thinking about our clients and their involvement in the process of therapy?

I am aware that in making these points about limits on the fluidity of self, I have been talking about the realness of the landscapes in which our selves emerge and exist, and the realness of the social and interpersonal contexts in which we live. In this way, the discussion is very directly related to my earlier discussion of reality and the question of the real, only here the spotlight is specifically on the landscapes in which we come to develop and know our 'selves', and on the realness of the experience of self.

This issue of realness and its sufficient acknowledgment has also troubled some narrative theorists. Michael Freeman from psychology has contributed significant ideas around narrative and the self, and has this to say as a rider in his work:

> What I have found in recent years, however – and I realize that this may sound entirely too 'personal' for some – is that many of the claims we have been considering do not do justice to the life I live: even if the furniture of the world doesn't exist apart from the words I use to speak it, I still bump into it all the time (Freeman 1993: 13).

He goes on to say with respect to the self:

> More to the point, even if my 'self', fleeting as it is, doesn't exist apart from my consciousness of it, from my own narrative imagination, indeed from my own *belief* in its very existence, it is nonetheless eminently real and – within limits – eminently knowable (emphasis in original, Freeman 1993: 13).

Closer to home in the family therapy literature, John Lannamann (1998b) gives a fascinating discussion of the problem of materiality in social constructionist ideas, and some of his arguments have already been discussed in Chapter 3. Lannamann begins his article with a description of his own Christian Science upbringing and the very real perils of negating material reality through insistence on the power of mind. He discusses resonances of this system of thinking with tendencies in systemic therapy and social constructionism to privilege the power of meaning without an adequate theory of power and materiality. Like Freeman, Lannamann's critique is hardly a call for a return to modernist ideas of self. Indeed, his own interest is specifically in the materiality of the body, and his project is to create some space within a social constructionist framework for an idea of relational embodiment. Lannamann's concerted attempt to theorise a relational idea of the body that does not negate its materiality has intersections with contemporary theorising within anthropology. Here one sees an engagement with the complexity of the lived body and its relation to the social experience of self and a thoroughgoing commitment to theorising the social dimensions of the body without denying its materiality (see Lock 1993).

The vexing issue in the concern for realness and materiality is the role of language and the way in which it is understood within narrative theory, and more specifically here, within the postmodern narrative self. Language and its role in the realness of self relates to the third and final question to be considered in this section: in what sense is the self narrative?

The third question

Language is central in narrative theory, for storying is a linguistic activity. Having said this, there are different ways in which language and its relation to the world may be understood, and major differences in understandings about this shows itself in the different versions of both social constructionist and narrative theory. In Chapter 3, a distinction was made between the idea that we can only ever know the social world and ourselves through language versus the idea that the social world and our-'selves' exist only within the confines of language. The first idea sees knowledge of the world being always mediated, constructed and expressed in language; the second idea sees language itself as providing the boundaries of the social world. This distinction was drawn in my first presentation of constructionist ideas – that one layer theorises how we come to know the world, while the other (far more contentious) layer theorises the limits and the nature of the social world itself.

As noted earlier, Gergen's work encompasses both layers, as does Anderson's popularisation of his ideas. To revisit a quote from Anderson, 'the self is a dialogical-narrative self' (Anderson 1997: 220), and as such 'self' exists within the bounds of language. Yet though this radical constructionist version is currently the primary influence in systemic discussions, the controversy shows in the wider constructionist and narrative milieu. The query precisely concerns the position of language in narrative – the relationship between 'word and world'. Anthony Kerby (1991), a philosopher, writes of the continuum in narrative theory between a position that sees language as expressing and constructing experience and a position that sees language as the definitive limits of what we call experience. He quotes Louis Mink as being at one extreme on this continuum. Here the argument is that stories are told, rather than lived, and it is in storying that we attribute beginnings, middles and ends, rather than this ordering occurring in our lived experience. Amongst others, Gergen stands at the other end of the continuum, and the painting of the postmodern narrative self reflects the view of life within language versus language within life.

If we accept with Gergen that 'theories of the self are, after all, nothing less than definitions of what it is to be human' (Gergen 1994: 211), and if we are interested in lived experience and the context of therapeutic practice, then there are many invitations to take a more qualified view of the role of language than the one which is dominant in much of the systemic narrative theorising. In wanting to hold out for a more complex relationship between world and word than extreme positions which privilege *either* word *or* world, I am not making a novel plea. Again, within narrative theory itself there is a struggle to meet this issue. Freeman wants to embrace the primacy of word 'without losing world in the process' (Freeman 1993: 16). Kerby (1991) tries to deepen narrative possibilities by allowing for implicit as well as explicit narratives and writes of 'pre-narrative experience', of 'quasi-narratives', and of the conditions of possibility of stories of the self.

In many ways, both Freeman and Kerby are extending narrative to allow some space for pre-languaged and unlanguaged experience, and one sees something of the same attempts beginning to emerge in the narrative discussions in family therapy. There has been little fanfare about these attempts, yet it is important to note that there is beginning to be some discussion of the idea of stories-not-yet told (see for example Anderson 1997). Kathy Weingarten's very recent work takes this a number of steps further, as she works with the ideas of silence and voice and the therapeutic task of witnessing the deep memory of trauma which may lie in the body rather than the zone of conscious and worded stories (see for example Weingarten 2000).

In many ways, these early moves are perhaps not too surprising, for in therapy practice I think one is hard-pushed not to acknowledge unlanguaged experience. Early patterns of attachment and separation are experienced outside words, and in contemporary attachment theory there are discussions of the way in which pre-languaged relational interactions become 'prototypes' of narratives of attachment (Stern 1998). Indeed, if for a moment we step outside the narrative interest in language as a social process, and think of language as also an emotional process, then we can recognise that developmentally there needs to be some early sense of 'I' in order for us to embark on the path of trying to represent experience through language.

Though it is rarely named, this other dichotomy of representation versus construction in language lies nestled in the narrative self. Representation in language is the process of trying to find words to describe and convey our experience – to 'wrap some words' around it. A recognition that the process of representation is itself a mediating and constructing experience need not wipe out a recognition of the human desire to name and communicate our experience. This momentum is centrally about self: we come to know and have a relationship with ourselves through our experience and the words we use to represent it. It is also centrally about others – in the process of representation in language, we use words to try to relate our experience to others. Again and again, we find ourselves facing a peculiar impoverishment in postmodern dichotomizing. Louis Sass in a critique of postmodernist and constructionist ideas in psychoanalysis speaks of the effect of a 'thinning or hollowing-out of existence' (Sass 1992: 178). The idea that language can both represent *and* construct experience holds far more possibilities than forcing a choice between the two.

To say that language remains throughout life a primary way of representing our experience and a primary way in which we 'hold' our knowledge and consciousness of the world, is not the same as saying there is no experience outside language. Many of us in therapy retain an interest in thinking about what psychoanalyst Christopher Bollas (1987) calls 'the unthought known', the awareness we hold outside consciousness of attachment patterns and the awareness of unconscious narratives. Existential crises, trauma and life-threatening times also bring emotional experience which, far from being only brought into existence by words, exist outside words and are often shared outside words with others even though we may also try to use words to represent those moments.

The family therapist, Anita Morawetz, wrote very movingly in the *Australian and New Zealand Journal of Family Therapy* of her own experience in this territory during the course of the illness of which she died (Morawetz 1987). There is beginning to be a tentative engagement with issues of spirituality in the family therapy literature (see the recent special feature in the *Journal of Marital and Family Therapy*[1]; Adams 1995, 1996; Aponte 1998; Walsh

1999). In its broadest sense we could think of spirituality as the domain of transcending meanings of existence. In one of the earlier discussions, Neil Adams (1996) entwined his interest in spirituality with his work with people with head injuries and their families. This linking is unlikely to be coincidental. Mortality, tragedy and absolute physical limits are often not well met by words. At one level, it is perhaps the very finiteness of our bodies and their capacities that speaks of an existence of self that does not reside solely within the territory of language.

But what does all this mean with respect to the question: in what sense is the self narrative? The consideration of language, its role in narrative, and its relation to the realness of our lived experience challenges the position of a postmodern narrative self in which the self only exists within narrative dialogue. Some narrative theorists try to meet the issue of unlanguaged experience by extending the very concept of narrative to include forms of narrative outside languaged narrative. To allow for unlanguaged and pre-languaged experience requires at the very least that we add a limit to the narrative self. The limit is this: rather than thinking of narrative as the sole source of creating and defining self, it may be more helpful (in therapy at least) for us to think of narrative as being one way in which we come to know self. With respect to the use of social constructionist ideas, this would be an argument for using it more as a theory of social knowledge rather than a theory of the nature of the social world.

To think of narrative as a way of *knowing* self rather than the exclusive way of *being* self is not to bounce back to a modernist idea of the essential self, for we can continue to think of knowledge as a powerful social process which in itself comes to construct experience, but which is also constructed by experience. To allow for a recursiveness of narrative knowing and experience gives much greater space for the lived experience of the realness of being human in all its complexity, fragility and finiteness.

Practice reflections

We come then to the end of the discussion prompted by questions of the postmodern narrative self, and this may be summarised fairly swiftly.

Must the relational self be always oppositionally positioned in relation to the autonomous self? No, not if we refuse to be bound by the oppositionality of postmodernism, and treat the autonomous and relational self as different kinds of descriptions of self which each meet something about the complexity of lived experience.

How fluid is self? The self is not boundlessly fluid, but our stories of ourselves, and our experience of ourselves, are both created and limited by the very real and very particular landscapes of people and events and social practices and ideas in which we live. The self is fluid, but it also bound by what Kerby (1991) calls the 'historicity and connectedness' of human experience.

In what sense is the self narrative? A lot of systemic narrative theorising has followed Gergen in taking a position that privileges languaged narrative, and which locates the existence of the social world and self within language. If in therapy we decide we want to allow for the domain of pre-languaged and unlanguaged experience, then there needs to be some qualification. Perhaps we could think of narrative as being one way in which we come to know self, rather than languaged narrative coming to define the total way of 'being' self.

At this point, I would like to remember the 13-year-old boy, his struggle with coming to claim and know himself in a hostile peer environment, his parents' struggle with their unconditional desire for him to be happy, and their bewilderment about what they should or could do for him.

I want to note that in the year I met with the family, a number of gay men were murdered. In fact, in that year in Sydney, in the category of 'murder by strangers', gay men outnumbered women as victims of murder. In some of the murders, the men were brutally killed by groups of teenage boys from different schools (public and private), and the killings were planned and took the form of a night out on the town. There was something extremely disturbing about all this when it emerged in the press, and some of the boys were finally charged and convicted. One of the boys was himself secretly gay, and this was reported during the trial.

But what am I saying here as a family therapist? I want to underline that there was a very real and a very complex landscape in this boy's life at the point at which he was coming to develop and know his own sexuality, and himself as a young man. The family landscape was real and complex. If he were to come to know himself as homosexual, would this come to be felt (/constructed) as another burdening tragedy within the family? What might it mean for him to claim a joyful and alive sexuality with his brother in an institution and his father still under threat of death? Who would it be disloyal to, and who might it be loyal to, in a family with very close and very loving connections? And in this family in which difference has been experienced and marked as tragedy, what might his own forms of masculinity and creativity come to mean?

The social landscape was also real and complex. How dangerous was the violence in his harassment at school, and how did it restrict and intimidate his capacity to develop and know himself? How damaging could that homophobia be to his private knowledge of self? How was he going to come to have the space to find and claim whatever form of sexuality was emerging in an environment of harassment by peers and reports of brutal gay murders by schoolboys?

Was the boy's self relational? Well yes of course, but he was also struggling to claim and hold onto a sense of individuality of self in a complex relational field: am I pushing it too much here to say that he may need some space to develop a sense of his autonomous self?

Could we speak of the fluidity of self? Well yes, but for goodness sake, there are not limitless stories available for this boy, but rather a quite hard task of coming to have a good story for himself in a very particular context. Contexts are not determining, but they do shape the form and possibilities of stories, and dangers and possibilities need to be navigated.

Does the self only reside in dialogue and narrative? Please, can we just take the 'only' out of this question! Disability and mortality do not only reside in dialogue and narrative, murder does not only reside in dialogue and narrative. And am I just being an incurable non-postmodernist romantic in thinking that human connectedness and love, and sexual desire and creativity and joy, do not only reside in dialogue and narrative?

Conclusion

This chapter has explored the ideas of the narrative self. In their departure from modernist conceptions of the self, social construc-tionist ideas draw a self which is relational rather than auto-nomous, fluid rather than fixed, and existing in narrative rather than as an interior self. These ideas open up a number of important possibilities, yet any exclusive reliance on them can impoverish our capacity in therapy to meet the complexity of the lived experience of self.

In this exploration of the self, a number of themes about the limits of postmodernist ideas came to be repeated. The problem of the oppositional framing of postmodernist ideas appeared once more, with the momentum to force choices in modernist-postmodernist dichotomies reducing the complexity of the experience of the self. The centrality of the issue of realness, and the difficulties inherent in negating realness and materiality, also reappeared. Yet in adding to the discussions of reality and truth, the examination of the difficulties of the narrative self threw into more striking relief the whole question of the limits of language.

This chapter ends the exploration of specific problematic areas in postmodernist ideas, and yet there is more to be said about the themes that have been emerging. The next chapter integrates the discussion of the critical limits of postmodernist ideas, referring back to the initial overview of postmodernism, and it also paves the way for the intersection of selected ideas from psychoanalysis as an alternate understanding of intersubjectivity.

Note

1 A number of articles were published as part of the special feature on 'Spirituality and Family Therapy' in the *Journal of Marital and Family Therapy* (2000) (26)2.

Chapter 7

Postmodernist limits and intersecting psychoanalytic ideas

So far I have chosen to approach the limits of postmodernist ideas through the specific explorations of reality and realness, truth, and ideas of self. These three different routes have led to some converging themes, as well as particular themes yielded by the topic at hand. In this chapter, I would like to draw these themes together and reflect back on the initial discussions of postmodernism and narrative and social constructionist ideas. This part of the work is both summary and synthesis, and allows me to clarify the focus of the remainder of the book.

The structure of the chapter is simple enough and in three parts. The first section takes on the task of synthesising the discussion of postmodernist limits. The second section argues for an appreciation of, rather than adherence to, postmodernist ideas in family therapy, and begs the question of alternate ways of theorising intersubjectivity which replicate neither the limits of modernist ideas, nor the restraints of family therapy's current use of postmodernist ideas. In the final section, as I intend to intersect very particular ideas from psychoanalysis in extending this discussion in the next chapters, I lay out the purpose and limits of my own use of psychoanalytic ideas and the specific choices I will be making in 'using' psychoanalytic ideas within the different therapeutic interests of systemic family therapy.

Postmodernist limits

At the risk of repetition, let me simply list core themes from each of the last three chapters, as preparation for ordering a discussion of the limits of postmodernist ideas.

Chapter 4 tackled the dichotomy of constructed versus independent realities and made the case that constructionist theory potentially negates the existence of independent realities. As well, though, and equally importantly in the field of therapy, these ideas have the possibility of negating the power of independent realities and the experience of realness in people's lives. Through the discussion, an argument was made for moving beyond the forced duality of constructed versus independent realities. At least for the purposes of knowledge for therapy, it may be useful to hold the space for theorising both constructed and independent realities, the relationship between them, and the relationship of these realities to the human experience of realness and the therapeutic task of witnessing realness.

Chapter 5 took up the postmodernist opposition to notions of truth and the implicit constructionist dichotomy of truth versus constructed meaning. Through a local exploration of the positioning of truth in the first order systemic therapies, an argument was made that pure modernist truth – objective, certain and universal – has never found an easy home in family therapy. This was seen to be a small reflection of the extent to which the modernist metaphor with its subject/object split has never adequately described the activity of psychotherapy where we are at one and the same time both subject *and* object. On the other hand, the construct of free-floating meaning as an alternative to (modernist) truth was also seen to be inadequate, as long as it remains insufficiently connected to independent realities and to the subjective experience of truth. An argument was made that if we move beyond the inadequacy of modernist truth and the inadequacy of subjectless/objectless meaning, we may be freed to begin to theorise truth as conditional and multi-levelled, and these kinds of understandings may be more finely tuned to the experience of therapy.

Chapter 6 addressed 'self' and the way in which it has been theorised within constructionist and narrative discourse. Here we ran head-on into another series of postmodernist-modernist oppositionalities, with the relational self being pitted against the autonomous self, the fluid self being held against the fixed self, and with the idea of the narrative form of self being opposed to the interior form of self. Each of these dualities was explored in turn, and a strong plea was made for allowing a both/and position in thinking about self in the field of therapy. It was also suggested that narrative may more usefully be cast as a way of 'knowing' self, and this is an alternative to the more grandiose claim that narrative defines self. Through this discussion, the constructionist/narrative privileging of language was encountered once again, and this time round, there was a clearer identification of the dichotomy created around language itself – does language construct or represent experience? Again, the impoverishment of this choice was highlighted, and I wanted to keep some space for thinking about the recursive way in which language both represents and constructs human experience, and in turn the way in which language itself both constructs and is constructed by experience.

So much for the summary, so let me now weave these themes back to the earlier presentations of postmodernism, and narrative and constructionist ideas. Here there are four major themes, and I will take each of them in turn.

The pattern of forced dualities in narrative/ constructionist discourse mirrors the oppositional parameters of postmodernism itself

In the explorations of reality, truth and self, we found ourselves confronting again and again the forced dualities of narrative and constructionist discourse. This pattern itself was one of the most striking aspects of the investigation, and it links very strongly with the history and positioning of postmodernism. If postmodernism has as its own social context the move beyond (and reaction against) modernism, then it is not surprising that postmodern theorising follows in its wake.

I had spoken of the springboard of postmodern theorising: what is postmodernism? not this, not modernism . . . then what? This is a springboard to the initial identification of postmodernist– modernist polarities, and then gives momentum for theorising the postmodernist side of the polarity. We saw this in the construction of the dualisms of independent versus constructed realities, (modernist) truth versus constructed meaning, the autonomous self versus the narrative self. Within each dualism, the narrative and constructionist theorising within family therapy has attended to the postmodernist polarity, with the modernist polarity being set up as the oppositional 'other'.

There is no question about the creativity of this form of theorising, and yet it also has limits. For when theory is generated from within an oppositional dualism, there is a paradoxical tendency for it to stay within the same parameters, indeed to continually recreate those parameters. Thus, one side of the polarity remains defined by the other, and it can become quite difficult to step outside the parameters of the polarity itself. Michel Foucault has made this argument very persuasively in his work on normalisation, as he traced the way in which the emergence and proliferation of practices and discourses of abnormality very powerfully created the governmentality of normalisation.[1] If you like, the abnormal creates and defines the normal, which creates and defines the abnormal.

As a pattern of theorising then, oppositional polarities create a circular movement that continues to reaffirm the polarities of the oppositional form. In this way, polarities themselves often create a surprisingly totalising field, and this can lead to what Maritza Montero refers to as the miseries of monism and dualism (Montero 1998: 120). Yet we are often stuck within polarities, precisely because we are ourselves part of the context that produces them. Nevertheless, it would be nice to struggle for a recursive rather than a circular movement, for a recursive movement allows a mutual and spiralling interaction that allows the possibility of something different to emerge. The idea of dialectics addresses this emergent potential and looking for the relationship *between* oppositionalities allows some relief from the ping-pong of the either/or. Thus, in thinking about knowledge for therapy, it may be more fruitful to explore the relationship *between* independent and constructed realities, truth and constructed meaning, and the autonomous self and the narrative self. Our core interest in human experience, indeed in the experience of the process of therapy, provides a continuous orientation to this endeavour.

A plea for avoiding radically anti-realist versions of constructionist ideas and the acontextual privileging of language

Having just made a plea for moving beyond oppositional polarities, I would also like to make a very particular plea for avoiding the more radically anti-realist versions of constructionist ideas. I began my exploration with reality and realness, and the concerns for the sufficient acknowledgement of independent realities and the power of the experience of realness. In exploring truth and self, these same concerns appeared again, and they remained central in each discussion. The shift from truth to free-floating meaning was identified as problematic exactly because it could negate realities and the subjective experience of claiming truth about realness. Ideas about the narrative self could slide into a territory where self was too fluid and too unhinged from the realities of social and emotional existence, and indeed we could begin to get a picture of self which flies in the face of the human experience of needing to hold on to continuity of self yet not be imprisoned by it. Thus, in terms of the overall investigation, it is the themes around reality and realness which form the heart of the critique.

In my initial presentation of narrative and constructionist ideas, I was interested in tracing the way in which these ideas have appeared and been used in the family therapy discussions. I drew a distinction between versions of social constructionism that primarily theorise the way in which we construct our *knowledge about* the world and the more radical emphasis within social constructionism which theorises that the social world itself lies fully within the ambit and processes of social construction. I also noted the influence in family therapy of Kenneth Gergen's ideas and the extent to which his theory elaborates a radically anti-realist version of social constructionism and offers a thoroughgoing critique of mainstream discourse. There is strong integrity in Gergen's ideas as critique, yet the extreme anti-realism embedded in his version of social constructionism does not seem especially well suited to the project of therapy and knowledge for therapy.

When I argued that we might do better to think of narrative as a way of knowing rather than being self, I was essentially arguing for the more limited use of social constructionist ideas and its focus on the way in which we come to know the world we are experiencing. However, there are also other theories and other debates within postmodernist social theory that draw attention to the problem of negating realness and realities. Indeed, the debates around the privileging of language and the way in which language is understood centre precisely on the problem of the relationship between 'world and word'. Following Gergen, much of the post-modernist family therapy discussion has privileged language and allowed it to take the weight of defining social and emotional existence. This is a limitation if we want to allow for the possibility of social and emotional life outside conscious languaged experience. The privileging also tends to reify language, as if it has some separateness to the social and emotional processes which create it. In a peculiar way, then, we can come to have an acontextual vision of language nestled in a theory which stresses context and relationship.

Missing objects, missing subjects: the postmodernist problem of fragmentation

We are at a point now of revisiting the earlier discussion of debates about postmodernist fragmentation and decentring the subject. The relationship of subject/object was addressed very explicitly in the chapter on truth, while the discussions of reality and self criss-crossed this territory.

In considering truth, the modernist assumption of truth was weighed against the idea of constructed meaning, where we found ourselves in danger of losing the connection between our constructions and the world, and down playing the emotional and social process of claiming 'truth'/knowledge about ourselves-in-the-world. From the modernist dilemma of splitting subject and object, we were now in the postmodernist dilemma of missing subjects and objects. This identification resonated with the previous discussion of reality and realness and the concern that the modernist assumptions of external reality left us with subjectless objects, while the negation of the idea of independent realities potentially left us with objectless subjects. The same theme appeared again in the discussion of ideas of self. The concern here was very directly with the possibility of losing the continuity of self and the realness of the relationship of the self to independent realities. Staying only on the narrative side of the narrative polarities of self risked a decentred and free-floating vision of the subject and of the experience of subjectivity.

Of course, the investigation of reality, truth and self was inspired by concerns about the 'fit' of postmodernism and the activity of therapy, and family therapy in particular. In turn, it produced very specific discussions which nonetheless resonate with the wider debates about postmodernism. If you like, we found the local version of the wider concerns about fragmentation and decentring the subject. We can now reflect these back and underline those concerns, having found their relevance for our own milieu.

Spinning out to the edges of postmodernist possibilities, decentring and dislocating subject and object, fragmenting the possibility of holding steady any relationships between – all this makes for profound disruptions to the modernist project. In other intellectual struggles, in other political environments, or as a politics of intellectual and cultural protest, we would have fewer concerns about it all. It is also possible to argue that postmodernism provides a useful description of the social conditions of postmodernity and the contemporary experience of fragmented subjectivities for those of us who are living within its time and space. I am easily persuaded by both arguments, and on most days I may be inclined to make them myself.

However, I am least likely to embrace these arguments when I am in the therapy room or confronting my own experience of the joys and pain and ordinariness of human relationships and the limits of my own existence. I might add that I am also not moved to embrace them when faced with the very real effects of abusive relationships, social injustice and political oppression. More specifically in terms of my project here about knowledge for therapy, I think that one really cannot afford to be missing subjects and objects. Thinking back again to the wider context of postmodernist debates discussed in Chapter 2, I am thus more drawn to the arguments for moving beyond fragmentation toward dialogue and for holding some space for being in relationship with postmodernism rather than immersing ourselves in it.

Reasserting the primacy of our interests in the experience of therapy

My last theme needs very little elaboration. I know it would be wrong to say that the investigation of reality, truth and self led to the 'conclusion' that we should allow the experience of therapy to act as a compass in guiding our engagement with postmodernist ideas, for it is quite clear that the investigation was launched from this position. It was therapy practice which challenged theory, not the other way round. Yet I think that when we followed through the challenge and explored constructionist and narrative ideas as they have been used in family therapy theory, we were left with a stronger argument for reasserting the primacy of our interests in therapy.

One could read the project of my investigation as critique, and to some extent it is just that. Yet I find this particular end point to be hopeful and, in an odd way, rather consoling. To choose to hold our position as therapists as central in approaching knowledge gives a guide to moving beyond theory-driven oppositionalities. It also allows a clearer space for holding human experience as a legitimate focus of our endeavours with knowledge and for retaining (rather than relinquishing) our central interest in the subject and subjectivity in all its messiness. When we talk of the idea of allowing a space for being in relationship with postmodernism and postmodernity, it allows us to claim the very particular space we occupy in this relationship when we face the task of generating understandings about the experience and process of therapy.

Appreciating postmodernism, addressing its limits

But let me draw a line now under the discussion of the limits of postmodernism. That it has been a critical discussion there can be no doubt, yet I have also been showing an ambivalence about labelling it as critique. I mentioned this ambivalence at the outset of the book, and am doing so again, because 'critique' can imply rejection, and I do not see an acknowledgement of the limits of postmodernist ideas in family therapy as leading to any wholesale rejection. I am not even too sure that it would be possible to reject postmodernism, given that it is on one level simply part of our wider intellectual and cultural context. More importantly, though, there is a real bind in claiming a critique, because the deeply embedded oppositionality means that it is too easy to assume that a critique of postmodernism is an argument for reclaiming modernist parameters.

I am hoping that it is clear enough by now that my project has not been about reclaiming modernism. I have no wish to return to the modernist fallacy of the split of subject and object, to the privileging of objective knowledge, to the search for certainty and universal truths, or indeed to the social relations of modernity and the power of expert knowledge. The postmodernist emphasis on context and relationship, the acknowledgement of the power of intersubjectivity and intersubjective processes, the demand that the complexity of subjectivity and its social context be theorised, the insistence on the only-ever-partial nature of knowledge, and the space for diversity: all these aspects of postmodernism enrich family therapy knowledge. My own investigation has proceeded from an appreciation of these aspects, while at the same time plotting the limits of the way in which the postmodernist metaphor is currently being used in family therapy.

It is possible to appreciate postmodernism yet be conditional about it and to work from within some of its parameters, while being alert to their limits. In short, I am indeed advocating that we stay in relationship with postmodernism, rather than immerse ourselves within postmodernism. More specifically, given the strategic place narrative and social constructionist ideas have occupied in expressing postmodernist ideas within family therapy, can we value a social constructionist perspective and the narrative metaphor while not being limited to them. Again, I would like to note that the idea of holding a position of conditional appreciation in relation to postmodernism is not really new, and I will simply add the conclusion of my explorations here to this emerging discussion.

That my own study has been bathed in postmodernist ideas, even if these ideas have themselves been the object of the study, is borne out by the extent to which this conclusion is harmonious with a postmodernist awareness of the context of knowledge and its limits. To say that I now would like to turn to ideas that move beyond the limits of the current use of postmodernism in family therapy is, in one way, simply to honour the postmodernist invitation to embrace diverse knowledges. And this is what I want to do. Having considered problematic aspects of constructionist and narrative ideas, I would like to consider alternate ideas that speak to some of the difficulties in our own local family therapy postmodernist discourse.

There is no prize for guessing the rough shape of the alternate theorisations which would be of interest here. We would be looking for different understandings of the processes of self and intersubjectivity, ones that 'meet' aspects of the experience of therapy, that do not preclude a recognition of the power of lived realities, and that are able to engage in some way with human experience beyond its conscious and languaged forms. There are no doubt many understandings that would travel in this direction. I have to say that I think it would be possible to stay within a primary commitment to narrative and constructionist ideas and attempt to extend them in this way. Previous mentions were made of John Lannamann's work (1998b) which addresses the issue of materiality in constructionist theory; of the difference of Michael White's use of Foucault rather than social constructionism; and of the beginning appearances of the ideas of unspoken narratives and voices-not-yet-heard, for example, in the work of Kathy Weingarten (2000) and Harlene Anderson (1997). However, my project is not about extending narrative and constructionist ideas, and instead I will be looking toward particular psychoanalytic ideas as a way of sketching some alternate possibilities.

My turn to psychoanalytic ideas at this point, then, is in part a sample discussion of alternate theorisations of intersubjectivity. Yet though it is true that I would welcome the range of other possibilities which could tackle this task (including the reworking and extension of the current constructionist and narrative projects), it would be disingenuous of me to suggest that I am alighting on psychoanalytic thinking as just an abstracted example of something different. I spoke in the introductory chapter of the exploration of postmodernism in systemic therapy as being the 'main frame' for the book and the intersection with psychoanalytic ideas being its 'secondary support'. It is time for me to be clearer about why I am choosing this particular secondary support.

I found myself laughing when I was writing this part of the chapter, because I really wanted to say that I picked psychoanalytic ideas because I liked them. Now I know that I cannot just say 'because I liked them', and I should take responsibility for naming the threads which lead to this choice. The door is certainly opened by the consideration of the limits of postmodernism and the desire to explore something different. But then I should add that I have found some psychoanalytic ideas to be enduringly useful in addressing aspects of the experience of therapy which are difficult to address within systemic thinking, and to call on psychoanalytic ideas in part simply reflects a continuity in my own personal history as a therapist. I should also probably add something about my experience as a client in analytic therapy and the way in which this has become woven into my use of self as a systemic therapist. I could also talk about the intersections that have been made across the last two decades between feminist interests and psychoanalysis, and it has been very interesting to follow contemporary psycho-analytic thinking from the outside, its continuing moves toward relational theory, and some of the parallels in the debates within psychoanalysis about the implications of postmodernist thinking.

I name these threads in the form of a personal narrative, which on one level it is. However, I do not think it is an unusual narra-tive. The introductory chapter quoted the recent survey of family therapists in Britain (Bor, Mallandan and Vetere 1998), who rated psychodynamic ideas as second only to Milan systemic ideas in terms of influence on their practice. This is a surprising result given the formal history of opposition to psychoanalytic ideas in family therapy. I wonder whether it reflects how common my own story is in terms of my development as a therapist and my experience as a client, and whether this is more common in Britain, not at all uncommon in Australia, and perhaps less common in North America. But I also named wider cultural and political influences – a particular feminist intellectual milieu and access through the wider therapy environment to an engagement with psychoanalytic ideas and practices. Again, these are contextual issues, and they point to the relationship between where we are and what we come to think about and be interested in.

Could I use these reflections to acknowledge that readers will be approaching the work of the next few chapters from a range of their own contexts and histories with psychoanalytic ideas? Some readers will not have a strong resonance with my personal narrative, and they may be more interested in engaging with the chapters simply as an exploration to sample other ideas. Other readers may share more similar histories and interests in psychoanalysis. My own passion for exploring particular psychoanalytic ideas intertwines an interest in the postmodernist debate, as well as a separate and longstanding practice interest. However, having two motivations running through a piece of work is not necessarily a problem, although it does quite rightly prompt me as a writer to recognise the diversity of positions of those of you who are reading this.

Intersecting psychoanalytic ideas

Having sketched in a general way my decision to draw on psychoanalytic ideas, let me use the last section of this chapter to outline more specifically how I will (and will not) be using them and the choice of topics for the next chapters.

I wrote in the first chapter of the traditional opposition within family therapy to psychoanalysis and the historical early circumstances of the differentiation of family therapy as a developing field from the dominance of the individual therapies, particularly psychoanalysis. I also noted the persistence of the tendency to call upon psychoanalysis as the discredited other, and the way in which this competitive practice has been used as a boundary-making technique in establishing systemic family therapy. In exploring the same issue, David Pocock (1997) argues that nonetheless there have been local knowledges within family therapy which have continued to show an involvement with psychoanalytic thinking, as well as work more within a systemic frame which has crossed borders with psychoanalytic knowledge and practice. I wrote that my own project in this book is a modest one, and in calling upon very particular psychoanalytic ideas, I am not attempting an integration, let alone any project of model building.

All this is by way of repetition, and I will continue the discussion now by saying that not only am I not attempting any integrative project, but my own use of psychoanalytic ideas falls outside the aims of integration. I have deliberately used the word 'intersection' as a description of how I am imagining my work in cross-linking different bodies of ideas, and although it is perhaps not the most accessible word to use, I hope that it flags the absence of a desire to build an integrative structure. Pocock's image of border crossings also has some resonance, although it suggests a neutrality about territorial distinctiveness that may be misleading with respect to my primary orientation as a systemic family therapist in approaching psychoanalysis in the project of this book.

There is no question that in looking toward psychoanalytic ideas, my feet are firmly in the territory of systemic therapy, and indeed this next part of the book is entwined very deliberately with the exploration of family therapy's use of postmodernist ideas. Of course, it would be quite a different orientation to be looking toward systemic therapy with my feet firmly in the territory of psychoanalysis. There have been very few such projects undertaken. Mary-Jo Gerson's work (1996) springs to mind as the most recent sustained example, as she mainly addresses psychoanalytically-minded therapists, intersecting ideas from systems thinking in her development of theory and practice in family therapy. Robyn Skynner's project of developing family therapy using group analysis (1976, 1987) should also be named here, as he quite extensively integrated systemic concepts in his work.

It would be a different orientation again to be looking from a commitment to psychoanalysis toward ways of applying these ideas to work with families rather than individuals. There is a solid body of work which has been established from this set of interests. It shows very little intersection with the developments within systemic therapy and, on the whole, it has developed quite independently. One thinks immediately of the project of elaborating an object relations approach to family therapy, and from North America, of the work of Samuel Slipp (1984, 1988), and David Scharff and Jill Scharff (Scharff and Scharff 1991; Scharff 1989). British psychoanalytic family therapists seem generally to have been less keen to build a 'model' of object relations family therapy and have produced instead some important collections that show the consistent development of a psychoanalytic approach to family therapy. I would particularly refer readers to edited collections by Sally Box et al. (1981, 1994), a collection by Roelene Szur and Sheila Miller (1991), and another edited book applying psychoanalytic ideas to community-based work with young children and their families by Judith Trowell and Marion Bower (1995). There are also some current articles in family therapy journals which use psychoanalysis as their main orientation (see for example Brodie and Wright 2002; Stiefel, Harris and Rohan 1998).

There is then a more disparate body of work which may be characterised using Pocock's 'border crossings' image. I have already mentioned the enduring influence in family therapy of Murray Bowen's ideas from North America (1978), and the intergenerational family therapy of Ivan Boszormenyi-Nagy (Boszormenyi-Nagy and Krasner 1986; Boszormenyi-Nagy and Spark 1973), and from Britain, the importance of John Byng-Hall's work on attachment and family scripts (1986, 1988, 1995a, 1995b, 1999). Staying within the North American context, I will add the work of Mike Nichols (1987), and Deborah Luepnitz (1988, 1997), who through her critique of the different systemic frameworks, moves to embracing a feminist object relations approach to work with couples and families. Within the British context, I will also add the work of Christopher Dare (1979, 1997) and Sebastian Kraemer (1994, 1997), as well as a number of others (for example Bentovim and Kingston 1991; Pinsof 1994). Moving somewhat further toward the systemic end of this border crossings group, I will name the work of David Pocock (1995, 1997) from Britain, and from Australia, Paul Gibney (1991, 1996) and Glenn Larner (1996, 2000), as well as some of my own work (Flaskas 1993, 1994, 1996, 1997a).

I have just given a very quick map of the psychoanalysis-family therapy field. Whereas in Chapter 1, I located the book's project within the re-emergence of an interest in psychoanalytic ideas in the postmodern context of systemic family therapy, here I have drawn the map in terms of the different kinds of orientation reflected in the linking of psychoanalysis and family therapy. If you like, I am giving a second set of bearings in terms of the location of my planned use of psychoanalytic ideas, this time placing myself on the cusp of the systemic end of the border crossings group.

Rightly or wrongly, I have felt the need to make my own position here as visible as possible, not the least because I do not want to disappoint readers who may be hoping for a more unconditional commitment to psychoanalysis and a wider-scale engagement with psychoanalytic ideas in the context of systemic family therapy. But I am not a psychoanalytic therapist wanting to bridge analytic theory and practices forged in the environment of an intimate and voluntary long-term therapeutic relationship, with the different therapeutic demands of seeing families in family therapy settings. Nor am I moving with equal freedom and commitment across psychoanalytic and systemic ideas. Instead, I am strictly limited in my engagement with psychoanalytic ideas, and I am 'using' them within my own set of interests within systemic therapy.

Having identified this orientation, I will now name the particular psychoanalytic ideas I will be calling on in the discussions in the next three chapters. Chapter 8 will consider attachment and the unconscious as relational processes, the way in which these processes show themselves in family therapy, and the extent to which they address languaged, unlanguaged and unlanguagable aspects of human experience. I am aware that psychoanalysis has itself been very ambivalent about attachment theory, but this will be discussed along the way, and within family therapy, ideas about attachment have certainly been associated with a psychodynamic perspective. Chapter 9 will continue the discussion of the unconscious by exploring transference, countertransference and projective identification, and I want to intersect these analytic ideas with a discussion of time and the experience of time. Transference, countertransference and projective identification are all ideas which address the intersubjective process of therapy, and Chapter 10 will further consider the therapeutic relationship in systemic family therapy. Building on the work of Chapter 9, I will extend the discussion of empathy and understanding in family therapy, and then I shall explore the idea of the space of not-knowing and the space of reflection, referring to some of the ideas of Wilfred Bion as well as the current systemic discussions.

As you can see, I plan to explore these psychoanalytic ideas within a broader discussion grounded in systemic interests. Once more, it is true that I am choosing these particular ideas because I like them! However, to say only this underestimates my belief in the usefulness of these ideas in practice and their capacity to sit quite comfortably alongside systemic commitments. If you were to push me some more and ask me again why I have chosen these ideas, then I would add something about my experience of supervising and being supervised in family therapy. For many years I had dual supervisions from psychodynamic and systemic orientations, and for many years I have been supervising family therapy in a context in which there is a parallel analytic supervision. The analytic ideas I have settled on to explore in the next few chapters are the ones that clinically have come to the fore in this experience of supervision. I will also add that across several involvements of regular analytic consultation in community-based child and family settings, it has consistently been the ideas of attachment and unconscious processes, and understandings of the therapeutic relationship using transference, countertransference and projective identification, which have been the key points of reflection. My choice then does indeed express my own practice experience, at the same time as using these ideas as examples of alternate possibilities in theorising intersubjectivity.

It is time, though, to move on to the next part of the book. In the same way that I layered the explorations of Chapter 4 through to Chapter 6 before synthesising the discussion in this chapter, I will move through the topics of Chapters 8 to 10 before integrating this work in the final chapter, which will then bring us full circle to the discussion of postmodernism and family therapy knowledge.

Note

1 I am thinking here particularly of Foucault's work in the first volume of *The history of sexuality* (1981).

Chapter 8

Attachment and the unconscious

This is the first of a set of three chapters to draw on selected psychoanalytic understandings that move beyond the confines of theories locating language in the central position of privilege. I am interested in particular psychoanalytic ideas that are relevant for systemic therapy and in harmony with its practices, and which meet and offer some thinking about processes that are not especially well met in the current systemic theorising. This chapter focuses on the process of attachment and introduces some ideas about the unconscious. Attachment and the unconscious are the first port of call because these ideas attempt to describe processes which I think show themselves again and again in the practice of therapy. I will use practice once more as a starting point, and then I will consider attachment and the unconscious in turn. This lays the basis for a discussion of the relationship of attachment and the unconscious to language, which brings the chapter back to practice.

Some practice experience

First Piece

A quick anecdote about the child I wrote about in Chapter 5, whom I had first seen when she was three in the context of a concern about sexual abuse. It is three years later and our second to last meeting. She draws a picture, borrowing an image from a TV commercial. A baby is in a pram which is rushing headlong down a hill toward a railway crossing, and there is a train coming full steam ahead up the track. The disaster is about to happen, but there are two good things which stop it. The very shape of the land protects the baby, for there is a dip at the bottom of the hill which brakes the speed of the pram and stops it going onto the railway track. There is also a friendly dog who is watching it all happen and barking a warning.

Second Piece

I see a family where the daughter who is eight has come to live with her father, his new wife and their baby. She has not lived with her father since she was one, and she has seen him only sporadically over the years. She has been living in a country town with her mother a long way from Sydney. Her mother seems to have some kind of untreated psychotic episodes from time to time, and the child has often been farmed out when her mother has been unwell. The family are coming, partly because the child welfare department who organised this placement suggested it, and partly because the stepmother is becoming increasingly angry with the child. The behaviours she finds infuriating are the child's lying and stealing, and generally her 'sneaky ways'. The stepmother had been looking forward to caring for her and giving her a stable home, but now she and the father fear that the girl may spoil their own family.

This is all emerging in the first session – it is a pretty sad story, and the future is not looking too rosy. At one point when I am talking to the father and stepmother, I look across at the child and recognise that she is sitting in exactly the same way that I am sitting, and then I realise that I had been half-noticing her matching my movements for quite some time in the session. In the moment of my recognition of this, I feel very moved, and it is also quite painful. Later on, I think that maybe I was moved by the overtness of her desire to join or be connected with me and that there was something painful about the impoverishment of her way of going about it – that she would try to connect with me by acting like me. Though I certainly did not experience this as sneaky, at the same time it gave me a glimpse into the territory which had become difficult and disappointing for the stepmother and father in their hopes and attempts to relate to, and care for, the child.

Third Piece

The third story. An 8-year-old Aboriginal boy is referred by one of the Aboriginal services. He lives with his auntie and her

5-year-old son, and she had become very alarmed when she found him down in the backyard by the big tree, practising knots from a book and fashioning a noose. He is assessed by a child psychiatrist who finds nothing remarkable, and the family is referred for family therapy.

The incident seems incomprehensible – now you see it, now you don't – and the boy is quiet and reserved but does not seem unhappy. There are some different themes in the therapy. His auntie raises his feelings about being left with her by his mother, and some work is done around that. We also do some work around his experience of racism in his school, and we work on strengthening his connections with others in his community who may guide and advise him.

The therapy finishes – some good work was done, and all seems well enough. Yet I was left with then, and still have now, a great concern for this child. If you were to ask me to name my worst fantasy, I would tell you that I fear that he could end up in jail as a young man and commit suicide there, becoming yet another Aboriginal-death-in-custody statistic from Australian jails. I also know that this is 'just' my worst fantasy, that this or another tragedy may not happen, and that the boy may well find some way through it and be okay.

I discuss these last two practice situations in a family therapy forum. Someone says 'well, dare we talk about the unconscious?', and someone else responds 'yes, but what kind of unconscious?' Let me add a second and parallel set of questions here: well, dare we talk about attachment? – yes, but what kind of attachment? These are the questions I would like to hold in mind in approaching attachment and the unconscious, not as internal qualities and properties but rather as processes eternally contextualised in relationships.

Attachment as a relational process

Attachment theory has the complexity of a research programme which now spans more than thirty years, and it could also provide one of the more interesting case studies of the twentieth century in terms of the social and political milieu of knowledge. John Bowlby's early work on attachment and loss in the 1960s was followed by his long period of collaboration with Mary Ainsworth, leading to theorising the attachment styles of babies and young children with their primary caregiver within a developmental frame. They identified the by now familiar primary distinction of secure and insecure attachment styles, with anxious/ambivalent and avoidant attachment styles being identified as different categories of insecure attachment. Later, the category of disorganised attachment style was added to this schema, which was an attempt to describe the observed dilemma of children (often in abusive situations) who showed the pattern of an anxious movement toward the parent, then a frozen moment of something like fear, followed by avoidance. A second strand of work, largely associated with Mary Main, has focused more on adult attachment styles, and some of the resulting research has targeted adult attachment styles in parent-child relationships as well as in couple relationships.[1]

I think it is fair to say that attachment theory has had quite bad press historically in family therapy, and there are a number of reasons for this. As a therapist, I find myself reacting against the general frame of the research program, particularly its momentum for the categorisation of attachment styles with the aim of attaching predictive power in terms of later abnormalities and pathologies. Of course, it is not just attachment research that has been in the business of nailing down prognostic indicators of pathology. Yet this kind of research programme scarcely represents 'news of difference' to therapists, who often know only too well that a difficult start to life can lead to problems later on, or that early childhood experience of sexual or physical abuse is likely to have negative effects. That this research can be very useful politically (for example, in arguing for preventive counselling and psychotherapy services) sits uneasily beside its objectifying and pathologising descriptions of very human situations. In this respect, Jane Akister (1998) gives a useful reminder that roughly 40 per cent of us may be classified as having an insecure attachment style and that there are many pathways to creative and productive lives.

The other off-putting aspect of attachment theory has been the very short step from the developmental focus on the early mother-infant relationship to sophisticated (and not so sophisticated) varieties of mother-blaming. Bowlby's original work on separation and loss was used very powerfully in the post-war years in Britain as an ideological rationale for moving women out of the workforce back into homes. Elsa Jones (1993) makes the point that prevailing economic and social conditions often allow for the emergence of knowledges which 'fit' – in this case, that the conservatism of the

1950s allowed the emergence of Bowlby's knowledge which was used to place the moral imperative of successful child-rearing squarely with mothers.

But though the retrospective social history of this period tends to highlight the conservative way in which Bowlby's ideas were used, there was at the same time a radical and progressive aspect to his work. Much of the political clout of the early observation of separation was fuelled by the researchers' outrage about prevailing institutional practices (for example, in hospitals and children's homes) which actively cut across children's attempts to create substitute attachment relationships in situations of loss. It is tempting to become complacent and think that these kinds of seriously 'anti-relationship' practices happened only in the past, yet I write this paragraph in the same week in which I hear a story of a baby being removed from his mother at two months on very shaky evidence of inadequate care. The baby is being breastfed, and the mother tries to keep expressing milk in the hope that she can continue breastfeeding when the baby is returned. The baby is returned – and I can assure you that this much is entirely predictable from the story of the circumstances of removal – but three months and three placements later, with the mother–baby relationship seriously undermined. So could we take on board this political contradiction of attachment theory – that though it may be used to blame parents and mothers in particular, it may also be used to protect and defend the preciousness of the earliest pre-verbal experiences of relating and the environment of parenting?

Attachment theory and Bowlby's work is associated with a psychoanalytic frame, although most of the empirical research has been undertaken outside psychoanalysis (mainly in psychology and infant psychiatry). Bowlby himself was an analyst, but the emergence of his interest in separation and loss, and attachment and 'real' relationships, set him apart from the dominant discourses in psychoanalysis at the time. Jeremy Holmes (1996) chronicles the history of the intense resistance to Bowlby's work within psycho-analysis, leading to the active exclusion of his ideas. Holmes argues that it was specifically his interest in the environment and the interpersonal which flew in the face of a psychoanalysis which was at the time taking an extreme anti-environmentalist position in the pursuit of knowledge of the intra-psychic (drawn in opposition to the interpersonal) world. In the retelling of this history, Holmes emphasises the strong resonance of Bowlby's work with Donald

Winnicott's ideas of the holding environment and good-enough mothering, and with Wilfred Bion's ideas on the importance of maternal reverie and emotional containment in the development of mind. Jonathan Pedder (1986) has also drawn links with the work of Michael Balint (see, for example, 1968). One can also underline the strong general resonance of Bowlby's work with the shift to a relational psychoanalysis.

In short, attachment theory has had bad press in psychoanalysis as well as in family therapy. Interestingly enough, we find now in both fields evidence of a re-engagement. The work of Holmes (1996, 1998, 2001) provides an excellent example here, and his 1998 article published in the *International Journal of Psycho-Analysis* was selected for a web site discussion forum. Peter Fonagy's research on attachment and reflective functioning is becoming increasingly influential within psychoanalysis (see Fonagy 2001, and Fonagy et al. 1991a, 1991b). From within family therapy, a recent introductory text (Dallos and Draper 2000) includes a discussion of attachment theory in a chapter on enduring issues in family therapy theory and practice. Gill Gorell Barnes (1995) also points to the harmony of an interest in attachment with the current systemic project.

Gorrell Barnes (1995) notes that mutual influence and systemic patterning are well established concepts in much of child development attachment research, and moreover theorising about attachment very directly places it as a process of intersubjectivity. Within this frame of intersubjectivity, the development and experience of patterns of attachment is seen to take place within the demystified context of micro-interactions in the physical intimacy of baby and parent. However, Gorrell Barnes also notes that this research points to a very finely tuned development of these patterns, in which meaning-making by baby and parent both shapes, and is shaped by, the interactions and communications of attachment. I probably do not need to labour the harmony of these themes with the systemic interests of mutuality, context, the centrality of meaning, and the idea of meaning as emerging in the space 'between'.

Working within this overlap of interest, John Byng-Hall has had a long-term commitment to extending the ideas of attachment theory in family therapy. His earlier work on attachment in families was produced against the mainstream currents of systemic therapy (Byng-Hall 1999). One of the main limits of attachment theory for family therapy has been that it has largely stayed within the parameters of dyadic relationships. Some of the more recent work has addressed the relationship context of the primary dyadic parent-infant relationship, and Daniel Stern's work in particular gives a very rich description of the relational complexity of the 'motherhood constellation' (Stern 1998). However, Byng-Hall has been interested in theorising not just the wider context of the dyadic attachment relationship but the way in which the relationship network of the family itself serves as a secure base of attachment (Byng-Hall 1995a). In effect, he argues that the experience of secure attachment is formed in the network of family relationships and well beyond the primary dyadic relationship.

Byng-Hall was also interested in the metaphor of storying long before it became popular in the family therapy literature. He published a number of articles using the idea of family scripts in family therapy (1986, 1988), and in his recent work, he has linked these practice ideas to some of the emerging research on narratives of attachment (1995b, 1997). He particularly uses the research by Mary Main (1991) on the coherence of parents' narratives of their primary attachment experiences, and the relationship of these narratives to the patterns of attachment with their children. This research suggests that it is not *per se* the goodness or badness of the parent's own experience of early attachment which unilaterally determines the attachment pattern with their own children, but that this experience can be mediated quite powerfully by the extent to which the parent has come to have a coherent narrative of their own experience as a child. If you like, the experience may be quite bad, yet there are transformative possibilities in the capacity for secure attachment if the person has been able to achieve a meaningful and congruent story about it.[2]

Holmes (1996) notes the intersection of narrative ideas and attachment theory that flows from Main's research, and the evidence of the transformative possibilities of coherent narratives is making an important contribution to the literature on resilience (see Rutter 1996; Walsh 1996). For rather obvious reasons, empirical research which tracks conditions of resilience and transformation is likely to be of far more immediate value to those of us who work as therapists. As Byng-Hall (1997) notes, Main's research on the significance of coherent narratives in allowing shifts in attachment patterns is very confirming of psychotherapies that have at their heart the attempt to draw meaning from difficult experiences.

Yet in this research, 'narrative coherence' is not a Pollyanna tactic of making a good story out of a bad experience. The idea of coherence in narrative form refers to the cohesiveness and plausibility of the story (see Main 1991). There is the criterion of internal consistency, for example, whether the specific illustrations a person gives of her or his attachment experience match the general description which is given of the relationship with the mother or father. But as well as the consistency of different parts of the story, a coherent narrative would also need to have consistency between the story and the available evidence of the (real) experience it attempts to represent.

In this research on narratives of attachment, then, there is no reneging on the idea of an independent reality, and it is not the languaged story itself which creates transformative possibilities. Rather, it seems to be the capacity to come to have a narrative in which parts of the story are related to other parts of the story, and very importantly, in which there is a congruent relationship between the content of the story and what we might call the 'reality' of the emotional experience it tries to describe. The critical aspects, then, seem to lie in the relationship *between* the story and the experience, the person's capacity and struggle to make meaning in reconstructing her or his own history, and the relationship of self and significant others.

It is becoming clear enough, I think, that a consideration of attachment as a relational process could lead very directly to a discussion of language and its limits, yet before I move to this, I would like to explore the idea of the unconscious.

The unconscious

In many ways, once we get over the historical distaste for attachment theory, I think it is not too difficult to accept its relevance for systemic family therapy. However, the idea of the unconscious is maybe more prickly. For despite the unconscious being perhaps the single most important contribution of psychoanalysis to the understanding of human experience, it has been eclipsed in successive frameworks of systemic therapy, and I would argue that it remains a problematic absence in narrative and constructionist therapies. At the same time, although the unconscious occupies a taken-for-granted centrality within psychoanalysis, how it may be thought about has been the subject of continuous development and redevelopment, often within a lively and contested debate.

That systemic therapy has chosen not to address the unconscious may be understood as part of its historical differentiation from psychoanalysis. Also, it is not difficult to comprehend our reluctance to embrace some aspects of the way in which thinking and practice around the unconscious have been configured within psychoanalysis. The core idea that the unconscious holds thoughts and emotions which we are unable to know at a conscious level, necessarily gets us into messy territory in therapy, and the small consolation here may be that this is a part of the messiness of human experience. Indeed, the position of the analyst in the unconscious interpersonal field of analytic therapy is the subject of considerable discussion in contemporary psychoanalysis (see for example Aron 1996; Natterson 1991; Orange 1995; Renik 1993; Schwaber 1996).

However, a nagging problem for family therapy in trying to 'import' analytic practices of interpreting the unconscious is this: a tentative interpretation shared in the intimacy of year three of an individual analysis may be enormously helpful, while the same kind of interpretation thrown into the interpersonal minefield of a second family therapy session is often likely to be a therapeutic non-event, and at worst it may be experienced as nonsensical and intrusive. All this is to say that there may be good reasons embedded in the reluctance of systemic family therapy to call too directly upon psychoanalytic practices, the integrity of which has been forged in a very different therapeutic environment.[3]

Yet separate to the issue of the different therapeutic context of analytic practices, systemic therapy has also reacted against the theory of the unconscious. In noting the absence of the idea of the unconscious in family therapy theory, the question 'what kind of unconscious?' still remains relevant. It is rather like trying to track the shadow of what we have come to exclude. Given the historical timing of family therapy's break with psychoanalysis, I think it is very likely that the idea that has been excluded is the stereotype of the Freudian unconscious as the territory of repression. This early idea of the unconscious went alongside Freud's understanding of human experience as shaped by instinctual desires, putting us in situations of impossible tensions between ego, superego and id, necessitating the process of repression. Thus, the Freudian unconscious is the repository of the repressed. I would be in very strong company in arguing that this framing of the unconscious and human experience as instinct driven is limited in terms of a systemic appreciation. However, it is not just limited for systemic purposes, and across time this early understanding of the unconscious has been challenged and changed as part of the development of psychoanalysis.

It is fair to say that as a whole, contemporary psychoanalytic theory shows a major shift to relational understandings of the unconscious, although of course there are many differences in the way in which relational processes are being understood and described. Bion's work, which has been profoundly influential particularly within post-Kleinian British psychoanalysis, marks a transformation from a simple understanding of the unconscious-as-repository-of-the-repressed to an understanding of unconscious processes as multi-layered, existing in complex relationship to emotional experience and the capacity to think (see for example Bion 1967; Grotstein 1983). Beginning with Winnicott's work (see for example 1971, 1986), the general move from a one person to a two person psychology also marks this shift, as does the popularity of the intersubjective and interpersonal perspectives that have emerged strongly in North America (see for example Mitchell 1988; Stolorow, Atwood and Brandchaft 1994). Across the divide of the differences represented in these theories, one is nonetheless seeing a commonality of the intensity of an engagement with understandings of the unconscious as relational. That this engagement is a struggle goes without saying.

However, to give some flavour of the struggle, I will mention a small and very particular slice of a debate given in a recent discussion by Karen Lombardi (Rucker and Lombardi, 1998). Writing within a commitment to relational psychoanalysis, she notes that some of the understandings of the unconscious that have emerged particularly from the North American interpersonal tradition have unwittingly replicated the limits of the theory of repression. She argues that in the move to a two person psychology, repression has largely been replaced by the idea of dissociation, and that within this version, unconscious experience becomes merely those meanings that are outside conscious existence. Though this alternate view still places a central emphasis on the relational context and process of meaning, and allows for the incorporation of social constructionist ideas, Lombardi notes that it nonetheless replicates the typography of the theory of repression. The unconscious, if you like, is simply that which cannot be conscious, and the relationship of conscious and unconscious experience stays within a linear and unidirectional mode (Rucker and Lombardi 1998).

Lombardi argues strongly for a dialectic of unconscious and conscious experience, and she goes on to describe the way in which creativity and transformative possibilities may lie in the relationship between conscious and unconscious processes. This is an interesting description and gives one way of understanding the dynamic of therapeutic change. Psychoanalytic therapy could be thought of as the form of therapy which most deliberately exploits the relationship of unconscious and conscious experience, for its momentum is to try to come to know unconscious experience, and there is no road to 'knowing' unconscious experience except through the way it shows itself in our conscious experience, in our lived bodies, in the language of dreams, and in our here-and-now relating to others. For all its contradictions, psychoanalysis is an attempt to create a space (and a relationship) within which the dynamic of unconscious and conscious experience may be lived through and thought about.

Perhaps a more immediate link here, though, is with the research on narrative and the transformation of attachment patterns. For, if we think of storying as a process in which the important element is not so much the story itself but the relationship between our experience, our struggle to give meaning to it and the story which emerges, then it may well be that part of this process involves the dynamic of unconscious and conscious experience. What may be known (and not known) about difficult experiences of attachment? And how may both the known and not-known come to have sufficient representation in what hopefully comes to be a coherent narrative?

In this section, I have been wanting to approach the question 'well, what kind of unconscious?', and let me sum up in a couple of sentences. It is *not* the Freudian unconscious as repository of the repressed which is of so much interest here, and it has probably been this earlier understanding of the unconscious which lies as the shadow exclusion in systemic therapy. The relational unconscious is of far more interest, particularly understandings of the relationship between conscious and unconscious experience. The next chapter continues a discussion of the territory between conscious and unconscious experience by exploring the processes of transference, countertransference and projective identification. Right now, though, I will continue it by considering language in relationship to attachment and the unconscious.

Attachment, the unconscious and language

This exploration is taking place in the context of the critique of theories of intersubjective processes that centrally privilege language. So what may be said, then, about attachment and the unconscious in terms of language? Just in case you think that I am about to go off into some bizarre argument that language has nothing at all to do with attachment and the unconscious, let me begin clearly by saying that in very significant ways, our experience of attachment and the unconscious takes place in, and is constructed by, language. In other very significant ways, though, this experience takes place outside language, for at different times and at different levels, the processes of attachment and the unconscious are pre-language and even beyond language. Let me unpack this argument more carefully, and then reconsider language, representation and storying.

In his description of attachment and parent-infant relationships, Stern (1998) stresses the dynamic between interaction and representation, and the conscious and unconscious. He is particularly interested in what he calls the parents' representational world, the way in which parental representations become enacted in interaction with the infant. Some of the representations that parents bring to bear may be conscious and framed in words. Other representations may be unconscious, though hardly less powerful for it. Stern stresses that there is nothing magical about conscious or unconscious representations: they do not float around the emotional stratosphere waiting to be 'caught by' or 'put into' the baby, but rather they come to be felt and to be seen in the moment-by-moment sequences of interaction between parent and infant which ultimately form the baby's 'schemas-for-being-with' and 'proto-narratives' of self-in-relation-to-others. This very early development of proto-narratives is part of a process in which the infant is already forming representations of the meaning of interactions and relationship.[4]

It seems unnecessary for me to write what I am sure we all know: that most babies are highly attuned to the parental environment and that the capacity for making meaning from our lived experience shows itself long before the capacity for language itself is developed. One sees this in the everyday intimacy and moment-to-moment interactions between parents and babies, and if one were to need evidence beyond the ordinary experience of relating to babies, attachment research closely documents the mutuality of the fine weaving of relationships between parents and infants. That all this is taking place in a landscape not far removed in time from when the baby was part of the mother's body is also recognised in the everyday awareness of parent-infant relationships. If we think of the human processes which attachment theory attempts to describe, then alongside acknowledging the reality of the baby-before-language, already making sense of the lived environment and relationships, we may need to acknowledge the unlanguaged and even unlanguageable landscapes of early life. These acknowl-edgements are quite compatible with a recognition of the critical importance of parents' languaged representations, and the power of (languaged) discourses and social practices that provide the social conditions of relating.

The unconscious is one part of all this discussion, for to think of the representations of attachment, the schemas-for-being-with and proto-narratives of attachment styles, is to find ourselves crossing the territory of the relationship of the conscious and the uncon-scious. Our schemas-for-being-with may be languaged and/or unlanguaged, consciously known and/or unconsciously known. There is the problem of trying to describe the relationship of unconscious knowledge and language, which Christopher Bollas (1987) tackles in his description of 'the unthought known' in the history and present of our landscapes of relating. In this sense, far from languaged stories and unconscious knowledge fitting together in a seamless construction, it is often the incongruence between conscious and unconscious that signals 'the unthought known'. Someone may know that his partner is just going away for three days to a conference in another town, yet still find himself picking a fight near the point of farewell, and then carrying a queasy anxiety and nursing a sense of being wronged which betokens another kind of story about relating that is much harder to put into words.

In this sense, our unconscious experience often disconcerts our conscious languaged stories. We find ourselves wondering about slips of the tongue or dream images or peculiar things we do in relationships precisely because *they do not fit* with our languaged stories. It is this jarring that challenges the story we have so far told ourselves about our experience and demands that we continue to restory our experience in a way that takes account of other things we are coming to know about ourselves in relation to others. If you like, when unconscious experience shows itself, it runs headlong into the limits of the language we have thus far consciously used to wrap around our experience.

This brings us back to the theme raised in Chapter 6 on the relationship of representation and language. There the discussion emphasised the role of language in representation – finding words to try to convey our experience is at the one time a process of both representation and construction. Here I will add that to stress the duality of this process is also to acknowledge the complex layering of experience itself. Narratives of attachment and loss and the development of conscious and congruent meanings are languaged activities. Language comes to construct how we know and think about our patterns and experience of attachment and relationships – and how we come to know and think about this experience has some transformational power, for good or ill. However, we also have the capacity to have unconscious knowledge outside conscious thought which often shows itself in incongruity, which we then try to make sense of and restory in a more congruent way.

What constitutes the 'real' experience here? The earliest experiences of attachment taking place before and beyond language? The way we represent and come to know this experience in language? The way in which the language we use and the story we come to have then constructs how we experience self and relationships? The way in which unconscious knowledge then confronts the adequacy of our own storying, prompting a continuous restorying? All these layers are real, and part of what we might choose to signal as 'lived experience'. In different kinds of psychotherapy, we may highlight and work with one layer rather than another, yet in human experience, they are all related.

But I will draw this section to a close, having made the argument that attachment and the relationship of the conscious and unconscious take place pre-language, in language and beyond language. This constellation gives great power to the process of representation and storying, yet the power lies not so much in the story itself but rather in the relationship between the story and the realness of experience, in all its layers. Let me take this back now to practice.

Practice reflections

First Piece

Toward the end of therapy, the 6-year-old girl draws a picture of a near disaster and a lucky escape. A baby in a runaway pram heads down a hill into the path of an oncoming train, but the very shape of the ground prevents the disaster, and there is a friendly dog watching what is happening and barking a warning. The child draws intently, then tells the story to her mother and to me very carefully, checking that we have it right.

Through all the murkiness of the sexual abuse and the pro-tracted welfare and court interventions, we come to a spot where the child produces this image. I am moved by the grati-tude in the drawing, and I smile to myself about the idea of the therapist-as-friendly-dog (I had not really been imagining myself in quite this way!). The image of the shape of the land holding and protecting the baby is very beautiful – a tribute, I think, to her relationship with her mother and the landscape of their connection.

Clearly these are just my own understandings of the child's image. Yet more powerfully I have a memory of the child's concentration in the session, her seriousness about wanting to convey something very important to herself and to her mother and to me. She uses the drawing to convey images and words which together represent a form of knowledge not entirely within language, and not entirely outside it. It is perhaps a state of knowledge to be respected and not battened down too firmly with words.

Second Piece

But what to say of the 8-year-old girl, newly arrived to live with her father, stepmother and their baby, with all her spoiling and sneaky ways? I spoke of being struck in the first interview by the realisation of her mirroring me, which at one level seemed hopeful about the aliveness of her desire to connect, and at another level seemed sad in the very earliness of the form of the connection. To use my own experience of that moment opens some doors to think about the girl's struggle in the territory of attachment – her difficulty, for all sorts of very good reasons, to feel connected with and to feel able to connect. To allow the possibility that this struggle is very real for her, if unlanguaged, also allows the possibility of thinking what it might be like for the stepmother and father in their everyday relating with her. And I begin to get some sense of the way in which her mirroring and attempts at compliance come to be experienced and languaged as sneaky, and the way in which her lying and stealing become one injury after another to the desire (however mixed and complicated) to parent her.

Some of this comes to be represented in the story that is all too quickly coalescing around the girl, but is it just the story that is the problem or the relationship between the story and the way it represents experience? I think here that the story relates to an unlanguaged emotional reality of attachment which is only too real. It comes to represent and construct this reality in a way that compounds and embeds the problems of attachment for the child and possibly adds to an unconscious story she may already have that she is the spoiler of mothers and families.

If you like, the languaged story is in relationship with the struggle around attachment, and the girl's capacity to be attached and experience attachment are in turn affected by the story which is being created in her 'new' family. For better or worse, real life, not just theory, is recursive.

Third Piece

What of the boy and the now-you-see-it-now-you-don't action of practising knots for a noose? We could say that there was a space in therapy constructed with his auntie and cousin which allowed a number of stories to be explored, and this led to some quite good things happening. Yet I am left with a fear. My construction as a therapist of my own fear – and I think there is an important question, albeit unanswerable, as to whether I am right or wrong – was that there was an emotional reality for this boy that was beyond words, and far from being constructed in language in an unhelpful way, it was not possible to construct much of it in language at all. It was instead seen at the tree, responded to with love by his auntie, thought about with concern by the Aboriginal service, looked at with care by the child psychiatrist, troubled over by me and his family in therapy, responded to by older Aboriginal members of his community and his teacher. Whether this, plus whatever happens from here on in, will be enough to hold the unspeakable I am not sure.

I think of the unconscious when I think of this boy, because there seemed to be a very powerful and potentially very dangerous struggle which was outside conscious languaged meaning for him. For all that, it was recognised by a number of connected people who continue to attempt some conscious and languaged interaction with him about it.

And I think of attachment in all its complexity and specificity – the loss of his mother, his difficulty in experiencing family and cultural belongingness, the extent to which the personal specifics of his history lie so profoundly in the very real history of the oppression of Aboriginal people, and the intergenerational legacy of the ruthless and systematic disruption of foundational attachments which has come to be known in Australia as 'the stolen generation'.

Do we really want to say that the many layers of this story I am telling you are created solely in language, exist solely in language and are transformable solely in language? It may be that I am in the throes here of some peculiar personal countertransference, but I must say that when I think of this boy, I cannot really fathom why in therapy we would be attracted to theories which are invested in reducing human experience to language.

Conclusion

Ideas of attachment and the unconscious have been largely excluded in the discussions of systemic family therapy, yet the processes they attempt to describe are powerful in shaping human experience. Some of the theorising of these ideas has been problematic, and yet in this chapter I have been wanting to emphasise the usefulness of thinking of both attachment and the unconscious as relational processes. However, not only are they relational processes, they are sites of transformation and change. Early patterns of attachment may be mediated by the stories we are able to create about our experience and the relationship of those stories to the experience they try to represent. The unconscious bears a kind of knowledge that is different to our conscious languaged stories, which can make itself known in the constant interplay of the conscious and unconscious and prompts a restorying which more fully acknowledges our lived experience.

We should not underestimate the power of language in constructing and representing our experience of these processes, and

neither should we underestimate the extent to which these processes have power in unlanguaged and sometimes in unlanguageable
spaces. To allow for these different possibilities potentially enables
another kind of engagement with our clients' lived experience and
our lived experience as therapists in the therapeutic relationship.

To begin to translate all this into the wider discussion of theory
that is the broader context of this chapter would be to say that the
processes of attachment and the unconscious allow a different
thinking about forms of subjectivity and intersubjectivity which
moves the parameters well and truly beyond the limits of language.

Notes

1 See Bretherton (1992) for a discussion of the Bowlby-Ainsworth
foundations of attachment theory, and Karen (1994) for a very
accessible review of attachment theory and research as it has unfolded.
2 There are intersections between Main's work on metacognition and
representation and the work of psychoanalyst Peter Fonagy and colleagues on the significance of the reflective self in mediating attachment
patterns (see for example Fonagy et al. 1991a, 1991b).
3 It is outside the scope of this chapter (and indeed, outside the scope of
this book) to give a full discussion of the attempt of object relations
family therapy to extend psychoanalysis to work with families (see for
example Slipp 1988; Scharff and Scharff 1991). However, I would argue
that some of the main difficulties from a systemic perspective around
object relations family therapy have been exactly the difficulties of
translating intrapsychic descriptions and dyadic therapy practices to
direct work with families.
4 The comments I am making here on Stern's work are elaborated in
Flaskas and Cade (1998).

Chapter 9

Transference, projective identification and time

Time is a marker in psychotherapy. Clients bring here-and-now concerns, yet current personal and familial concerns are part of a human landscape which bridges past, present and future time. The last chapter explored attachment and the unconscious. Transference, countertransference and projective identification are particular psychoanalytic ideas that describe aspects of the meeting of conscious and unconscious experience in relationships and the shaping of past experience in the present. These ideas are tailored to understanding the therapeutic leeway of psychoanalysis, yet they also give broader understandings of relational patterns, and they link to themes about the lived experience of time.

This chapter begins again with practice experience, then moves through a discussion of transference, countertransference and projective identification. The second part of the exploration focuses on time. Themes here include the lived experience of time, the dimensions of past and future time in present time, 'stuck' time and narrative closure, and repeating patterns. This constellation of ideas is then used to reflect on the practice experience.

Some practice experience

First Piece

I see a woman and her two daughters, the older one seven and the younger one five. The 7-year-old wakes at night with abdominal pain and becomes very upset and often ends up in tears during the day. In the second session, this child brings me a picture of herself as a baby being held by her father. Her parents have never lived together, and their ongoing contact around the girls still makes her mother very unhappy. The child also tells me she thinks it would be good if they came to see me every day. Nonetheless, she proceeds to make a remarkably rapid recovery, and her mother's everyday distress becomes clearer. We agree that I will see the mother a few times, then see them all together again.

The woman's story is difficult. Her own mother had an untreated psychotic illness; her father was not around; she and her younger sister were put in a home when she was five, and she tried to look after her; her younger sister made a number of suicide attempts as a young adult, and one of these attempts left her with a severe disability; she has always hoped for more from the children's father and gets distressed each time this does not happen; and she hates the children being hurt and feeling that their father does not care about them.

Our talking about this is painful, yet it flows quite easily. Despite the easy flow, I find myself becoming increasingly fearful in the sessions, and I keep thinking about closing off the work when the family meets again. From the outside, the work would look a 'success' – the presenting problem is 'cured' – yet at another level I am quite clear that there is more therapeutic work to be done for the 'cure' to hold.

Second Piece

A mother contacts me under pressure very angry about her 6-year-old son. She is herself just 23 and has a new 6-month-old baby girl and a semi live-in relationship with the baby's father. The boy has been a problem 'since before day one', and they have been to counselling twice before, and each time it was 'useless'.

This is all in the intake notes, and it is not an easy first session. It is as if the mother needs to prove just how bad the boy really is, and there is a relentless attack. To witness it feels like collusion with abuse, yet I also know that any move on my part to rescue the child is likely to escalate the attack. Things finally begin to settle, and I am asking them to describe what it is like at home when the fights are really bad. We are going through the sequence, and in one of those peculiar Pollyanna moments that can take hold of you in such a session, I say to the child: 'so after your Mum shouts and yells at you, you go to your room and have a good cry'. He looks at me and says: 'no, I don't have a good cry, I have a bad cry – a very bad cry'. Later in the session, the mother tells me about her attempts to get help in the past. One time, they saw a counsellor who just let the child 'twist her around his little finger – he really had her fooled'. The other time they went to a hospital service which was 'terrible'. The mother was asked a lot of questions that they did not have a right to know, and it made her cry. It was quite clear that it was not a good cry but a very bad cry.

In a session with the mother and her partner, I hear the story of the boy's birth. The mother was 16 and determined to have him adopted. She had told them she did not want to see the baby. But then they brought him to her, and she felt pressured into keeping him. In the telling of the story, there was a sense that the very physicality of her son as a tiny baby had trapped her, and the story was told with anger.

In the first period of the work, progress is made steadily if slowly. Then, seemingly out of the blue, the mother's anger skyrockets again, and she begins to talk seriously about putting her son in foster care. I become very worried that the momentum to reject could easily spin out of control, with potentially disastrous consequences for the boy.

Transference, countertransference and projective identification

Transference, countertransference and projective identification are cornerstone concepts in psychoanalytic theory and practice. While Freud developed the early ideas of transference and counter-transference from 1910, projective identification was first theorised in the work of Melanie Klein and her contemporaries in Britain from the late 1940s. As you would expect, there have been major developments of these ideas since then. Gregorio Kohon (1986), Thomas Ogden (1982), Douglas Orr (1988), Joseph Sandler (1989), and Michael Tansey and Walter Burke (1989) all give interesting sample discussions of the development of these ideas and some of the debates which have been significant in this history.

Though transference, countertransference and projective identification serve as a means of understanding intrapsychic and unconscious experience, it would be wrong to characterise them as linear concepts. They offer intersubjective understandings, and the notion of the intrapsychic self that is constructed is of self-in-relationship.

Indeed, in this sense these ideas have always been relational in their orientation. More specifically, the momentum for theorising has been part of the challenge of understanding the analytic relationship and the transformational possibilities that may be created within the analytic frame between analyst and patient.[1] This is not to deny the struggle within psychoanalysis to comprehend the intense mutuality of the analytic process. In reading contemporary analytic theory, one almost gets the sense that psychoanalysis has itself been taken by surprise by the 'sudden' recognition of this intense mutuality and its implications for thinking and practice. Again and again there is an underlining of the relationality of the analytic process, and one assumes that this underlining speaks to the 'other' historical conception of psychoanalysis as a linear process with the 'blank-screen' analyst.

John Klauber, for example, argues that 'the most neglected feature of the psychoanalytic relationship still seems to me to be that it is a relationship' (Klauber 1986: 200). Neville Symington notes that 'with the exception of Winnicott . . . most analysts operate on the assumption that people are separate entities' (Symington 1986: 270), and he emphasises that 'at one level the analyst and patient together make a single system' (Symington, 1986: 262). Meanwhile Kohon writes:

> The analyst is never an 'outsider'; he is part and parcel of the transference situation. In fact, one could argue that the transference is as much a function of the countertransference as the countertransference is a result of the transference (Kohon 1986: 53).

Donna Orange (1995) echoes Kohon's thinking when she advocates the use of the idea of co-transferences rather than transference and countertransference.

These quick references are meant simply to give a flavour of the recognition of the mutuality of the analytic relationship and the construction of transference, countertransference and projective identification as relational concepts. But I am in danger here of my commentary running too far ahead, so let me take a step back and describe transference, countertransference and projective identification in turn.

Freud's early idea of transference evolved from his practice of psychoanalysis, where he began to theorise the way in which the analyst and the analytic relationship could be used by the patient to 'transfer' a foundational relationship, with all the unconscious fantasies and feelings associated with it. Freud's central interest in sexuality and the oedipal complex led to the early ideas of the analyst coming to represent, for example, the (oedipal) father in the context of the analysis. Within the ambit of a primary concern with the oedipal complex, transference tended to be 'read' in this more concrete form of the analyst coming to symbolise the (oedipal) mother or father of the patient's unconscious world.

However, though transference may sometimes be just as specific as this, current understandings have moved beyond these more literal ideas of transference. The focus remains steadily on the patient's unconscious fantasies and emotions, but within contemporary analytic thinking, transference is used more to describe the process of a person recreating her or his patterns of emotional experience in the context of the present analytic relationship. Transference, then, is about an individual's patterns of relating. As such, it can occur only in the context of a relationship, and it occurs in any significant relationship, not just the therapy relationship. As 'the living history of ways of relating' (Scharff and Scharff 1991: 203), transference patterns are able to show core emotional dilemmas and struggles, and it is for this reason that the transference of the patient in the analytic relationship is seen as centrally valuable in showing the way for the analytic work. In this way, one could think of transference as representing the bridging of the past-in-the-present, and this point is made very well by Ruth Riesenberg Malcolm when she writes:

> . . . transference is an emotional relationship of the patient with the analyst which is experienced in the present, in what is generally called 'the-here-and-now' of the analytic situation. It is the expression of the patient's past in its multiple transformations (Riesenberg Malcolm 1986: 433).

If transference refers to the patterns of experience that the patient brings and enacts in the analysis, countertransference refers to the involvement of the analyst in the relationship, and the emotions, attitudes and patterns of relating that the analyst may begin to experience and enact in the context of the therapeutic relationship. The circular nature of transference and countertransference cannot be escaped, precisely because both the (patient's) transference and the (analyst's) countertransference are constructed in relation to each other and in the context of the analytic frame.

That it is simply not possible to avoid countertransference is also an uncontroversial idea. However, historically there have been different positions taken about the implications of countertransference for the analyst's position. On the one hand, countertransference has been seen as something which the analyst must overcome if the analytic space is to be preserved for the patient. On the other hand, countertransference has been seen as a valuable medium of analytic work, providing the source of rich information about the patient's unconscious dilemmas.

Tansey and Burke (1989) note that these two seemingly contradictory positions on countertransference were both present in Freud's early discussions. In some of the contemporary applications of these analytic ideas to the broader psychotherapies, there is a tendency to allow both positions on countertransference simply to sit side by side. Michael Kahn (1991), for example, takes a pragmatic position on whether countertransference is to be overcome or used, and he grounds this in the specifics of the particular transferences and countertransferences that are being evoked. One could think generally of countertransferences coming primarily from the analyst's own experiences and emotional dilemmas, which though they may be triggered in the process of interacting with the patient's transference, nonetheless speak more loudly of the analyst's own conscious and unconscious struggles rather than the patient's. However, there is another layer of countertransference experience that is more closely linked to the analyst's involvement in the patient's transference and unconscious experience. Contemporary analytic thinking would now locate this kind of countertransference experience at the heart of analytic practice.

Indeed, in current discussions, transference itself is approached and inferred via the reflection of the analyst on her or his own countertransference. Nina Colthart (1986) gives a finely textured discussion of this process and the use of countertransference in thinking the unthinkable and tracing the shape of transference as it emerges in the analytic relationship. Projective identification is an analytic concept which over time has become more and more important in the understandings of this territory of countertransference. Again, we can note that this concept describes a relational process, and it addresses a particular kind of unconscious interaction between patient and analysis.

Projective identification may occur when the patient is struggling with emotions or dilemmas that are too difficult to sustain or know at a conscious level. Within this understanding, the unbearable and unconscious thought or feeling or impasse becomes split off and projected outwards and away from self. However, projection is only one part of the relational process of projective identification, and it requires that another person takes on board the projection through the process of identification. The conditions for this identification involve a sufficiently connected relationship and the ability of the other (/the analyst) to find sufficient resonance within her or his own emotional possibilities for the identification. As with transference, projective identification is part of the complexity of human experience within relationships, and it by no means lies solely within the province of the analytic relationship.

But is projective identification primarily an unconscious defence, or a form of communication that has as part of its momentum the desire to be known and understood by another? Ogden (1982) would argue that it is at the one time a defence, a form of communication and a pathway to psychological change. Yet both within psychoanalysis and in its application in other therapeutic contexts, an appreciation of projective identification as a form of communication allows a therapeutic connectedness which would otherwise be hard to gain by staying within the boundaries of conscious communication. In this respect, there has been considerable discussion (particularly within the interpersonal tradition of psychoanalysis) of the role of projective identification in allowing empathic connection, and Tansey and Burke (1989) would certainly see it as a form of generative empathy.

Thus, the idea of projective identification as a form of unconscious communication has the capacity to be used to generate empathy, and this is one of its strongest appeals for other therapeutic frameworks. Yet projective identification is not a simple idea in either theory or practice. Its very nature – that someone else's experience may be felt for a time as if it were your own – means that it is necessarily confusing, and practice reflection about the nature of specific instances of projective identification should always be tentative. Indeed, the whole terrain of transference, countertransference and projective identification should be approached tentatively, and I would argue that this is particularly important when these ideas are being used outside an analytic frame.

Kohon would warn even other analysts about the dangers of misusing these ideas. He singles out a tendency in some analytic practice to systematically attribute everything that goes on in the analysis to the patient's transference, noting that this can lead to the 'creation of a distinctively stagnant psychoanalytic product: the "you mean me" interpretations' (Kohon 1986: 72). In a similar vein, he notes that the ideas of countertransference and projective identification may be (mis)used by the analyst to defend against the patient's transference, and indeed to defend against the analyst's own experience of pain in the analysis. There is then a reverse projection, with the analyst's experience being disowned and passed to the patient. The danger here is that the analyst could become cut off from the realness of the patient's experience, and the potential of these ideas to serve in understanding and connection could be seriously negated.

It would be untrue to say that I have just been giving the kind of account of analytic ideas that would be given within psychoanalysis, for my purposes here are quite specific and lie within the interests of extending ideas in systemic therapy. Nonetheless, to this point I have tried to stay within the frame of the way in which these ideas have been shaped as understandings of the analyst-patient relationship and the therapeutic momentum of the analytic situation. I will now take a step sideways and consider transference, countertransference and projective identification as particular kinds of descriptions of patterns-across-time, bringing them into constellation with other ideas of the lived experience of time.

On time, narrative and patterns

If we think of transference as being the relational expression of the past in its 'multiple transformations' (to repeat Riesenberg Malcolm), then inevitably we are dealing with the lived experience of time. Transference within psychoanalysis comes to be taken as an expression of the past as it lives in the present. To think of the lived experience of time, though, evokes not just the living past, but also the expectation of the future and times-to-come.

Time is inescapable – we exist in it and live through it, and it continues regardless of our consciousness of it, and indeed regardless of our mortality. Therapy itself sits in present time, and the therapeutic process continually straddles the past-in-the-present and the future-in-the-present. Current relationship dilemmas bear the living past, and yet the very frame of therapy assumes a hopefulness about something being different in the future. Time may be at its simplest when taken for granted, for to begin to address it at a theory level quickly raises a number of complexities. For all that, its centrality to the process of therapeutic change makes it fruitful to explore. My discussion in this section will be restricted to three themes – the reflexivity of past, present and future time; the experience of 'stuck' time and narrative closure; and patterns and sequences in time.

Luigi Boscolo and Paolo Bertrando (1992, 1993) give a fascinating discussion of the way in which understandings of time may lend a new perspective to the theory and practices of systemic therapy. They discuss the different layers of time, from the time of things and objects to the interior sense of time, or the individual's own 'internal' sense of time. Moving from the premise that different lived experiences of time require different explanations and metaphors, they distinguish interior time from social or interactional time, and from cultural time across generations. Boscolo and Bertrando focus particularly on interactional time as family time, and the possibilities for bringing both the past and the future into the present time of therapy. These ideas are then used to elaborate the conceptualisation of a reflexive loop of past, present and future time.

Boscolo and Bertrando also explore the idea of 'frozen' time as one way of describing the situation of families who find themselves repeating problematic sequences in an attempt to meet a past traumatic event. Discussions of therapeutic rituals (Boscolo and Bertrando 1993; Imber-Black 1993) and particularly rituals addressing family grief and loss, give very moving accounts of practices that are aimed quite specifically at addressing the past-in-the-present in the attempt to unfreeze time. Time can also become frozen around individual trauma, and indeed research on memory and early trauma is beginning to chart the effects of trauma on the physiological development of the brain. Flashbacks can be a particularly painful experience of the living-through of the effects of trauma, and they represent a form of frozen time that shows the intimate relationship of body, mind and emotions.

I have also been struck by the way in which timelessness is so often a feature of chronicity in family problems. It is as if the problem comes to be experienced in an undifferentiated 'always' frame – a sense of an unchanging past and the despair of an unchangeable future seem to collapse the family's experience of the problem into a timeless present. As a therapist, I have often found myself losing the capacity to distinguish time in relation to the family's struggles. I begin to become involved in the experience of timelessness, and then have to remind myself to hold on to time with the family, to not lose the 'before', 'after', 'when', 'for the moment', 'down the track', 'as it was then' language of therapeutic conversation.

Stuck time and the experience of timelessness are invariably accompanied by narrative closure, for the very nature of a story is that it unfolds through time, as the past moves to the present and anticipates a future. Stories cannot move on when personal or relational time is stuck, and the frustration of this is often very directly expressed in therapy – 'we sound like a broken record', one father told me; 'I'm so sick of this story I'm even boring myself', a woman said.

Narrative theory in its broader intellectual traditions has made a major contribution to understandings of time. Paul Ricoeur's philosophical work locates narrative time as a deeper experience beyond linear chronological sequence (Ricoeur 1981, 1984). Working from Heidegger's concept of within-time-ness and becoming, Ricoeur notes that 'becoming' mediates the dimensions of past, present and future time – the time of 'becoming', then, is a unity of coming-forth, having-been and making-present. It is interesting to think that this is precisely the kind of time that the activity of psychotherapy tries to evoke, and that although there is the frequently used description of creating therapeutic 'space', there is no common description for the process of evoking therapeutic time.

Narrative ideas have also been very influential in psychotherapy in debates around the time of the historical past versus the narrative past. These debates have been waged strongly within psychoanalysis where the question of what kind of past is represented in the experience of transference and projective identification is of critical importance. Some psychoanalysts have argued that to engage with the unconscious through transference and counter-transference is to engage in the process of narrative (see Morris 1993; Schafer 1992; Spence 1987; Szajnberg 1992; Wyatt 1986). These analysts would be working with an idea of unconscious narratives, and it is worth underlining that this is a radical departure from other theorisations of narrative.

The challenge of narrative within psychoanalysis has seen counter-arguments which reassert a positivist idea of the past as being a literal 'real' past (see Dunn 1995; Leary 1989). However, other counter-arguments have stressed the relational form of intrapsychic experience and the extent to which the activity of psychoanalysis addresses the realness of the past as it exists now in the patient's intrapsychic world, in all its mediations across time (see Bouchard 1995; Britten 1995; Cavell 1998). It is probably quite clear from my earlier discussions on reality and realness that my own sympathies would lie more with this second counter-argument.

Yet throughout this discussion of time and the therapeutic context, I have found myself thinking of family patterns, and the now rather old-fashioned systemic concept of sequences. The practice concept of sequences grew from the strategic therapies, and the strategic emphasis on present behaviour has in many ways limited its potential value. The traditional definition of sequences is that they are patterns of behaviour across time (Breunlin and Schwartz 1986), yet as I have argued in other places (Flaskas 1996, 1999), this reduction of interactional patterns to behaviour is unnecessarily limiting. In human interaction, behaviour is always in relationship with meaning and emotional experience. When viewed in this way, the lens of meaning and stories is not in opposition to a broader lens of sequences which encompasses the relationship of stories to behaviour and emotion.

Moreover, though an idea of sequences which is restricted to present time tends to offer a linear chronological view, extending sequences to patterns across past time and into the expectations of future time allows much greater leeway for engaging with the complexity of present time. The work by Douglas Breunlin and Richard Schwartz (Breunlin and Schwartz 1986; Breunlin, Schwartz, and MacKune-Karrer 1992) gives some pointers to this way of enhancing the concept of sequences. They look for patterns across different time frames, from minutes to hours, from days to weeks, from months to years, to intergenerational and cultural time. Their argument is that the immediate relationship patterns around presenting problems (e.g. the sequence of a couple's fighting, or of a young woman's self-harming behaviour) are usually supported by patterns of longer duration in the present, and understanding the level of embeddedness of current patterns in the past patterns of family time can help to shape the therapy work.

Viewed from this angle, transference, countertransference and projective identification are sequences that take place in the immediate therapeutic environment of the analytic hour, bound in time and space. However, the therapeutic leeway they offer depends on the connection of patterns across time – their richness, if you like, lies in bringing the living past into the present of the therapy process itself.

One of the drawbacks of the concept of sequences is that it relies heavily on the idea of repeating patterns. Of course, patterns and stories sometimes do repeat themselves almost exactly. However, the time from birth to death allows many different points for repetition, and although patterns may be closely repeated, more often they provide opportunities for mediating experience. In narrative terms, they provide opportunities for revising experience and for elaborating different themes in a continuing restorying.

For example, one might come to know that a father has been physically abused, not by the repetition of abuse with his children (when it is only too clear), but rather by his difficulty in setting any limits with them and the fights he has with his wife when she tries to do this. A woman who has been sexually abused as a child might find herself in situations in which she feels exploited again and again, yet though there may be a familiar tune repeating itself, it is worthwhile considering what is different, and what elements of the repetition show repair work. A mother whose own mother died when she was four might find herself, as each of her own children moves towards four, in the grip of an anxiety that quickly turns into a depression with suicidal thoughts. These times of repetition – acutely painful, with spiralling effects and involvement of all the family – are nonetheless important times of reparation and growth, although they are also times in which the landscape of the family and of each child changes. Thus, the idea of repetition in sequences underemphasises the way in which current patterns often show not so much direct repetition as the history of transformations of the past. In this way, the complexity of repetition in mediating and shaping experience can easily be lost.

But it is time to gather the different threads of this part of the discussion. The psychoanalytic ideas of transference, counter-transference and projective identification, and the way in which they are used to try to engage the living past, led to a broader consideration of time, and the dimensions of the living past, the present, and the future-in-the-present. Therapeutic time is present time as it bridges the living past and the expected future. The difficulty of stuck time in the experience of individuals and families was tied to the idea of narrative closure and narrative time. Finally, the idea of sequences as patterns-across-time was explored, with a plea for moving beyond patterns of behaviour to encompassing the emotional and meaning dimensions of relational patterns and for allowing for the complexity of transformation in repeating patterns.

Though not a seamless whole, I plan to use this body of ideas in reflecting on the earlier practice descriptions.

Practice reflections

First Piece

Let me pick up again on working with the family where the 7-year-old girl comes with abdominal pain during the night and crying during the day, and her mother tells me of a painful background of loss and rejection. Two things stand out about my own experience here. The first is the quite noticeable feeling of anxiety I came to have in the first few sessions; the second is the persistent thought that developed that I should take the first opportunity to finish early with the family. With respect to the family's experience, I am struck by the ease with which the girl gave up her symptoms, and also by the freshness of the mother's everyday distress about her ex-boyfriend's comings and goings, and her even greater distress about the girls being hurt by his unreliability.

My anxiety comes to make some sense when I think about the interactional sequence in the therapy. To give a description based on the emotions rather than the behaviour of the presenting problems, we could think of the girl as presenting with distress (daytime tears), and anxiety/fear (night-time abdominal pain). In the therapy sequence, the child quickly gives up her symptoms, and her mother expresses more distress, and I come to feel alarmed and anxious. One description of this sequence is that the mother and I take back the difficult emotions, and this frees up the child. A second (and not incompatible) description would be to think of my experience of the anxiety as an example of projective identification. The pain and distress were consciously known about in this family, and the mother very readily took this over from her daughter; however, there were no words about fear in circulation in the family, and indeed fear had come to be expressed physically by the girl waking up in pain. I came to experience an emotion which was very hard for the family to know about at a conscious level or to language, and yet they were very much living with its effects.

The thought I had about finishing was fed in part by my anxiety, the simple enough countertransference of wanting to solve it by closing off the work! But I do not think it was just a personal reactivity that was triggering the thought, which continued to occur despite my clarity that more therapeutic work was needed. And although I never really felt in danger of acting on it, the thought went on nagging me. To be curious about it as a fantasy, I can not help but wonder about the momentum to prematurely give up on this family in terms of a resonance with the mother's actual experience of being 'given up' prematurely as a child when she and her sister were taken into care. The mother's early experience was so much a part of her emotional landscape, and the pain of being rejected was very much part of her living past. This living past was showing itself in some way in my thought about finishing too early.

The theme of the past-in-the-present runs through this discussion of the transference and projective identification, as it was running through the family's struggles. The mother found it very painful to watch her daughters being hurt when their father let them down. It produced a kind of timeless distress for her about rejection, and a despair that she was unable to protect her daughters from being hurt.

There was indeed an aspect of stuck time and narrative closure in the family around this issue. For through her sensitivity to the girls' experience of rejection, the mother had come to have only a story of rejection about her daughters' relationship to their father, and they had found it hard to tell her about the other parts of their experience with him. The older girl puts this on the therapy agenda when she brings me the photo of herself as a baby being held by her father. She and her little sister come to talk about the fun they have with him, and how nice it is to go to Nanna's (his mother's), and their auntie and cousins' place. Various practical things come of this, and the mother adds something to her story of their rejection, and she begins to see her persistence with their father as something good she is offering them, even if it means that they all at times feel hurt. Her orientation as a mother to the future of her children is part of the future-in-the-present, and she begins to become more hopeful of the possibility of being less distressed herself.

Second Piece

Work with the second family was more difficult. The mother's anger and attacks on her 6-year-old son have all the hallmarks of long-term emotional abuse, and certainly her negative story-ing of him feels set in concrete. There was nothing particularly surprising about my own countertransference, as I struggled with my anger toward the mother as she attacked her son, and I persisted in trying to find the therapeutic space in which I could feel genuinely in touch with her dilemmas. This became possible in the session in which I saw her with her partner, and she talked about her son's birth when she was 16 and her sense of being forced to keep him. Words were not wrapped around her own history of abuse in this session, and it seemed important to respect her censorship at the time. However, this history was palpable, and my sense was that she had a physically and emotionally very abusive childhood, and the conception of and pregnancy with her son was experienced by her as a continuation of the abuse.

I feel the usual hopelessness in witnessing the intergenera-tional repetition of abuse and the stuckness of patterns and stories. This becomes easier when the positive changes begin, and then without warning the mother wants her son put into foster care. The momentum to reject him is very strong, and I fear it is quite possible that she will act on it. I am horrified at the prospect for the boy, and yet I also hang on to the idea that the mother needs some time and space to think about whether she really wants her son, and whether she thinks she can mother him. This all happens across a number of sessions, and her attacks on the boy become more contained in almost direct proportion to her freedom in considering her choice. She decides she will keep him, and there is no question that this was a significant turning point in her relationship with her son.

Where abuse is overt, one's own countertransferences are usually pretty impossible to miss. That I would struggle with feeling hopeless about the family and angry with the mother is not very difficult to understand, nor is it hard to understand the lack of equanimity I feel when it seems that the mother might in fact reject the boy and foster him out of the family. Yet to stay only with the level of the reasonableness of my emotional responses may miss something about the connectedness of my own experience and the family's experience. The anger in the family was quite conscious, but feeling 'rotten through-and-through' (the mother's words about the son) was a more toxic emotion which moved in and out of conscious experience. It surfaced in the 'bad' crying, and when the mother threw the badness at her son in her attacks on him, he would reciprocate to get back at her. When I felt most outraged and most inadequate in sessions, I would find myself needing to censor the desire to attack the mother, who in that moment in my fantasy was bad. This pattern in the therapy – the need to defend against feeling bad by disowning it and throwing it on to someone else – was embedded in the pattern of abuse between mother and son, and I think almost certainly repeated the mother's own experience of abuse as a child.

We could say that time and stories were stuck in the family's presentation, and I am sure I was not the only one feeling a hopelessness about it all. Yet an important repetition occurs within the boundaries of the therapy: will the mother keep the child, or will she give him up? It is in reality a dangerous process, and yet the mother creates this opportunity, seven years later, to make a choice. The past had entered the therapy room in a very present and active way.

But what were the conditions that made this reclaiming of time and re-enactment of choice possible? There were some things about the therapy that helped, and yet I think that the more significant factors in the mother's readiness to use the therapy in this way, at this time, lay in the unfolding of her family's life. The circumstances of the birth of her second child – a wanted child, whom she was far more easily able to love, with a father who was still around – presented a serious challenge to her relationship with her son. I am inclined to think that the new baby fuelled her anger with her son whom she had not felt able to love, and yet at the same time challenged her as a mother about the negativeness of her relationship with him. In the process of actively claiming her son, she began to have a much more detailed and compassionate story about herself as a very young mother and about her son as a baby and as he was now, and she was able to compare what was happening for her then to what was happening for her now. Thus, the repetition of choosing enabled an important step of reparation and a different marking of time.

I have not tried to use the above discussions to neatly box the ideas laid out in this chapter. Rather, I have taken the opportunity to draw out the themes as they seemed relevant in reflecting on my experience in each of these therapies. For both families, the living past was firmly embedded in the current struggles, and stuck time and stuck stories and stuck patterns were all a challenge. In the therapeutic movement, hopelessness and hope were represented in the families' future orientation, and it was the future as well as the present that mobilised change. In the second therapy, there is a repetition which allows an active reworking of the past-in-the-present, and the past is mediated as some important reparation takes place in the present.

Re-reading the last paragraph, I am struck by how easy it is to write about family therapy as if you were not there! But of course I was very much there, and the discussion also brought out patterns in the therapeutic relationship and in my own emotional process as the therapist. This discussion used the ideas of transference, countertransference and projective identification, though with different emphases in the two different pieces of work. I was not working psychoanalytically, and precisely because I am using these ideas in the different framework of systemic therapy, I applied them quite pragmatically at points that seemed most useful for my own work.

With the first family, the anxiety and wanting to finish early are parts of my own experience which stand out precisely because they do not seem to make sense with my conscious experience of the family. For what it is worth, at a practice level, I think the moments in therapy when your own emotional process disconcerts your conscious understandings are often very useful points to consider the family's unconscious experience and your own fit with it as the therapist. Reflecting on my own experience with the first family in terms of transference and projective identification allowed me to have a different kind of connectedness with the family's experience and a stronger sense of therapeutic collaboration with their struggles. With the second family, I experience the ordinary countertransferences of working with abuse. However, reflecting on the relationship between my countertransference and the family's experience again allows me to have a stronger sense of connectedness and empathy, and in this way it both protects and enriches the therapeutic relationship.

Conclusion

The last chapter introduced the relational unconscious, and in this chapter the more specific ideas of transference, countertransference and projective identification were explored alongside a broader consideration of the lived experience of time. Transference, countertransference and projective identification are particularly geared toward understanding the intersubjective process of analysis and the way in which the patient's living past comes to be expressed within the boundaries of the analysis and the analytic relationship. These ideas engage with unconscious processes and the analyst's own involvement in the analysis, and they have the capacity to generate understanding and empathy. When used outside an analytic frame, they are particularly useful in offering understandings about the therapeutic relationship and the therapist's experience, and in strengthening empathy and allowing a different kind of therapeutic connectedness.

The analytic ideas addressed the living past as it is expressed in the therapy and also opened the issue of time and the therapeutic process. Present time in therapy can be thought of as expressing the past-in-the-present as well as the future-in-the-present, and different therapy frameworks engage with these dimensions of time in different ways. Stuck time is often part of the presentation of individual and family difficulties, and stuck time goes with stuck stories and stuck patterns. The issue of narrative closure and narrative time and the repetition of patterns were explored, and attention was drawn to the significance of repetition in mediating the past and allowing the revision and development of storying.

In reflecting on the two pieces of practice experience, all these ideas found some place in describing the therapies. The discussion raised my own experience as therapist as well as my understandings of the families' experiences. Given that the ideas of transference, countertransference and projective identification all address the intersubjective processes of therapy, it is not surprising that both the theory and practice discussions of this chapter have begun the work of the next chapter, which directly explores ideas about the therapeutic relationship in systemic therapy.

Note

1 I have decided to retain the use of 'patient' when discussing psychoanalytic practice, because I think it is misleading to substitute the term 'client' in this different context and misrepresents analytic discourse. However, when I am using psychoanalytic ideas in the context of systemic thinking and practice, I will revert to the use of 'client'.

Chapter 10

Further thoughts on the therapeutic relationship

In effect, the concluding paragraph of the last chapter becomes the introduction to this chapter, for the discussions of transference, countertransference and projective identification offer one way of understanding aspects of interactional patterns in the therapeutic relationship. This chapter will simply assume these discussions and move to a fuller consideration of the therapeutic relationship in the systemic context. Some themes already discussed will be further elaborated, other intersections will be made with analytic thinking, although in this chapter my central focus will be on developing themes which are emerging in the family therapy discussions. This is the last of the three chapters to draw on psychoanalytic ideas, and the synthesis of this work with my earlier investigation of postmodernism remains for the final conclusion.

After a long period of neglect, the therapeutic relationship has been more openly addressed in family therapy in recent years. There have been a number of discussions of the topic (see, for example, Pocock 1997; Reimers 2001; Rober 1999; and the collection edited by Flaskas and Perlesz 1996) and of the related topic of the therapist's use of self (Hardham 1996; Hildebrand and Speed 1995; Paterson 1996). However, there are also the beginning signs of a greater readiness to 'paint in' the therapist in family therapy discussions, and I think this reflects the ripples of postmodernism, and the extent to which narrative and social constructionist ideas have the capacity to lead to a greater awareness of the importance of the therapist in the therapeutic process and therapist-present practices. One sees this in Michael White's most recent book *Narratives of therapists' lives* (1997), and for example, in the way in which Harlene Anderson (1997), Lynn Hoffman (1993, 1998) and Kathy Weingarten (1998, 2000) all make themselves more visible in their writing. We are perhaps also seeing here the influence of feminist politics with respect to acknowledging authorship.

I also have written in other places about the therapeutic relationship (Flaskas 1989, 1994, 1996, 1997a), but in this chapter I am crafting the discussion around themes that relate more closely to my project in this book. The chapter will once more take practice as its starting point, and then move from the themes of the last chapter to a fuller discussion of understanding and the process of empathy. The next section will consider the idea of the therapeutic position of not-knowing as it has developed in family therapy, and the intersections which are being made with contemporary psychoanalytic thinking following the ideas of Wilfred Bion. The final section begins with the argument that there needs to be flexibility in using the space of not-knowing alongside the space of reflection, then develops a discussion of the space of reflection with respect to therapeutic impasse. This will then lead back to the practice.

Some practice experience

First Piece

I see a couple following family work where they move on from a focus on one of the children's behaviour to issues in their own relationship around parenting. It is a stepfamily, and the three children are from the mother's previous marriage. Access issues and the stepfather's relationship to the children's father had been part of the family work. In the privacy of the couple sessions, the therapeutic net widens, and the wife's unhappiness and disappointment with her husband and his anger about this, very quickly come to be put on the table.

Threes are an interesting relationship combination, no less in a therapy triangle than anywhere else. The issues are almost out of a textbook on gender and heterosexual relationships. The wife is emotionally very quick and very good with language. The husband is uncomfortable around the language of emotions and relationships, gets twisted up in it, and usually both in and out of sessions ends up either becoming overtly angry and aggrieved or else he goes on a kind of verbal strike. The wife is strongly committed to the therapy, and the husband is ambivalent. I think at the time that my role as the therapist would be much easier if I were a man, and if you had asked me where the difficulties in the therapeutic relationship lay, I would have said in my engagement with the husband.

Yet after a few of these sessions I have a dream. I am looking at the woman, and though she seems very together, I know she is having a breakdown of the mad variety as opposed to the sad variety. In the dream I am surprised, although the madness is so crystal clear, and I think 'ah yes, but of course'. Now we all know that dreams are the territory of self. Much as I would like to grace this dream with the frame of pure professional altruism – 'she dreamt only for her clients . . .' – I think I do have to own the fact that it does remain always my dream! Yet at the same time, it is interesting when we create dreams using images of particular clients, settling associations or thoughts or feelings on them, and cross-linking some unconscious puzzle about our own dilemmas and our clients'. At any rate, the next session after this dream, the couple do not come back. The husband rings me very upset about this, and he tells me that it is his wife who does not want to continue the therapy.

Second Piece

A mother contacts for therapy, concerned about her 8-year-old son and his ongoing problem with soiling. The parents have two other children – a 6-year-old girl, and a 10-month-old. It is an unusual first session. Both parents are quite shy, and by contrast the boy is bright and forthcoming, verbally very articulate, and at the mere suggestion of an invitation, embarks in a very cheery way on describing and drawing (in glorious detail) all the problems associated for him with soiling. I am not sure what it is like for the parents and other children, but I begin to feel sidelined, rather like a member of the audience, and I have to work quite hard to hold on to being 'the therapist' in the session.

This is all interesting enough, and I go into the next session expecting to build on some of the first session work and introduce Michael White's 'sneaky poo' frame.[1] This plan is immediately derailed, as the parents start by telling me that the boy had stopped urinating the day after the first session. After two days packed with various emergency appointments with various specialists, he was pronounced physically okay and things were now back to normal – still soiling but alright 'in the other department'. Through the first part of this second session, I feel lost and as if I am operating in a thick fog with near zero visibility. I am not even sure what my own reaction is to the rather spectacular sequel, and I cannot gauge either the mother's or father's reaction, and efforts to try to wonder about the child's experience feel distant and impoverished.

Unsure about my own judgement, I nonetheless decide to introduce the sneaky poo work. I do this after acknowledging that I feel flummoxed by what had happened, and after a rather fulsome discussion about what 'flummoxed' means, we all do some wondering about the sequence, who thought and felt what, and it is quite a difficult discussion. I also say that I am not sure if it is too early to start the sneaky poo work and that I would need the boy and his parents to guide me about whether they thought it really was the right time.

Over the next few sessions, there is a major improvement, and the child revels in his success while his parents are delighted and relieved. There is a break over the holidays, and they return with a minor setback which is quickly overcome, and the work finishes. Over the next three years, the family come back twice. The first time they bring their concern about rivalry and fighting between all three children (but especially the older two); and the second time, the parents want to address their differences in parenting, and their difficulties in maintaining a 'united front'.

Understanding and empathy

Understanding and empathy emerged strongly as concluding themes in the last chapter. Transference, countertransference and projective identification are the medium through which analytic work takes place, although in the different context of systemic family therapy practice, these ideas do not occupy the same position. However, they provide a valuable resource for thinking about the therapeutic relationship and the therapist's experience in a way that can generate and strengthen empathy and allow a different kind of therapeutic connectedness. Let me pick up at this point and continue the discussion about the process of empathy and understanding.

I doubt that I need to give an extended justification of the relevance of these processes to the therapeutic relationship, or indeed of the relevance of considering the therapeutic relationship itself. There is an increasing familiarity within family therapy with the gist of what is by now three decades of research on successful therapy outcomes (see for example Grunebaum 1988; Hubble, Duncan and Miller 1999; Lambert 1992). David Pocock summarises this research by noting that generally it is the similarities rather than the differences between therapeutic frameworks which figure in the investigation of positive therapeutic change. He also notes that of the factors associated with positive outcomes, it seems to be client variables rather than therapist variables that have the greater significance. And of the therapy and therapist variables, it seems that factors associated with the therapeutic relationship are the next most important grouping, roughly twice as important as the third grouping of variables associated with therapeutic model and technique (see Pocock 1997).

Empathy and the process of feeling understood are central to clients' experience in the therapeutic relationship, and this shows up again and again in research and practice. Empathy is a relational concept. From one side of the relationship, it is about the experience of feeling understood by another. From the other side, in the context of therapy, it is about the capacity of the therapist to attempt to understand the other's experience, as well as the ability to convey something of that understanding. A number of discussions in the family therapy literature relate to empathy (Harari 1996; Nichols 1987; Perlesz et al. 1996; Perry 1993; Pocock 1997; Rober 1999; Wilkinson 1992). I would like to acknowledge here two articles that have strongly influenced my own thinking in this area. The first is an article by Australian family therapist, Ron Perry (1993), entitled 'Empathy – still at the heart of therapy: the interplay of context and empathy'. The second, by David Pocock (1997), is entitled 'Feeling understood in family therapy', and I have made a number of references to this and other work by Pocock throughout this book.

Perry gives an excellent review of empathy and carefully delineates between particular methods for trying to convey empathy and the experience of empathy itself. He notes that the dominant way of teaching how to convey empathy has been through the 'reflecting back' technique, and in counselling training this has tended to become the standard of empathy rather than being taught as just one method of showing empathy. We can note here that though reflecting back is very useful in individual work when there are only two of you in the room, it is often quite problematic when used with families. With families, there may be, say, five people in varying degrees of unhappiness or conflict having quite different experiences of (and stories about) the presenting concern. As a therapist, one has to sustain a higher level of uncertainty, and the task of developing a free therapy space is often more complex and protracted. One is also often initially working 'blind' in a minefield of loyalties and alliances, and reflecting back can throw you unwittingly into alliances, risking neutrality when you still very much need it.

What I have just said is all commonplace practice knowledge, and Perry's discussion underlines the distinctiveness of therapeutic context, the challenge of trying to understand and convey understanding in work with families, and the way in which different methods and techniques meet this challenge. He explores a number of family therapy practices – questioning, opinions, interventions, tasks, reflecting teams – in terms of their capacity to convey understanding. Thus, Perry's work invites us to think of family therapy techniques as a means of empathy, and he helps us to have a sharpened awareness of the continuous process of empathic engagement in the practices we use. Through the discussion particularly of questioning, he offers a fuller understanding of the empathic impact of the therapeutic position of curiosity, which is common to the second order therapies.

I think it is interesting to think about the differences in approaching empathic connection from a position of curiosity, rather than the kind of therapeutic orientation one uses in reflecting back methods. Empathy involves listening and it also involves a preparedness to imagine. In trying to think about another's experience and reflect it back in words, the creative imagining of empathy uses an identification with the client – if you like, one positions oneself in fantasy as the-same-as, and hence, the very common expression 'putting yourself in the other's shoes'. On the other hand, when one is listening from a position of curiosity, the creative imagining of empathy is from a point of difference – even foreignness – that is held alongside an unswerving focus on trying to understand the other's experience. 'Think Martian', said my training supervisor in family therapy when trying to teach us questioning from a position of curiosity, and I have to say that I found this very liberating.

Different contexts of work may call for different emphases in moving between the empathic orientations of sameness or difference: for example, in the way that seeing families calls more heavily on curiosity and an orientation of difference. Yet therapeutic flexibility lies in being able to move between the two, to go back and forth using ourselves in imagination as identified with the client, as well as searching for ways of understanding the difference. This is a subtle and yet an ordinary process in the therapist's use of self. It sounds clumsy to put it in the more abstract language of subjects and objects, but I still want to say that in this back-and-forth movement, the therapist uses self as subject then object then subject then object in orienting to the client's experience, as well as in orienting to her or his own capacities for identification.

The ideas of transference, countertransference and projective identification could be thought of at one level as particular descriptions of the way in which analytic practice uses this therapist movement between subject and object. That the ideas address the unconscious experience of both the patient and the analyst may make it harder to see the movement. And yet, in essence, these ideas privilege being-in-relationship-with as the pathway to empathic engagement with the patient's subjectivity. Here the unswerving focus is on the patient's unconscious experience, but approaching this involves a readiness to sustain an immersion in this experience, while always struggling for the space to think about it. Transference comes to be understood through the analyst's countertransference and experience of the patient's projective identification, and in trying to think about this, the analyst moves from using herself(/himself) as subject to then trying to understand her(/his) own experience as object. All this is in the interests of generating understandings of the patient's subjective experience. Thus, the therapeutic process that relies on this complex use of self sees a continual relationship of the territories of subject and object, not just for the patient but for the analyst as well.

To use these analytic ideas as part of the process of understanding in the different context of systemic therapy also involves exploiting this movement. However, precisely because family therapy is quite a different business to individual analysis, the net is thrown much wider. Pocock (1997) makes this point in relation to what it is we might be trying to understand in family therapy. He holds some postmodernist ideas of understanding alongside contemporary psychoanalytic ideas. In particular, he uses Derrida's idea of *différance* as a way of thinking about what it is we try to understand in the hidden or unspoken parts of stories. This is of course much broader than the primary analytic interest in unconscious emotional experience. Pocock writes:

> In family therapy, the *différance* may include the patterns of mutual influence not yet thought about, the unappreciated strengths, the unacknowledged injustice, the cultural influences not yet recognised, the parts of the story that remain untold, or the unconscious wish of family members (Pocock 1997: 290).

We can also note that this net is cast much wider than the traditional emphasis of discussions of empathy, which have tended to focus on individual emotional experience.

Pocock also argues that in moving toward understanding in family therapy, we should embrace multiplicity in the use of theory, rather than being confined by the discipline of only one set of ideas. In short, he advocates that we 'use theory lightly' (Pocock 1997: 294) in generating empathic understanding. His conclusion about the process of understanding is this:

> . . . feeling understood is more than just useful knowledge; more too than a better story. It is an experience of being more known to and appreciated by others and, through them, to a greater appreciation of oneself. It is a celebration of both our common humanity and of our differences (Pocock 1997: 298).

However, this last point probably moves us on too far for this chapter's discussion. So let me finish this section by underlining the themes of the need to broaden our understanding of empathic engagement in family therapy – of the flexibility of using an empathic orientation of sameness (/identification) and difference (/foreignness/curiosity); of the interplay of using ourselves as subject and object in empathic connection; of the pattern of this in analytic work; and of the wider net we cast in family therapy in searching for understandings of the 'beyond language' in stories people bring.

Considering the idea of not-knowing

The discussion so far about curiosity and empathy from an orientation of difference raises another layer of themes around the idea of the therapeutic position of not-knowing. Despite the very different theory and practice contexts, there has been a strong resonance here between contemporary psychoanalytic theory and family therapy discussions. In this section, I am interested in tracing the appearance in family therapy of the idea of not-knowing and linking it to the position of curiosity. I would also like to introduce not-knowing within psychoanalysis and the use of Bion's ideas on emotional containment and the capacity for thinking, and I will do this by following through some of the discussion developed by Glenn Larner (2000).

The elaboration and advocacy of the therapeutic position of not-knowing within family therapy is largely associated with the work of Harry Goolishian and Harlene Anderson (Anderson and Goolishian 1992), and Anderson's subsequent work (1997). This work has been very influential as one of the main counterpoints to the more directive models of structural and strategic family therapy and the more directive interview style associated with the earlier Milan model. Anderson has continued to develop her ideas on not-knowing in a collaborative environment that includes the work of Norwegian family therapist Tom Anderson and his colleagues, and this connection is fully acknowledged by Anderson herself (1997), as well as by others (see for example Hoffman 1993).

The work of Goolishian and Anderson has been discussed before at some length in this book in terms of the importance of their contribution to social constructionist ideas within the postmodern developments in family therapy. Elaborating the idea of the therapist approaching the conversation of therapy from a position of not-knowing is for them a development of the implications of social constructionist ideas. Within this frame, therapy is about the process of generating meaning, and this is an activity that takes place in the languaging of the therapeutic conversation. The therapeutic conversation is understood as a mutual and collaborative endeavour between client and therapist, and in this dialogue, it is the client's experience which is privileged. To engage with the client's understanding of her or his own experience, the therapist needs to suspend her or his own preconceptions and commitments. Thus, the therapist approaches the work from a position of not-knowing, as a way of creating maximum space for the emergence of the client's reality, and as a way of creating the conditions for a collaborative conversation which becomes the therapeutic environment for the generation of new meaning (Anderson and Goolishian 1992).[2]

One hears in this description the rejection of the therapist-as-expert position that postmodernist discussions usually associate with modernist politics. The work of Goolishian and Anderson, and indeed White's narrative therapy, show a very clear commitment to approaching therapeutic work from the assumption of the client as expert of her or his own experience. In terms of the discussion of understanding and empathy, I would also like to say that the idea of not-knowing is in harmony with the idea of curiosity, and it could be thought of as one expression of an empathic orientation using an imagination of difference. In this sense, it is not surprising that it has come to have a broad influence in the current systemic therapies, for it is very much at home in second order thinking about curiosity.

I also noted much earlier on in this book that Anderson's practices 'look' quite similar to some of the practices of the humanistic therapies, for they give therapeutic power to the experience of listening and being listened to. Of course, within a social constructionist frame, the acts of listening and being listened to are significant beyond their impact as an emotional experience, for in this understanding, listening-and-being-listened-to becomes the environment of the social construction of self and meaning. There is a strong theme of embracing social otherness within this social constructionist framing of listening-and-being-listened-to, and this theme is made quite overt in Weingarten's discussion of radical listening (1995).

There are a number of interesting practice issues which relate to the idea of the therapeutic position of not-knowing, not the least being the tension inherent in the very idea of attempting to be helpful from a 'not-knowing' position. Just how not-knowing is not-knowing? And if it were to mean really abandoning all one's preconceptions, knowledge and skills as a therapist, how could this be helpful? Goolishian and Anderson (Anderson and Goolishian 1992) themselves addressed this tension by arguing that the therapist does not renege on knowledge and skills and takes responsibility to learn to be something like a 'master conversationalist'. The use of the word 'master' seems politically out of place here, and Anderson has developed the discussion of this tension using different metaphors (see Anderson 1997), as have other writers. Joan Laird (1998), for example, argues that we need to be 'highly informed' in our not-knowing. Barry Mason (1993) draws the importance of the difference between the experiences of safe and unsafe uncertainty, on both sides of the therapeutic relationship. This leads him to write of the need for the therapist to hold 'authoritative doubt' while working toward allowing a position of safe uncertainty.

Glenn Larner (2000) also explores the tension of knowing not-to-know, and he does this in a discussion in which he locates the parallel influences of postmodernist thinking within both family therapy and psychoanalysis. Larner outlines the resonances of the idea of not-knowing as it has emerged in family therapy and psychoanalysis, and in mapping its emergence within psycho-analytic theory, the common background of the postmodernist shift is thrown into clear relief. He points to the range of contem-porary psychoanalytic theory showing this influence, and then he traces the movement from Donald Winnicott to Wilfred Bion's work in transforming the interest from an individualised concept of mind to the relational context of knowing and being known, and indeed to the relational context of the capacity for thinking.

Bion's work has been mentioned before in the discussion of the unconscious, and it is central to the landscape of contemporary psychoanalytic theory (see for example Grotstein 1983; Symington and Symington 1996). He is best known for his ideas about thinking, and his theorising traces the dynamic of conscious and unconscious experience in the individual's attempts to come to know, and the way in which the capacity for thinking itself is part of an emotional and relational process (see for example Bion 1967, 1970; Symington and Symington 1996). It would be wrong to say that Bion is not interested in truth, because he is very much interested in the truth of the individual's experience, but it is important to note that his theory is devoted more to understanding the dynamic of approaching or avoiding thinking about truth, and the process of the linking and breaking of links in thinking rather than truth itself. For Bion, trying to find and hold the capacity for thinking is a process that both requires and achieves emotional containment. He uses the developmental metaphor of the baby's experience of unlanguaged and unlanguageable distress, which comes to be emotionally held by the parent's capacity to try to make some meaning out of the baby's experience and to have the baby and the baby's experience 'in mind'. To learn to know how to know, then, requires the precondition of a relationship with another who wants to know us and respond from that knowing, and it is in the containment of this relationship that the capacity for thinking and reflecting emerges.

Outside psychoanalysis, Bion's work is probably best known for his development of this idea of containment as it applies to the analytic relationship, and in particular the space for thinking that the analyst tries to create in the immersion of the analytic work. This is also the idea that Larner focuses on in developing his discussion of the common ground of not-knowing within family therapy and current psychoanalytic theory which reflects and develops Bion's ideas. Bion's development of the idea that the analyst needs to suspend memory and desire has become a central reference point in his work (Bion 1970, 1988), and some of the ongoing analytic discussions of this idea track a similar tension to the discussions within family therapy of the complexity of not-knowing (see for example Spillius 1988; Symington and Symington 1996).

Larner moves well beyond noting the commonality of the influence of postmodernist ideas and the similarities of the ideas around knowing-not-to-know in family therapy and psychoana-lysis. He argues that the stance of not-knowing needs to be held alongside the desire for knowing, and not-knowing and knowing together provide a frame for the development of meaning within the therapeutic process. Further, he argues that this narrative movement can itself function as an emotional container in the psychoanalytic sense, and this process within the therapeutic relationship helps clients develop and 'hold' their own knowing.

Without too much discussion here, can I simply flag some inter-sections between the idea of the process of narrative-as-container and some of the ideas explored earlier as part of the exploration of attachment. In particular, the transformative possibilities of coming to have coherent narratives of attachment lie in a similar territory. I emphasised in that chapter that it was not the narrative itself that seemed to be the important factor, but rather the relationship between the story and the realness of experience and the person's capacity to struggle to make meaning. In a similar way, it is important to underline here that it is not the content of the narrative itself which is containing within a therapeutic context, but rather it is the emotional and interpersonal process of meaning-making, in which coming to know something more fully is struggled with within a therapeutic relationship in which knowing and not-knowing is held. And I find myself coming again to a point where I want to say that it is the relationship between the realness of experience, how we come to know (as both represen-tation and construction of that experience), plus the relational context of this knowing which is important, rather than the 'product' of knowledge itself.

This section has been considering the therapeutic position of not-knowing. The exploration of the emergence of the idea of not-knowing within family therapy was prompted by the previous discussion of empathic orientations of sameness and difference and the therapeutic position of curiosity, and I have cast the position of not-knowing as being one expression of a position of curiosity. The common ground of the development of psychoanalytic ideas of not-knowing was then discussed using Larner's work. His inter-sections between Bion's ideas of not-knowing, emotional contain-ment and the process of narrative within therapy prompted some further discussion about reflection and meaning-making in the context of the therapeutic relationship.

The space of reflection and some thoughts on impasse

A notion of therapeutic flexibility has been a theme developing throughout the discussion so far. When thinking about approach-ing empathy from the orientations of sameness (/identification) and difference (/foreignness/curiosity), I spoke of the flexibility of the movement of the therapist back and forth, of using oneself as both subject and object in trying to connect with the family's experience. In thinking about not-knowing as an expression of curiosity, we moved to the idea of not-knowing being held together with know-ing in the therapeutic process.

'Knowing' here is shorthand for 'desiring or wanting to know and understand'. There is the danger that something may be con-fused if this translation is not made, for 'knowing' can easily be heard as making a claim on certain and definitive (modernist) knowledge. Let me be very clear that this is not the idea in Larner's discussion or indeed in the contemporary psychoanalytic discus-sions. However, because of the possibility of this confusion, I wonder whether it might be better to think about the 'knowing' part of the not-knowing/knowing dynamic as being the space for reflection that the therapist tries to create, both for herself (/himself) and the family in the therapeutic conversation. If it were to be reframed in this way, then we could think of the space of not-knowing being held alongside the space of reflection.

To think of trying to create and hold open the space for reflec-tion could be linked to Bion's ideas about the capacity for thinking and the process of containment. It could also be linked to ideas about the openness of the development of narrative, and perhaps more particularly to the difficulties of 'stuckness' in thinking and narrative closure. In the last chapter there was a discussion about timelessness, repetition and narrative closure in family relationships, and let me build on these ideas by adding here that timelessness, repetition and narrative closure may be used to describe impasses in therapeutic work and the therapeutic relationship, in much the same way as they may stand as descriptions for personal and relational impasse.

I am aware that this exploration so far has all been in a rather abstracted realm. So could I note that the idea of trying to hold the space of not-knowing alongside the space of reflection perhaps has its greatest pragmatic value in systemic work in thinking about impasse and failure. Impasse and failure are remarkably under discussed given their regularity and frequency in therapeutic work and given the everyday difficulties we face as therapists in trying to meet and hold through the times when the therapy gets stuck or simply does not contribute very much to change. Indeed, David Spellman and David Harper (1996) have written of failure, mistakes and regrets in family therapy as subjugated stories in our own discourse, and they wonder about their persistent non-appearance in formal family therapy discussions. At the same time, there have been some notable if sporadic attempts over time (see for example Coleman 1985; Kaffman 1987), and some recent glimmerings that may suggest that we are perhaps ready to tackle the less heroic aspects of our work (see for example Butler and Bird 2000; Johnson, Makinen and Millikin 2001; Rober 1999; Spellman and Harper 1996; the recent special feature in *Context*).[3]

Though it is beyond my project here to do justice to the topics of failure and impasse, I would like to note very briefly some ways in which impasse in particular comes to affect the therapeutic relationship and the therapist's use of self within that relationship. Neither families nor therapists face seriously stuck times in therapy with equanimity. Impasse usually travels in the company of difficult emotions: anxiety and fear of failure, guilt, blame, frustration, anger, shame, hopelessness and despair. And of course it is not just the families we work with who have difficulties riding through these times and the accompanying emotional territory. Although sometimes the impasse has been created solely by what has (or has not) happened in the therapy itself, often it is part of the family's process in struggling with change and the issues which brought them to therapy, and it is not uncommon for a 'fit' to emerge between the kind of issues in the therapeutic relationship and the family's struggle. Regardless of how this is falling, though, I believe that impasse is always *felt* in the therapeutic relationship, and it always *affects* the therapeutic relationship.

At the very least, in times of impasse, it pays to attend to the interactional sequence in the therapeutic relationship and to the expression and the effects of one's own countertransference and emotional reactivity. The very practical question in a particular instance of impasse is whether the therapist's responsiveness is creating space for movement in the impasse or compounding the stuckness. The therapist's involvement here may simply show a triggering of her or his own usual patterns of relating, or some kind of (more or less) unwitting joining of the family's sequences, or a conscious or unconscious identification with struggles which belong more to the family or to a particular family member. These points in therapy are notorious for the possibilities of unhelpful thera-peutic enactments of the family's difficulties, and it is very hard to remain unaware of this danger particularly when one is working with abuse.

My discussion in the last chapter tracked some of this territory using the psychoanalytic ideas of transference, countertransference and projective identification, and I gave a particular discussion of how these ideas may be helpful. However, beyond the content of these ideas – exactly how one might think of transference or projective identification – they are useful as a way of reflection in times in which the capacity to reflect begins to be lost. This is precisely the situation of impasse, where one becomes sufficiently bewildered or confused or fearful or rattled or reactive to find it difficult to hang on to the orientation of curiosity. In Bion's sense, we could talk of situations in which we as therapists lose the capacity to think. In terms of narrative, we are talking of situations in which there is a closure of narrative for both family and therapist. However impasse is described, the first task is to try to hold on to, and often struggle to regain, some space of reflection.

Peter Rober (1999) makes some similar arguments very per-suasively in his discussion of the self of the therapist, therapeutic impasse and the process of reflection. He does so within a general commitment to social constructionist ideas, and he characterises the therapeutic conversation as a circle of meaning constructed by therapist and family in which the therapist participates in the 'outer' conversation of the therapy as well as her or his own 'inner' conversation. The therapist's inner conversation – about memories, thoughts and emotions evoked by the therapy and the family – becomes one way of trying to move through the paralysis of meaning which characterises impasse. Rober also discusses the specificity of how one might use one's own inner conversation in work with families and the range of direct and more indirect ways in which it may inform and influence the ongoing conversation of the therapy.

When I read Rober's article, I was struck by the resonance between his descriptions and what I would often choose to think of as the processes of transference and countertransference. I am not saying here that Rober is talking about transference and countertransference, rather, I think he is talking about the same territory of experience that the ideas of transference and counter-transference may also be used to address. Thus it is not the theory which is the same, but the experience it addresses. Or put another way, one is seeing similarities between different maps of the same territory of the experience of impasse in family therapy.

The similarity that is striking between Rober's ideas and the way in which I have been using the psychoanalytic ideas is the common emphasis on creating and holding the space of reflection, and although Rober would use different words to describe the relation-ship between the space of not-knowing and the space of reflection, it is clear that he sees these as simultaneous rather than alternating processes. Moreover, in writing about the constructive and respectful use of therapists' reflections about their own process in the ongoing outer therapy conversation, he locates the first task of reflection as internal reflection. If we were to think of the emotional process of containment, then we might be considering the way in which as therapists we use the space of reflection to first contain ourselves, before we move from that space to try to nurture a containing space of reflection in our conversations with families.

It is clear enough from all this discussion that I am wanting to broaden the consideration of the therapeutic relationship to include the emotional process of therapy and to be more inclusive of the therapist's experience in considering the therapist-family relation-ship. In exploring some ideas about holding the space of reflection alongside the space of not-knowing, I have wanted to link the space of reflection with the task in therapy of trying to emotionally hold the therapeutic work. Along with Rober, I have also been arguing that our first (and most available) 'object' in difficult therapeutic times is our own self, as we struggle to give some meaning to what is often a complicated experience in relationship to our own and the family's dilemmas and to use (rather than censor) the richness of our connectedness to the family in the therapeutic process.

That we are doing this in the service of trying to understand the family's experience should go without saying. That it is in practice very important to do this becomes evident enough when we face impasse which can easily become the prefiguring of therapeutic failure. And could I also say as part of this summary that I think that good theory ideas – regardless of the exact nature of their content – are often used as part of the process of emotionally holding ourselves as therapists in trying to think about our work. This is perhaps another pragmatic reason for being open to different theory ideas and 'holding theory lightly' in our practice in family therapy.

Practice reflections

First Piece

It can be difficult to navigate the shift from family therapy to couple therapy. One already has an engagement with the couple through the family work, yet the therapeutic relationship has emerged in a different context, and it has been formed around the different goals and the different emotional territory of the family work. A good-enough therapeutic relationship for one context of therapy may not be good-enough in another.[4] With the couple I wrote about, I felt like we were in an established therapy, yet the move to couple work threw us into quite a different territory of intimacy and relational difficulties, requiring different understandings and a different kind of therapeutic connectedness.

The family work had been a success. The couple work was not, and there is no question that the impasse in engagement in this different context prefigured the therapeutic failure. My understandings of the impasse changed from the way I was thinking about it when I was immersed in it to the way I reflected on it afterwards. In the sessions, I had been taken up with the interactional process around the husband's anger and verbal strikes, and my conscious reflections and attempts to understand and relate circled around this. Yet I come to have a dream with an image of the wife, and a thought about a break-down and her surprising yet understandable madness. Unfortunately, my own process was too slow, and the dream came too late. The therapy was broken off in a sudden way, and I am left suspecting that this would probably make it harder for the couple to use therapy again. And because I knew the family and the children, I am left 'knowing' something more about the possible interaction of the couple's difficulties with the struggle of the youngest child who had initially been presented in the therapy.

What can I say? I think now that it was easier for me to 'know' the husband's resentment and anger than it was to 'know' the wife's predicament and all that this emotionally entailed for her. In retrospect, I think I engaged more (and identified less) with the husband and engaged less (and identified more) with the wife, and this became inflexible and unbalanced. It is usually complex when this kind of thing happens in a therapeutic relationship. Something about my own countertransference in the identification with the wife is perhaps now only too transparent; we can all guess who the woman in the dream was, but as a boundary issue, I think it would be only polite if readers pretended that it was not me! The effect of this counter-transference was that I lost my curiosity about the wife, and the space for reflection and thinking became compromised as I got 'stuck' with the couple. However, my stuckness and the very pattern of my not-thinking also has a resemblance to something that was being played out between the couple. The husband's anger and strikes had become very visible to both of them and took up the relational space between them. Yet the wife's dilemmas, and whatever 'madness' was experienced by her, became an invisible story to the couple outside words (and perhaps outside consciousness). Thus, the pattern of my own countertransference and my own not-thinking paralleled something about the couple's situation

Of course, I do not 'know' any of this, yet to own that my own understandings are uncertain and always partial does not strike me as any good reason to stop thinking and reflecting. To do so would simply be to cut off my own involvement in the therapy and thus negate the power and the usefulness of therapeutic connectedness, even if in this case it all comes too late.

Second Piece

To return to my description of the therapeutic relationship with the family who presented three separate times, with the work spanning a few years. Stern (1998) in his discussion of parent-infant psychotherapy writes of the pattern of serial bouts of brief therapy across years and developmental phases and argues that this pattern of therapy is not a lesser form of long-term psychotherapy, but rather one which more closely fits the developmental realities of families with young children. I am reminded of Stern's discussion by the work with this family and of the need to see therapy and our involvement as always just part of the family's ongoing process. I hope it does not show an unremittingly modernist streak in me to note my admiration for the parents in this family, the way in which they used therapeutic work, and the healthiness of the sequence in the presenting problems. The first presentation of the split-off and unlanguaged individual symptom of soiling moves to the more languaged territory of relationship (the children's fighting and their aggressiveness and competition), which moves to the parents being able to more clearly identify and think about their own issues and differences.

But it is part of the first piece of work which I described – the very first session and the boy's overly cheerful performance about his soiling, my struggle not to become part of the family audience, and the way in which I needed to remind myself that I was meant to be the therapist and that I shouldn't just leave the child to conduct the session. There is then the sequel to the session – the boy now stops weeing as well as pooing, and there is the emergency trip to the hospital, the urologist, the x-ray department and various other medical tests and appointments. His parents admit to having felt very worried, his mother says she was frustrated when it turned out there was nothing wrong (she had spent the best part of two days traipsing around hospitals with the boy and the 10-month-old baby in tow), and the boy now wants to see it as all very interesting, although he can admit that he was 'a bit scared'. We have this quite difficult discussion in the second session, when I finally begin to come out of the fog which enveloped me in the beginning part of the session. In their telling of the story about what had gone on between the sessions, I had felt rather like an unknowing witness and also carried a vague sense of shame about how publicly wrong things had gone.

All this leads me to be unsure about whether I should continue with the sneaky poo frame. I find myself weighing up the belief that it might be important not to be thrown off course by the boy's reaction (to hold steady, to not be intimidated by the problem), and a concern that the externalisation of sneaky poo and mobilising the boy's autonomy could in this situation continue to eclipse the more difficult languaging of the experience of smallness, fear, vulnerability, anger, or whatever it is that is hard to see behind the powerfully cheerful bravado. However, the sneaky poo frame works well enough, and in the meetings after the holiday break and the relapse, the boy is able to be more open about how bad he feels about it. His parents are also able to be more open about themselves while maintaining their support of their son.

What is the role of my own reflection (or, as Rober would say, my internal conversation) during this first piece of work? In the end, it did not 'show' too much, except perhaps in my readiness to have a secondary conversation with the family alongside the main externalising frame. This secondary conversation invited a safe naming of the more difficult experiences of the different family members. However, holding the space for my own thinking helped me hold on to my own position as therapist. Thus, my struggle to understand and think about the work had the effect of containing me, even if this did not show directly in exactly what I did in the therapy room.

In terms of the family, though, I think that the invitation in the first piece of work to think more about their experience led to the possibility of the development of the therapeutic conversation in the succeeding pieces of work. And it was in the last piece of work, talking with the parents about their own histories and what had been difficult for each of them as parents and as a parenting couple, that I appreciated something more about the form of my connectedness in the very early work. The parents spoke of how young they had been when their first child (the boy who was soiling) was born, how overwhelmed they had felt, and how alone. They felt like they were just watching him, not knowing what to do. That something of this landscape was still continuing when I first saw them became clear enough in the parallels I heard between their description and my own experience. That they were deeply ethical in their parenting had had its downside in that it had made these feelings of inadequacy very hard, and there had been a sense of shame.

Conclusion

This chapter has explored a number of themes with respect to the therapeutic relationship in the systemic context of family work. Beginning with a discussion of empathy and understanding, there was an identification of the flexibility we use as therapists in orienting from sameness and difference, with our capacity for identification being linked to an orientation of sameness, and our capacity for curiosity being linked to an orientation of difference. There was a discussion of the therapist's use of self as both subject and object, and this movement was noted in the analytic descriptions of the processes of countertransference and projective identification. A second intersection was made with analytic thinking through the exploration of the idea of not-knowing, and I explored the idea of therapist flexibility in holding the space of not-knowing alongside the space of reflection. The final part of the theory discussion considered the space of reflection and the problem of therapeutic impasse in terms of some of Bion's ideas on thinking and containment, and in terms of narrative closure.

I think all this was signposted clearly enough along the way. In using these ideas to reflect on the examples of practice, there was as usual some weaving in and out. Yet hopefully, in the reflection of practice, the relevance of the theory ideas gained more shape. The first situation described a therapeutic failure, which was prefigured by an impasse in the therapeutic relationship and a closing-down of my own capacity for thinking and understanding. Something was out of balance in my identification and engagement, and yet there seemed to be a relationship between the barrier of my own countertransference and the more invisible parts of the wife's experience within the couple's relationship. The second situation described a peculiar start to family therapy and then an unfolding across a few years through three separate lots of work. Though the initial difficulty did not develop into an impasse, keeping hold of the space of reflection was important in containing myself and allowing me to orient in my thinking to both the strengths and fragilities in the family. The conversation and languaging became richer with each contact, and it was only with time that I came to see the parallels between my initial experience as the therapist and the parents' experience of relating to their first-born child.

There are other comments that spring from these reflections – comments on the preciousness of trying to know through reflection, however uncertain and partial that knowledge may be; the richness of the therapeutic relationship, and the challenge of developing understandings which acknowledge and honour this richness; and the question of whether in postmodernist times we somehow try to abandon being subjects and objects, or instead embrace the flexibility of using ourselves as both subjects and objects in our relationship as therapists with the families with whom we work. But these discussions are more properly part of the integration of the ideas of the past three chapters, and the synthesis of this work with the wider project of the book. So let me draw the line here, and move on to the concluding comments.

Notes

1 Michael White first introduced the practice of externalisation in his earlier work with children and families, which had a strategic flavour. It is a shame that these ideas have become passé in the current narrative practices, because they are finely tuned to children's developmental desire for autonomy, and their capacity for using the transitional as-if space of play, which 'sneaky poo' and similar externalisations use (see White 1984).
2 I am aware that I have just used the singular 'client' throughout this paragraph, which evokes the context of one-to-one therapy. This is a faithful reflection of the use of the singular in the discussion by Goolishian and Anderson, which does perhaps raise some issue about the extent to which their ideas are more finely-crafted to individual therapy.
3 See *Context*, Number 39 (1998).
4 See Flaskas (1997a) for a further discussion of the idea of a good-enough engagement in the context of family therapy practice.

Chapter 11

Concluding comments

In the last part of this book, I want to work back through its different layers. First, I will integrate the intersections made with psychoanalytic ideas in the last three chapters and then revisit the discussion of postmodernism in family therapy. This conclusion then returns full-circle to the initial themes of experience and conditional knowledge, ending with the plea to allow the space for theory diversity in enriching family therapy knowledge and practice.

Reflecting on the intersections with psychoanalytic ideas

In integrating the intersections I have made with psychoanalytic ideas, I will again very quickly summarise each chapter's discussion and then draw together the themes which emerge from this work.

Chapter 8 introduced the relational processes of attachment and the unconscious. Attachment theory addresses the development of patterns in relationship, and the unconscious may be thought of as a layer of experience that exists alongside our conscious, languaged understandings of the world. When it shows itself in our lived experience, it disconcerts our conscious understandings and challenges the limits of our languaging about ourselves. Current attachment research is beginning to link the capacity to develop coherent narratives about attachment experience with the possibility of transforming attachment patterns. The unconscious also has the capacity for transformation, for in confronting the limits of our conscious stories, it challenges us to re-story our experience in a way that brings a richer coherence to our under-standings of ourselves. In considering specifically the relationship of these processes to language, I argued that attachment and the unconscious address territories of human experience that are languaged, unlanguaged and at times unlanguageable. This chapter also raised once more the theme of the realness of experience.

Chapter 9 moved to a discussion of the psychoanalytic ideas of transference, countertransference and projective identification, bringing them into alignment with a broader discussion of the lived experience of time. These ideas primarily address the unconscious interaction of the process of therapy and the way in which the patient's living past is brought into the time and space of the analytic relationship. Therapeutic time bridges the past-in-the-present as well as the future-in-the-present, and the idea of narrative closure was used in considering the 'stuck' time of personal and familial impasse. This in turn led to a discussion of sequences and repetitions, as points in time when the living past can be mediated and re-storied, for better or worse. These ideas are all useful in systemic family therapy, and using the ideas of transference, countertransference and projective identification generates a different level of empathic connection and enriches therapeutic connectedness.

Chapter 10 further explored the therapeutic relationship. A fuller discussion was given of empathy and understanding in the context of family therapy, and I wrote of therapeutic flexibility in using the empathic orientation of sameness (/identification) and difference (/curiosity/foreignness). The movement within analysis where the analyst becomes subject then object in the experience of, then reflection on, countertransference and projective identification was used to consider this to-and-fro movement of the use of self in systemic therapy. The idea of not-knowing in family therapy was held alongside some of Bion's ideas within psychoanalysis of not-knowing, and this led to an argument for holding both the space of not-knowing and the space for reflection in our work with families. I particularly considered therapeutic impasse in terms of narrative closure and the closing down of the therapist's capacity for thinking and reflection.

In synthesising the development of the work across these chapters and the way in which selected psychoanalytic ideas were woven into the discussion, I will draw together four related themes. This set of themes is more about the idea of using psychoanalytic ideas than the content of the investigation just summarised, and I will list them one by one.

It is possible to call on psychoanalytic ideas and retain our primary interest in a systemic orientation to family therapy practice

I would like to use the form of the investigation of the last three chapters to reinforce the possibility of calling on psychoanalytic ideas in the systemic context of work. The particular intersections that I have made have not been about building a psychoanalytic practice but instead about furthering our capacities in systemic family therapy. I wrote in Chapter 7 of the different orientations one might take in linking psychoanalysis and family therapy, and following the work of the last three chapters, I feel that I am now in a better position to add to that discussion.

Listening for resonance versus constructing competitiveness

In thinking about the way I have just used psychoanalytic ideas, I am more aware that I have worked from a frame of listening for their resonance with systemic themes and dilemmas, rather than approaching them through a construction of competitiveness. I had real trouble coming up with another word for 'resonance' in the last few chapters, fearing that readers might be getting bored with it, yet it was hard to find a suitable substitute. To say that something has resonance with something else evokes an image of hearing a common chord in different descriptions.

It does not mean that one thing is the same as the other, in the way that attachment theory is not the same as the systemic concept of patterning, and the unconscious is not the same as the idea of silent voices or unspoken stories, and Bion's idea of not-knowing is not the same as the discussion which has emerged in family therapy. Yet I think one hears a common chord which invites further exploration, and in the further exploration of an idea that is different yet has some similarity, it is possible to generate understandings that would not be possible if you stay only within one frame or approach the other frame with a view to competition. Am I being too optimistic in thinking that the common chord one hears is the integrity of different frameworks trying to relate theory to human experience and the process of therapy? Perhaps this is overly optimistic, but nevertheless, I still want to say that different therapy frameworks – in this case, systemic therapy and psychoanalysis – relate in different ways to the same territory of human experience, and this is the compelling reason to listen for resonance.

The freedom to be strategic and conditional in using psychoanalytic ideas: exploring areas of thinking and practice which are not well met in family therapy

In listening for resonance, though, we can hold the freedom to be strategic and conditional. We are not in an either/or situation. We do not have to take psychoanalysis on board holus-bolus, which in itself would be a peculiar thing to be aiming for given the very specific contexts of family therapy practice and most family therapy practitioners. Providing we are not searching here for a universal knowledge base, we can be selective, and in thinking about the process of my own selection and intersections in this project, I will suggest that we can be strategic in calling on psychoanalytic ideas which speak to processes which are under-theorised in systemic therapy. This is not to say that only psycho-analytic ideas can enrich our theory and practice – even in a modernist world it was always rather embarrassing to evoke the image of 'gaps' in knowledge that needed to be 'filled'! And so, in approaching, for example, attachment theory and the unconscious, I do not think it is a matter of 'filling gaps' in our thinking and practice. Instead, these psychoanalytic ideas can be used more conditionally to generate different kinds of thinking and reflection around our systemic interests in experience and relationship patterns which are outside words.

Opening out possibilities of different kinds of reflection, and using the richness of our experience in therapy and the therapeutic relationship

We have reached the last of this set of themes. The momentum of the work of the last three chapters has been to generate other reflections, moving from the work of Chapter 8 to the more narrowly focused work of Chapters 9 and 10 and the topic of the therapeutic relationship. Chapter 10 emphasised the importance of holding open the space for reflection in the process of therapy, and

I am really saying the same thing again here, only this time with respect to our thinking about therapy and knowledge for family therapy.

In the final practice reflections, I alluded to a contortion that has slipped into the postmodernist discourse in family therapy. Having recognised that knowledge is only ever partial, contextual and conditional, it is sometimes almost as if we then have no right to our own thoughts – or if we struggle for mutual and respectful relationships with our clients in the interests of staying with their experience, then we should not acknowledge or think about the messy and less heroic and less respectful aspects of our relationships. These implications are contorted because they censor thinking about experience, and this steers us away from using the richness of the therapeutic relationship and our experience as therapists in the process of therapy. Again, I am not suggesting that only psychoanalytic ideas offer an alternative here, though it is certainly the perspective I have chosen to explore.

This brings us to the end of this set of themes. In Chapter 7, I wrote of the dual interest I had in exploring psychoanalytic ideas from the point of view of my own long-term interest in using them in systemic practice, as well as using them as sample other ideas in the postmodernist debate. What I have just discussed belongs more to the first point of interest, and I would like now to consider the work of the last three chapters in terms of the limits of postmodernism in family therapy.

Revisiting the postmodernist limits in family therapy

A different kind of summary is needed in considering the critique of the limits of postmodernism in family therapy's current use of social constructionism and the narrative metaphor. Following the synthesis in Chapter 7 of the first part of the book, I suggested that to move beyond these limits we could look for different understandings of the processes of self and intersubjectivity, ones that meet aspects of the experience of therapy, that do not preclude a recognition of the power of lived realities, and that are able to engage in some way with human experience beyond its conscious and languaged forms. I have chosen to use psychoanalytic ideas in this project while again recognising that other kinds of ideas could have similar potential.

Four themes were brought together about the limits of family therapy's use of postmodernism. These were: the pattern of forced dualities in narrative/constructionist discourse mirrors the oppositional parameters of postmodernism itself; a plea for avoiding radically anti-realist versions of constructionist ideas and the acontextual privileging of language; missing objects, missing subjects and the postmodernist problem of fragmentation; and reasserting the primacy of our interests in the experience of therapy. The fourth theme is really the subject of the last part of this conclusion, and so in this section I will concentrate on the first three concerns.

Moving beyond forced dualities

Ultimately, I think it is impoverishing to craft our knowledge solely within the parameters of the forced duality of the (rejected) modernist position and the oppositional 'other' postmodernist position. Calling on psychoanalytic ideas from within systemic interests is one way to move beyond this restriction. Of course, psychoanalysis is scarcely immune from the restrictions of forced dualities within its own theory, but it is not psychoanalysis itself that has been the subject of the exploration of the last three chapters but rather particular psychoanalytic ideas brought to bear on examples from my own practice in family therapy.

In moving through the psychoanalytic ideas of attachment and the unconscious, transference, countertransference and projective identification, and ideas about not-knowing and the space for thinking, I have very deliberately tried not to engage in a description of how things ought to be. In the practice reflections, I have used the ideas to think about the experience of the different therapy situations, both the clients' and my own, and the psychoanalytic ideas have been woven in and out. The current postmodernist dualities in family therapy discourse simply did not appear in the same form in this different kind of discussion. Independent versus constructed reality, truth versus languaged meaning, the autonomous self versus the relational self – we could say that each side of these dualities appeared in different ways in the theory and practice discussions, yet there seemed no need to use one side of the duality to exclude reflection on the other. And the different analytic ideas allowed an engagement with subjective experience and independent realities, context and meaning, self and relationship. In this way, they allowed for an engagement with the individual's experience and subjectivity in the context of relationships, and also offered understandings of intersubjective processes, including the therapeutic relationship.

Allowing for realness, and experience beyond language

The concern for realness was at the heart of the exploration of the limits of postmodernist ideas, and it was linked to the concern about radical versions of social constructionist ideas which understand social and emotional realities as (only) languaged realities. These themes were very directly addressed in Chapter 8, and I drew the appeal of the ideas of attachment and the unconscious by exploring the way in which they allow for a more complex relationship between experience and language. The theme emerged very strongly that human experience is, in different ways and at different points in time, languaged, unlanguaged and even at times unlanguageable, and the ideas of attachment and the unconscious more adequately acknowledge this complexity. Moreover, in exploring the transformative possibilities of coherent narratives of attachment and the interaction of conscious and unconscious experience, we found understandings that allow for the power of independent realities as well as the power of our constructions of those realities. This move beyond a forced duality of independent versus constructed realities leaves the door open for the possibility of thinking of the relationship between.

The way in which I called on analytic ideas in Chapters 9 and 10 was rather different, for the ideas of transference, countertransference and projective identification, and Bion's ideas on thinking, are all theorised within the psychoanalytic project of understanding the unconscious and unconscious processes. In this sense, in the intersections of these last two chapters, the unconscious was taken as given, and the psychoanalytic ideas were used alongside other ideas (for example, about the experience of time, impasse and narrative closure, and family therapy discussions of empathy and not-knowing). The practice reflections shaped the way in which these ideas were used, and this blending of ideas allowed discussions of particular practice situations that enabled some thinking about realness, the experience of realness, and processes for both clients and therapist that may be outside language.

Remaining interested in subjects and objects, and the relationship between

The argument that postmodernism potentially decentres the subject and fragments subjectivities was echoed in the specific exploration of current family therapy discussions of truth, reality and the self. After its rejection of the modernist splitting of subject and object, postmodernism is not too interested in theorising subjects and objects, and thus it cannot hold firmly the commitment to theorising the complex relationship between. It is clear enough by now that I remain very sceptical of the idea that it is even possible to abandon the interest in subjects and objects, and I cannot easily understand why we would be attracted to this idea in the context of therapy and knowledge for therapy.

This does not mean that I want to reclaim the modernist splitting, nor do I want to be caught up in the postmodernist problem of missing subjects and objects. I argued in the first part of the book that in human experience we are both subjects and objects, and this is just as much the case in therapy as anywhere else. There I was talking more of the experience of being a client, and the last chapter raised the experience of being a therapist. Thus, rather than reverting to the modernist conception where the client becomes object and the therapist is subject, I am arguing strongly that in the process of therapy, we are all (therapists and clients) subject and object.

The work in Chapter 8 (particularly on attachment) reinforces the argument of the human experience as subject and object. However the work in Chapters 9 and 10, which tracked the psychoanalytic conception of the analyst's involvement through countertransference, considered the subtlety of the analyst's use of self as both subject and object. In extending this thinking to the therapeutic relationship in systemic therapy, I argued that the same to-and-fro movement happened in the therapist's use of self. We move flexibly between empathic orientations of sameness and difference and, in times of impasse, we treat our own subjective experience as the first object of reflection in the struggle to regain the capacity to think and connect back with the clients' experiences.

I have reached the end of summarising the work of the last three chapters and its synthesis with my project on postmodernism. Yet there remains one further discussion which was begun in the first chapter and has been threading its way throughout the book in one form or another. It is the final discussion of the relationship of knowledge and experience, and its implications for our approach to using knowledge in family therapy.

On knowledge and experience: a final argument for theory diversity

In the introduction, I wrote of the embedded commitments that have shaped the project of this book. These commitments have been to lived experience and a conditional approach to knowledge, and I am returning now to these ideas.

I have said very little so far in this conclusion about the way I have used practice discussion, despite the fact that practice has been a substantial part of more than half the chapters. The particular parts of different therapies I have chosen to present have ranged from quick snapshots to a more detailed outline of part of the therapy, and the kind of reflections have ranged from discussions of the way in which the theory themes of the particular chapter show themselves in the experience of therapy to using the theory themes to develop understandings of the therapeutic situation under discussion. I have chosen ordinary examples from my own practice and allowed myself the freedom to use situations that came to mind in the context of the topics of each chapter. The discussions have not been programmatic in the sense of aiming to illustrate ideal practice, and I have tried not to write myself out of the descriptions, as if as therapist I have no real involvement or subjectivity in the process of the therapy. The method of book-ending chapters with practice has been in line with the idea that it is practice that provokes and challenges theory development, which in turn feeds back into how we understand practice.

The chapters that have relied on practice discussion have had different aims in their theory development, most noticeably in the difference between the discussion of the limits of postmodernist ideas and the last three chapters using psychoanalytic ideas. In Chapters 4 to 6, the practice drew attention to critical issues in our use of postmodernist ideas; with the last three chapters, the challenge of practice was more focused on ways of understanding, intertwining the psychoanalytic ideas with other ideas. Particularly in Chapters 9 and 10, the discussion flowed freely in and out of the engagement with the psychoanalytic ideas, and the practice reflections were prompted by other ideas as well.

When I was first planning the book, I had in mind a more singular use of psychoanalytic ideas in the last three chapters. Yet as is often the way with writing, when you sit down and start doing it, you realise the flaws in the plan. In this case, I realised that though it would be neater for me to hold the focus more fully on the use of psychoanalytic ideas, this project did not match how I think about practice or what I do in practice. Hence the decision in Chapters 9 and 10 to develop additional themes from systemic discussions – the discussion of time, sequences and narrative closure in Chapter 9, and the discussion of empathy and understanding and the family therapy version of not-knowing in Chapter 10.

You could say that I found myself voting with my feet for calling on a diversity of theory ideas, even in the discussion which prioritised the intersections with psychoanalysis. I could call upon the discussion about postmodernist limits to explain this decision, but I have to admit that though this influences me in the direction of eclecticism, I am far more powerfully influenced by the demands of practice.

Thus, though I respect the creativity and commitment of colleagues who choose to immerse themselves in one particular way of working and strive to develop a consistency of theory and practice, it is not a project that I embrace. But it is also true that I feel uneasy about the history of competitiveness between family therapy frameworks as well as feeling uneasy about the politics of demands that force us to squash our thinking and practice into one box. However wonderful that box may be it will never contain the richness of human experience.

At the end of this book, I find myself thinking of the comment of the narrative theorist, Mark Freeman, whom I quoted in Chapter 6. Despite his clear commitment to narrative ideas, he writes that many narrative claims 'do not do justice to the life I live' (Freeman 1993: 13). This is how I feel about the limits of postmodernism and social constructionist and narrative ideas in family therapy. It is not that I do not find these ideas useful, it is not that I do not think that how we construct the world in language is powerfully influencing, and it is not that I do not ally myself with the aims of collaborative and respectful practice. It is simply that to stay solely within the confines of these ideas does not do justice to the life I live. It does not do justice to my sense of my own life or my clients' lives, or my experience of self and relationships. Moreover, it does not do justice to my experience as a therapist of the everyday realities of therapy practice and the richness of my involvement in the therapeutic relationship.

So let me finish here, arguing once again for allowing the space for theory diversity in family therapy, an argument that comes as much from a commitment to honouring experience as it does from the theory arguments developed throughout this book.

Bibliography

Abadi, M. and Rogers, S.H. (1995) *Reality and/or Realities*, Northvale, NJ: Jason Aronson.

Adams, N. (1995) 'Spirituality, science and therapy', *Australian and New Zealand Journal of Family Therapy* 16, 4: 201–8.

—— (1996) 'Positive outcomes in families following traumatic brain injury (TBI)', *Australian and New Zealand Journal of Family Therapy* 17, 2: 75–84.

Akister, J. (1998) 'Attachment theory and systemic practice: Research update', *Journal of Family Therapy* 20, 4: 353–66.

Amundson, J.K. (2001) 'Why narrative therapy need not fear science and "other" things', *Journal of Family Therapy* 23, 2: 175–88.

Amundson, J., Stewart, K. and Valentine, L. (1993) 'Temptations of power and certainty', *Journal of Marital and Family Therapy* 19, 2: 111–3.

Anderson, H. (1997) *Conversation, Language and Possibilities: A Postmodern Approach to Therapy*, New York: Basic Books.

—— (1999) 'Re-imagining family therapy: Reflections on Minuchin's invisible family', *Journal of Marital and Family Therapy* 25, 1: 1–8.

—— (2001) 'Postmodern collaborative and person-centred therapies: What would Carl Rogers say?', *Journal of Family Therapy* 23, 4: 339–60.

Anderson, H. and Goolishian, H. (1988) 'Human systems as linguistic systems: Preliminary and evolving ideas about the implications for clinical theory', *Family Process* 27, 4: 371–93.

—— (1992) 'The client is the expert: A not-knowing approach to therapy', in S. McNamee and K.J. Gergen (eds) *Therapy as Social Construction*, London: Sage.

Anderson, T. (1987) 'The reflecting team: Dialogue and meta-dialogue in clinical work', *Family Process* 26, 4: 415–28.

—— (1990) *The Reflecting Team: Dialogue and Dialogues about Dialogues*, Broadstairs, Kent: Borgman.

—— (1992) 'Relationship, language and pre-understanding in the reflecting processes', *Australian and New Zealand Journal of Family Therapy* 13, 2: 87–91.

Anderson, T. (1995) 'Reflecting processes; acts of informing and forming: You can borrow my eyes, but you must not take them away from me!', in S. Friedman (ed.) *The Reflecting Team in Action: Collaborative Practice in Family Therapy*, New York: Guilford.

Aponte, H.J. (1998) 'Love, the spiritual wellspring of forgiveness: An example of spirituality in therapy', *Journal of Family Therapy* 20, 1: 37–58.

Aron, L. (1991a) 'Interpretation as expression of the analyst's subjectivity', *Psychoanalytic Dialogues* 2, 4: 475–507.

—— (1991b) 'The patient's experience of the analyst's subjectivity', *Psychoanalytic Dialogues* 1, 1: 29–51.

—— (1996) *A Meeting of Minds: Mutuality in Psychoanalysis*, Hillsdale, NJ: The Analytic Press.

Balint, M. (1968) *The Basic Fault*, London: Tavistock Publications.

Barratt, B.B. (1993) *Psychoanalysis and the Postmodern Impulse: Knowing and Being Since Freud's Psychology*, Baltimore: Johns Hopkins University Press.

Bateson, G. (1972) *Steps to an Ecology of Mind: Mind and Nature*, New York: Ballantine Books.

—— (1980) *Mind and Nature: A Necessary Unity*, London: Fontana/Collins.

Baynes, K., Bohman, J. and McCarthy, T. (eds) (1987) *After Philosophy: End or Transformation?* Cambridge, MA: MIT Press.

Bentovim, A. and Kingston, W. (1991) 'Focal family therapy: Linking systems theory with psychodynamic understanding', in A. Gurman and D. Kniskern (eds) *The Handbook of Family Therapy, Volume II*, New York: Brunner-Mazel.

Berger, P.L. and Luckman, T. (1966) *The Social Construction of Reality: A Treatise in the Sociology of Knowledge*, New York: Doubleday/Anchor Books.

Bertrando, P. (2000) 'Text and context: Narrative, postmodernism and cybernetics', *Journal of Family Therapy* 22, 1: 83–103.

Best, S. and Kellner, D. (1991) *Postmodern Theory: Critical Interrogations*, Basingstoke: Macmillan.

Bion, W.R. (1967) *Second Thoughts: Selected Papers on Psycho-Analysis*, London: Maresfield Library, Karnac Books.

—— (1970) *Attention and Interpretation*, London: Tavistock Publications.

—— (1988) 'Notes on memory and desire', in E.B. Spillius (ed.) *Melanie Klein Today – Volume 2: Mainly Practice*, London: Routledge.

Bollas, C. (1987) *The Shadow of the Object: Psychoanalysis of the Unthought Known*, New York: Columbia University Press.

Bor, R., Mallandain, I. and Vetere, A. (1998) 'What we say we do: Results of the 1997 UK Association of Family Therapy Members Survey', *Journal of Family Therapy* 20, 4: 333–51.

Borbeley, A.F. (1998) 'A psychoanalytic concept of metaphor', *International Journal of Psycho-Analysis* 79, 5: 923–36.

Bordo S. (1990) 'Feminism, postmodernism and gender-scepticism', in L.J. Nicholson (ed.) *Feminism/Postmodernism*, New York: Routledge.

Boscolo, L. and Bertrando, P. (1992) 'The reflexive use of past, present and future in systemic therapy and consultation', *Family Process* 31, 2: 119–30.

—— (1993) *The Times of Time: A New Perspective in Systemic Therapy and Consultation*, New York: W.W. Norton.

—— (1996) *Systemic Therapy for Individuals*, London: Karnac Books.

Boszormenyi-Nagy, I. and Krasner, B.R. (1986) *Between Give and Take: A Clinical Guide to Contextual Therapy*, New York: Brunner-Mazel.

Boszormenyi-Nagy, I. and Spark G.M. (1973) *Invisible Loyalties: Reciprocity in Intergenerational Family Therapy*, Hagerstown, MD: Harper & Row.

Bouchard, M.-A. (1995) 'The specificity of hermeneutics in psychoanalysis: Leaps on the path from construction to recollection', *International Journal of Psycho-Analysis* 76, 3: 533–46.

Bowen, M. (1978) *Family Therapy in Clinical Practice*, New York: Jason Aronson.

Bowker, G. and Sankey, H. (1993/4) 'Truth and reality in social constructivism', *Arena Journal* No. 2, 1993/94: 233–52.

Box, S., Copley, B., Magagna, J. and Moustaki, E. (eds) (1981) *Psychotherapy with Families: An Analytic Approach*, London: Routledge & Kegan Paul.

—— (eds) (1994) *Crisis at Adolescence: Object Relations Therapy with the Family*, New York: Aronson.

Bretherton, I. (1992) 'The origins of attachment theory: John Bowlby and Mary Ainsworth', *Developmental Psychology* 28, 5: 759–75.

Breunlin, D.C. and Schwartz, R.C. (1986) 'Sequences: Toward a common denominator in family therapy', *Family Process* 25, 1: 67–87.

Breunlin, D.C., Schwartz, R.C. and MacKune-Karrer, B. (1992) *Metaframeworks: Transcending the Models of Family Therapy*, San Francisco: Jossey-Bass.

Britten, R. (1995) 'Psychic reality and unconscious belief', *International Journal of Psycho-Analysis* 76, 1: 19–23.

Brodie, F. and Wright, J. (2002) 'Minding the gap not bridging the gap: Family therapy from a psychoanalytic perspective', *Journal of Family Therapy*.

Brook, A. (1995) 'Explanation in the hermeneutic science', *International Journal of Psycho-Analysis* 76, 3: 519–32.

Brown, S.D. and Pujol, J. with Curt, B.C. (1998) 'As one in a web?

Discourse, materiality and the place of ethics', in I. Parker (ed.) *Social Constructionism, Discourse and Realism*, London: Sage.

Bruner, E.M. (1986) 'Ethnography as narrative', in V.W. Turner and E.M. Bruner (eds) *The Anthropology of Experience*, Urbana, IL: University of Illinois Press.

Burbatti, G.L., Castoldi, I. and Maggi, L. (1993) *Systemic Psychotherapy with Families, Couples and Individuals*, Northvale, NJ: Jason Aronson.

Butler, M.H. and Bird, M.H. (2000) 'Narrative and interactional process for preventing harmful struggle in therapy: An integrative empirical model', *Journal of Marital and Family Therapy* 26, 2: 123–42.

Byng-Hall, J. (1986) 'Family scripts: A concept which can bridge child psychotherapy and family therapy thinking', *Journal of Child Psychotherapy* 12, 2: 3–13.

—— (1988) 'Scripts and legends in families and family therapy', *Family Process* 27, 2: 167–79.

—— (1995a) 'Creating a secure family base: Some implications of attachment theory for family therapy', *Family Process* 34, 1: 45–58.

—— (1995b) *Re-writing Family Scripts: Improvisation and Systems Change*, New York: Guilford.

—— (1997) 'Toward a coherent story about illness and loss', in R.K. Papadopoulos and J. Byng-Hall (eds) *Multiple Voices: Narrative in Systemic Family Psychotherapy*, London: Duckworth.

—— (1999) 'The unfashionable Byng-Hall: A conversation on family therapy in the millennium – interview with Glenn Larner', *Australian and New Zealand Journal of Family Therapy* 20, 1: 34–9.

Cavell, M. (1991) 'The subject of mind', *International Journal of Psycho-Analysis* 72, 1: 141–54.

—— (1998) 'Triangulation, one's own mind and objectivity', *International Journal of Psycho-Analysis* 79, 3: 449–67.

Coleman, S. (ed.) (1985) *Failures in Family Therapy*, New York: Guilford Press.

Collier, A. (1998) 'Language, practice and realism', in I. Parker (ed.) *Social Constructionism, Discourse and Realism*, London: Sage.

Colthart, N. (1986) '"Slouching toward Bethlehem" . . . or thinking the unthinkable in psychoanalysis', in G. Kohon (ed.) *The British School of Psychoanalysis: The Independent Tradition*, London: Free Association Books.

Combs, G. and Freedman, J. (1998) 'Tellings and retellings', *Journal of Marital and Family Therapy* 24, 2: 405–40.

Crago, H. (1998) 'Editorial: The unconscious of the individual and the unconscious of the system', *Australian and New Zealand Journal of Family Therapy* 19, 2: iii–iv.

Dallos, R. and Draper, R. (2000) *An Introduction to Family Therapy: Systemic Theory and Practice*, Buckingham: Open University Press.

Dallos, R. and Urry, A. (1999) 'Abandoning our parents and grand-parents: Does social constructionism mean the end of systemic family therapy?', *Journal of Family Therapy* 21, 2: 161–86.

Daniel, G. (1998) 'Broadening the gap or narrowing the vision', *Journal of Family Therapy* 20, 2: 211–8.

Dare, C. (1979) 'Psychoanalysis and systems in family therapy', *Journal of Family Therapy*, 1, 1: 137–152.

—— (1997) 'Chronic eating disorders in therapy: Clinical stories using family systems and psychoanalytic approaches', *Journal of Family Therapy* 19, 3: 319–52.

Dell, P.F. (1985) 'Understanding Bateson and Maturana: Toward a biological foundation for the social sciences', *Journal of Marital and Family Therapy* 11, 1: 1–20.

Doan, R.E. (1998) 'The king is dead; long live the king: Narrative therapy and practicing what we preach', *Family Process* 37, 3: 379–85.

—— (2000) 'Some reflections for "The Virtual Symposium"', *Australian and New Zealand Journal of Family Therapy* 21, 3: 130–2.

Doherty, W.J. (1991) 'Family therapy goes postmodern', *Family Therapy Networker* 15, 5: 19–25.

Downey, L. (2001) 'Intimacy and the relational self', *Australian and New Zealand Journal of Family Therapy* 22, 3: 129–36.

Dunn, J. (1995) 'Intersubjectivity in psychoanalysis: A critical review', *International Journal of Psycho-Analysis* 76, 4: 723–38.

Eagleton, T. (1996) *The Illusions of Postmodernism*, Oxford: Blackwell.

Efran, J. and Lukens, M.D. (1985) 'The world according to Humberto Maturana: Epistemology and the magic kingdom', *Family Therapy Networker* 9, 3: 23–8, 72–5.

Elliott, A. (1995) 'Psychoanalysis and the seductions of postmodernity: Reflections on reflexive thinking and scanning in self-identity', *Psychoanalysis and Contemporary Thought* 18, 3: 319–61.

—— (1996) *Subject to Ourselves: Social Theory, Psychoanalysis and Postmodernity*, Cambridge: Polity Press.

Epston, D. and White, M. (1989) *Literate Means to Therapeutic Ends*, Adelaide: Dulwich Centre Publications.

—— (1992) *Experience, Contradiction, Narrative and Imagination: Selected Papers of David Epston and Michael White 1989–1991*, Adelaide: Dulwich Centre Publications.

Faimberg, H. (1995) 'Misunderstanding and psychic truths', *International Journal of Psycho-Analysis* 76, 1: 9–13.

Falicov, C. (1998) 'Commentary on Hoffman: From rigid borderlines to fertile borderlands: Reconfiguring family therapy', *Journal of Marital and Family Therapy* 24, 2: 157–63.

Falzon, C. (1998) *Foucault and Social Dialogue: Beyond Fragmentation*, London: Routledge.

Finlay, M. (1989) 'Post-modernising psychoanalysis/psychoanalysing post-modernity, *Free Associations* 16, 1: 43–80.

Fish, V. (1993) 'Poststructuralism in family therapy: Interrogating the narrative/conversational mode', *Journal of Marital and Family Therapy* 19, 3: 221–32.

Fishbane, M.K. (2001) 'Relational narratives of the self', *Family Process* 40, 3: 273–91.

Fitzpatrick Hanly, M. (1996) '"Narrative", now and then: A critical realist approach', *International Journal of Psycho-Analysis* 77, 3: 445–57.

Flaskas, C. (1989) 'Thinking about the emotional interaction of therapist and family', *Australian and New Zealand Journal of Family Therapy* 10, 1: 1–6.

—— (1992) 'A reframe by any other name: On the process of reframing in strategic, Milan and analytic therapy', *Journal of Family Therapy* 14, 2: 145–61.

—— (1993) 'On the project of using psychoanalytic ideas in systemic therapy: A discussion paper', *Australian and New Zealand Journal of Family Therapy* 14, 1: 9–15.

—— (1994) 'Exploring the therapeutic relationship: A case study', *Australian and New Zealand Journal of Family Therapy* 15, 4: 185–90.

—— (1995) 'Postmodernism, constructionism and the idea of reality', *Australian and New Zealand Journal of Family Therapy* 16, 3: 143–6.

—— (1996) 'Understanding the therapeutic relationship: Using psycho-analytic ideas in the systemic context', in C. Flaskas and A. Perlesz (eds) *The Therapeutic Relationship in Systemic Therapy*, London: Karnac Books.

—— (1997a) 'Engagement and the therapeutic relationship in systemic therapy', *Journal of Family Therapy* 19, 3: 263–82.

—— (1997b) 'Re-claiming the idea of truth: Some thoughts on theory in response to practice', *Journal of Family Therapy* 19, 1: 1–20.

—— (1999) 'Limits and possibilities of the postmodern narrative self', *Australian and New Zealand Journal of Family Therapy* 20, 1: 20–7.

—— (2000) 'Narrative and family therapy: On passion, pragmatism and politics', *Australian and New Zealand Journal of Family Therapy* 21, 2: 121–4.

Flaskas, C. and Cade, B. (1998) 'Of apes and infants: The cutting edge of psychoanalytic thought?', *Australian and New Zealand Journal of Family Therapy* 19, 2: 75–80.

Flaskas, C. and Humphreys, C. (1993) 'Theorising about power: Intersecting the ideas of Foucault with the "problem" of power in family therapy', *Family Process* 32, 1: 35–47.

Flaskas, C. and Perlesz, A. (1996) 'Introduction: The return of the therapeutic relationship in systemic therapy', in C. Flaskas and A.

Perlesz (eds) *The Therapeutic Relationship in Systemic Therapy*, London: Karnac Books.

Fonagy, P. (2001) *Attachment Theory and Psychoanalysis*, New York: Other Books.

Fonagy, P., Steele, H. and Steele, M. (1991a) 'Maternal representations of attachment during pregnancy predict the organization of infant-mother attachment at one year of age', *Child Development* 62, 5: 891–905.

Fonagy, P., Steele, M., Steele, H., Moran, G. and Higgitt, A. (1991b) 'The capacity for understanding mental states: The reflective self in parent and child and its significance for security of attachment', *Infant Mental Health Journal* 12, 3: 200–17.

Foucault, M. (1979) *Discipline and Punish*, New York: Vintage Books.

—— (1981) *The History of Sexuality: Volume 1*, Harmondsworth: Penguin.

Fraser, N. and Nicholson, L. (1993) 'Social criticism without philosophy: An encounter between feminism and postmodernism', in T. Docherty (ed.) *Postmodernism: A Reader*, Hemel Hempstead: Harvester Wheatsheaf.

Fraser, R. (1984) *In Search of a Past: The Manor House, Amnersfield 1933–1945*, London: Verso.

Freedman, J. and Combs, G. (1996) *Narrative Therapy: The Social Construction of Preferred Realities*, New York: Oxford University Press.

Freeman, M. (1993) *Rewriting the Self: History, Memory, Narrative*, London: Routledge.

Friedman, L. (1995) 'Psychic reality in psychoanalytic theory', *International Journal of Psycho-Analysis* 76, 1: 25–8.

Frosh, S. (1995) 'Postmodernism vs psychotherapy', *Journal of Family Therapy* 17, 2: 175–90.

—— (1997) 'Postmodern narratives: Or muddles in the mind', in R.K. Papadopoulos and J. Byng-Hall (eds) *Multiple Voices: Narrative in Systemic Family Psychotherapy*, London: Duckworth.

Gadamer, H.-G. (1975) *Truth and Method*, New York: Seabury Press.

Geertz, C. (1973) *The Interpretation of Cultures*, New York: Basic Books.

—— (1983) *Local Knowledge*, New York: Basic Books.

Gergen, K.J. (1991) *The Saturated Self: Dilemmas of Identity in Contemporary Life*, New York: Basic Books.

—— (1994) *Realities and Relationships: Soundings in Social Construction*, Cambridge, MA: Harvard University Press.

—— (1998) 'Commentary: The place of material in a constructed world', *Family Process* 37, 4: 415–19.

Gergen, K.J. and Kaye, J. (1992) 'Beyond narrative in the negotiation of therapeutic meaning', in S. McNamee and K.J. Gergen (eds) *Therapy as Social Construction*, London: Sage.

Gerson, M.-J. (1996) *The Embedded Self: A Psychoanalytic Guide to Family Therapy*, Hillsdale, NJ: Analytic Press.

Gibney, P. (1991) 'Articulating the implicate: An invitation to openness', *Australian and New Zealand Journal of Family Therapy* 12, 3: 133–6.

—— (1996) 'To embrace paradox (once more, with feeling): A commentary on narrative/conversational therapies and the therapeutic relationship', in C. Flaskas and A. Perlesz (eds) *The Therapeutic Relationship in Systemic Therapy*, London: Karnac Books.

—— (1999) 'Family therapy: Out from behind the hero narrative', *Australian and New Zealand Journal of Family Therapy* 20, 1: 28–33.

Gilligan, S. and Price, R. (eds) (1993) *Therapeutic Conversations*, New York: W.W. Norton.

Goldberg, A. (1994) 'Farewell to the objective analyst', *International Journal of Psycho-Analysis* 75, 1: 15–25.

Goldner, V. (1985) 'Feminism and family therapy', *Family Process* 24, 1: 31–7.

—— (1991) 'Toward a critical relational theory of gender', *Psychoanalytic Dialogues* 1, 3: 249–72.

—— (1992) 'Making room for both/and', *Family Therapy Networker* 16, 2: 55–61.

—— (1998) 'The treatment of violence and victimization in intimate relationships', *Family Process* 37, 3: 263–86.

Goldner, V., Penn, P., Sheinberg, M. and Walker, G. (1990) 'Love and violence: Gender paradoxes in volatile attachments', *Family Process* 29, 4: 343–64.

Gordon, C. (ed.) (1980) *Power/Knowledge: Selected Interviews and Other Writings 1972–1977 by Michel Foucault*, New York: Pantheon.

Gorrell Barnes, G. (1995) 'The intersubjective mind: Family pattern, family therapy and individual meaning', in M. Yelloly and M. Henkel (eds) *Learning and Teaching in Social Work: Towards Reflective Practice*, London: Jessica Kingsley.

Green, A. and Stern, D. (2000) *Clinical and Observational Psychoanalytic Research: Roots of a Controversy*, London: Karnac Books.

Grotstein, J. (1983) 'Wilfred R. Bion: The man, the psychoanalyst, the mystic. A perspective on his life and work', in J.S. Grotstein (ed.) *Do I Dare Disturb the Universe: A Memorial to W.R. Bion*, London: Maresfield Library, Karnac Books.

Grunebaum, H. (1988) 'What if family therapy were a kind of psychotherapy?', *Journal of Marital and Family Therapy* 14, 1: 195–9.

Habermas, J. (1981) 'Modernity vs postmodernity', *New German Critique* 22, 1: 3–14.

Hamilton, V. (1993) 'Truth and reality in psychoanalytic discourse', *International Journal of Psycho-Analysis*, 74, 1: 63–79.

Hanly, C. (1990) 'The concept of truth in psychoanalysis', *International Journal of Psycho-Analysis* 71, 2: 375–83.

Harari, E. (1995) 'The longest shadow: A critical commentary', *Australian and New Zealand Journal of Family Therapy* 16, 1: 11–13.

—— (1996) 'Empathy and the therapeutic relationship in systemic-oriented therapies: A historical and clinical overview', in C. Flaskas and A. Perlesz (eds) *The Therapeutic Relationship in Systemic Therapy*, London: Karnac Books.

Hardham, V. (1996) 'Embedded and embodied in the therapeutic relationship: Understanding the therapist's use of self systemically', in C. Flaskas and A. Perlesz (eds) *The Therapeutic Relationship in Systemic Therapy*, London: Karnac Books.

Hare-Mustin, R. (1986) 'The problem of gender in family therapy theory', *Family Process* 26, 1: 15–27.

Hart, B. (1995) 'Re-authoring the stories we work by', *Australian and New Zealand Journal of Family Therapy* 16, 4: 181–9.

—— (1996) 'The construction of the gendered self', *Journal of Family Therapy* 18, 1: 43–60.

Harvey, D. (1990) *The Condition of Postmodernity: An Enquiry into the Origins of Cultural Change*, Cambridge, MA: Blackwell.

Held, B. (1995) *Back to Reality: A Critique of Postmodern Theory in Psychotherapy*, New York: W.W. Norton.

Hildebrand, J. and Speed, B. (1995) 'The influence of therapists' personal experience on their work with couples', in J. Van Lawick and M. Sanders (eds) *Family, Gender and Beyond*, Heemstede: LS Books.

Hoffman, I.Z. (1991) 'Discussion: Toward a social-constructivist view of the psychoanalytic situation', *Psychoanalytic Dialogues* 11, 1: 74–105.

Hoffman, L. (1990) 'Constructing realities: An art of lenses', *Family Process* 29, 1: 1–12.

—— (1993) *Exchanging Voices: A Collaborative Approach to Family Therapy*, London: Karnac Books.

—— (1998) 'Setting aside the model in family therapy', *Journal of Marital and Family Therapy* 24, 2: 145–56.

Holmes, J. (1996) *Attachment, Intimacy and Autonomy: Using Attachment Theory in Adult Psychotherapy*, Northvale, NJ: Jason Aronson.

—— (1998) 'The changing aims of psychoanalytic psychotherapy: An integrative perspective', *International Journal of Psycho-Analysis* 79, 2: 227–41.

—— (2001) *The Search for a Secure Base: Attachment Theory and Psychotherapy*, Hove: Brunner-Routledge.

Hubble, M.A., Duncan, B.L. and Miller, S.D. (1999) *The Heart and Soul of Change: What Works in Therapy*, Washington: American Psychological Association.

Huyussen, A. (1986) *After the Great Divide: Modernism, Mass Culture, Postmodernism*, Bloomington: Indiana University Press.

Imber-Black, E. (1986) 'Maybe "lineal causality" needs another defence lawyer: A feminist response to Dell', *Family Process* 24, 4: 523–5.

—— (ed.) (1993) *Secrets in Families and Family Therapy*, New York: W.W. Norton.

Jameson, F. (1993) 'Postmodernism, or the cultural logic of late capitalism', in T. Docherty (ed.) *Postmodernism: A Reader*, Hemel Hempstead: Harvester Wheatsheaf.

Johnson, S.M., Makinen, J.A. and Millikin, J.W. (2001) 'Attachment injuries in couple relationships: A new perspective on impasses in couple therapy', *Journal of Marital and Family Therapy* 27, 2: 145–55.

Jones, E. (1993) *Family Systems Therapy: Developments in Milan-Systemic Therapies*, Chichester: Wiley.

Kaffman, M. (1987) 'Failures in family therapy: And then what?', *Journal of Family Therapy* 9, 4: 307–28.

Kahn, M. (1991) *Between Therapist and Client: The New Relationship*, New York: W.H. Freeman and Company.

Karen, R. (1994) *Becoming Attached: First Relationships and How They Shape Our Capacity to Love*, New York and Oxford: Oxford University Press.

Keeney, B.P. and Sprenkle, D.H. (1982) 'Ecosystemic epistemology: Critical implications for the aesthetics and pragmatics of family therapy', *Family Process* 21, 1: 1–19.

Kelly, G. (1983) *A Theory of Personality*, New York: W.W. Norton.

Kelly, M. (ed.) (1994) *Critique and Power: Recasting the Foucault/ Habermas Debate*, Cambridge, MA: MIT Press.

Kerby, A.P. (1991) *Narrative and the Self*, Bloomington, IN: Indiana University Press.

Klauber, J. (1986) *Difficulties in the Analytic Encounter*, London: Free Association Books.

Kogan, S.M. (1997) 'The politics of making meaning: Discourse analysis of a "postmodernist" interview', *Journal of Family Therapy* 20, 3: 229–51.

Kogan, S.M. and Gale, J.E. (1997) 'Decentering therapy: Textual analysis of a narrative therapy session', *Family Process* 36, 1: 101–26.

Kohon, G. (1986) 'Introduction', in G. Kohon (ed.) *The British School of Psychoanalysis: The Independent Tradition*, London: Free Association Books.

Kraemer, S. (1994) 'The promise of family therapy', *British Journal of Psychotherapy* 11, 1: 32–44.

—— (1997) 'What narrative?', in R.K. Papadopoulos and J. Byng-Hall (eds) *Multiple Voices: Narrative in Systemic Family Psychotherapy*, London: Duckworth.

Krause, I.-B. (1995) 'Personhood, culture and family therapy', *Journal of Family Therapy* 17, 4: 363–82.

Laird, J. (1998) 'Theorizing culture: Narrative ideas and practice principles', in M. McGoldrick (ed.) *Revisioning Family Therapy: Race, Culture and Gender in Clinical Practice*, New York: Guilford Press.

Lambert, M.J. (1992) 'Implications of outcome research for psychotherapy integration', in J.C. Norcross and M.R. Goldfried (eds) *Handbook for Psychotherapy Integration*, New York: Basic Books.

Lannamann, J.W. (1998a) 'Rejoinder: The place of the constructed in a materially responsive world', *Family Process* 37, 4: 421–3.

—— (1998b) 'Social constructionism and materiality: The limits of indeterminacy in therapeutic settings', *Family Process* 37, 4: 393–419.

Larner, G. (1994) 'Para-modern family therapy: Deconstructing postmodernism', *Australian and New Zealand Journal of Family Therapy* 15, 1: 11–16.

—— (1995) 'The real as illusion: Deconstructing power in family therapy', *Journal of Family Therapy* 17, 2: 198–217.

—— (1996) 'Narrative child family therapy', *Family Process* 35, 4: 423–40.

—— (2000) 'Toward a common ground in psychoanalysis and family therapy: On knowing not to know', *Journal of Family Therapy* 22, 1: 61–82.

Laub, D. (1992) 'Bearing witness or the vicissitudes of listening', in S. Felman and D. Laub (eds) *Testimony: Crises of Witnessing in Literature, Psychoanalysis, and History*, New York: Routledge.

Launer, J. (1996) '"You're the doctor, Doctor!": Is social constructionism a helpful stance in general practice consultations?', *Journal of Family Therapy* 18, 3: 255–67.

Leary, K.L. (1994) 'Psychoanalytic "problems" and postmodern "solutions"', *Psychoanalytic Quarterly* LXIII: 433–65.

Leary, K.R. (1989) 'Psychoanalytic process and narrative process: A critical consideration of Schafer's "narrational project"', *International Review of Psycho-Analysis* 16, 2: 179–90.

Levine, D.P. (1999) 'Identity, the group, and the social construction of reality', *Journal for the Psychoanalysis of Culture and Society* 4, 1: 81–91.

Lloyd Mayer, E. (1996) 'Subjectivity and intersubjectivity of clinical facts', *International Journal of Psycho-Analysis* 77, 4: 709–37.

Lock, M. (1993) 'Cultivating the body: Anthropology and epistemologies of bodily practice and knowledge', *Annual Review of Anthropology* 22: 133–55.

Lovibond, S. (1993) 'Feminism and postmodernism', in T. Docherty (ed.) *Postmodernism: A Reader*, Hemel Hempstead: Harvester Wheatsheaf.

Luepnitz, D.A. (1988) *The Family Interpreted: Feminist Theory in Clinical Practice*, New York: Basic Books.

—— (1992) 'Nothing in common but their first names: The case of Foucault and White', *Journal of Family Therapy* 14, 3: 281–4.

Luepnitz, D.A. (1997) 'Feminism, psychoanalysis and family therapy: Reflections on telos', *Journal of Family Therapy* 19, 3: 303–17.

MacKinnon, L.K. and Miller, D. (1987) 'The new epistemology and the Milan approach: Feminist and sociopolitical considerations', *Journal of Marital and Family Therapy* 13, 2: 139–55.

McFadyen, A. (1997) '*Rapprochement* in sight? Postmodern family therapy and psychoanalysis', *Journal of Family Therapy*, 19, 3: 241–62.

McLeod, J. (1997) *Narrative and Psychotherapy*, London: Sage.

McNamee, S. and Gergen, K.J. (eds) (1992) *Therapy as Social Construction*, London: Sage.

McNay, L. (1992) *Foucault and Feminism: Power, Gender and the Self*, Cambridge: Polity Press.

Madison, G.B. (1988) *The Hermeneutics of Postmodernity*, Bloomington, IN: Indiana University Press.

Madson, P. (1992) '"Postmodernism" and "late capitalism": On terms and realities', in J. Shotter and K.J. Gergen (eds) *Texts of Identity*, London: Sage.

Main, M. (1991) 'Metacognitive knowledge, metacognitive monitoring, and singular (coherent) vs. multiple (incoherent) model of attachment: Findings and directions for further research', in C.M. Parkes, J. Stevenson-Hinde and P. Marris (eds) *Attachment across the Life Cycle*, London: Routledge.

Maloney, B. and Maloney, L. (1996) 'Personal relationships in systemic supervision', in C. Flaskas and A. Perlesz (eds) *The Therapeutic Relationship in Systemic Therapy*, London: Karnac Books.

Markova, I. (1987) 'Knowledge of the self through interaction', in K. Yardley and T. Honess (eds) *Self and Identity: Psychosocial Perspectives*, Chichester: Wiley.

Mason, B. (1993) 'Toward positions of safe uncertainty', *Human Systems* 4: 189–200.

Minuchin, S. (1991) 'The seductions of constructivism', *Family Therapy Networker* 15, 5: 47–51.

—— (1998) 'Where is the family in narrative family therapy?', *Journal of Marital and Family Therapy* 24, 4: 397–403.

—— (1999) 'Retelling, reimagining and re-searching: A continuing conversation', *Journal of Marital and Family Therapy* 25, 1: 9–14.

Mitchell, S.A. (1988) *Relational Concepts in Psychoanalysis: An Integration*, Cambridge, MA and London: Harvard University Press.

Montero, M. (1998) 'The perverse and the pervasive character of reality: Some comments on the effects of monism and dualism', in I. Parker (ed.) *Social Constructionism, Discourse and Realism*, London: Sage.

Morawetz, A. (1987) 'Speaking personally', *Australian and New Zealand Journal of Family Therapy* 9, 1: 71–8.

Morris, H. (1993) 'Narrative representation, narrative enactment, and the psychoanalytic construction of history', *International Journal of Psychoanalysis* 74, 1: 33–54.

Natterson, J. (1991) *Beyond Countertransference: The Therapist's Subjectivity in the Therapeutic Process*, Northvale, NJ: Jason Aronson.

Nichols, M.P. (1987) *The Self in the System: Expanding the Limits of Family Therapy*, New York: Brunner-Mazel.

Nicholson, L. (1992) 'On the postmodern barricades: Feminism, politics and theory', in S. Seidman and D.G. Wagner (eds) *Postmodernism and Social Theory: The Debate over General Theory*, Cambridge, MA: Blackwell.

Nicholson, S. (1995) 'The narrative dance: A practice map for White's therapy', *Australian and New Zealand Journal of Family Therapy* 16, 1: 23–8.

Norris, C. (1990) *What's Wrong with Postmodernism: Critical Theory and the Ends of Philosophy*, Hemel Hempstead: Harvester Wheatsheaf.

Ogden, T.H. (1982) *Projective Identification and Psychotherapeutic Technique*, Northvale, NJ: Jason Aronson.

—— (1994) 'The analytic third: Working with intersubjective clinical facts', *International Journal of Psycho-Analysis* 75, 1: 3–19.

O'Hara, M. and Anderson, W.T. (1991) 'Welcome to the postmodern world', *Family Therapy Networker* 15, 5: 19–25.

Orange, D.M. (1995) *Emotional Understanding: Studies in Psychoanalytic Epistemology*, New York: Guilford Press.

Orr, D.W. (1988) 'Transference and countertransference: A historical survey', in B. Wolstein (ed.) *Essential Papers on Countertransference*, New York: New York University Press.

Papadopoulos, R.K. and Byng-Hall, J. (eds) (1997) *Multiple Voices: Narrative in Systemic Family Psychotherapy*, London: Duckworth.

Parry, A. (1991) 'A universe of stories', *Family Process* 30, 1: 37–54.

Parry, A. and Doan, R.E. (1994) *Story Re-Visions: Narrative Therapy in the Postmodern World*, New York: Guilford Press.

Paterson, T. (1996) 'Leaving well alone: A systemic perspective on the therapeutic relationship', in C. Flaskas and A. Perlesz (eds) *The Therapeutic Relationship in Systemic Therapy*, London: Karnac Books.

Pedder, J.R. (1986) 'Attachment and new beginning: Some links between the work of Michael Balint and John Bowlby', in G. Kohon (ed) *The British School of Psychoanalysis: The Independent Tradition*, London: Free Association Books.

Penn, P. (1985) 'Feed-forward: Future questions, future maps', *Family Process* 24, 3: 299–310.

Perelberg, R.J. and Miller, A.C. (eds) (1990) *Gender and Power in Families*, London: Routledge.

Perlesz, A. (1999) 'Complex responses to trauma: Challenges in bearing witness', *Australian and New Zealand Journal of Family Therapy* 20, 1: 11–19.

Perlesz, A., Furlong, M. and the 'D' family (1996) 'A systemic therapy unravelled: In through the out door', in C. Flaskas and A. Perlesz (eds) *The Therapeutic Relationship in Systemic Therapy*, London: Karnac Books.

Perry, R. (1993) 'Empathy – still at the heart of therapy: The interplay of context and empathy, *Australian and New Zealand Journal of Family Therapy* 14, 2: 63–74.

Pilgrim, D. (2000) 'The real problem for postmodernism', *Journal of Family Therapy* 22, 1: 6–23.

Pinsof, W.M. (1994) 'An overview of integrative problem centred therapy: A synthesis of family and individual psychotherapies', *Journal of Family Therapy* 16, 1: 103–20.

Pocock, D. (1995) 'Searching for a better story: Harnessing modern and postmodern positions in family therapy', *Journal of Family Therapy* 17, 2: 149–74.

—— (1997) 'Feeling understood in family therapy', *Journal of Family Therapy* 19, 3: 283–302.

Puget, J. (1995) 'Psychic reality or various realities', *International Journal of Psycho-Analysis* 76, 1: 29–34.

Quadrio, C. (1986a) 'Analysis and system: A marriage', *Australian and New Zealand Journal of Psychiatry* 18, 3: 184–70.

—— (1986b) 'Individuation as a life process – The interface of intrapsychic and systems theories', *Australian and New Zealand Journal of Family Therapy* 7, 4: 189–93.

Redekop, F. (1995) 'The "problem' of Michael White and Michel Foucault', *Journal of Marital and Family Therapy* 21, 3: 309–18.

Reimers, S. (2001) 'Understanding alliances. How can research inform user-friendly practice?', *Journal of Family Therapy* 23, 1: 46–62.

Renik, O. (1993) 'Analytic interpretation: Conceptualizing technique in light of the analyst's irreducible subjectivity', *Psychoanalytic Quarterly* LXII: 553–71.

Ricoeur, P. (1981) 'Narrative time', in W.J.T. Mitchell (ed.) *On Narrative*, Chicago: The University of Chicago Press.

—— (1984) *Time and Narrative, Vol. 1*, London: University of Chicago Press.

Riesenberg Malcolm, R. (1986) 'Interpretation: The past in the present', *International Review of Psycho-Analysis* 13, 3: 433–43.

Rober, P. (1999) 'The therapist's inner conversation in family therapy practice: Some ideas about the self of the therapist, therapeutic impasse and the process of reflection', *Family Process* 38, 2: 209–28.

Rorty, R. (1980) *Philosophy and the Mirror of Nature*, Princeton: Princeton University Press.

Rosenau, P.M. (1992) *Post-Modernism and the Social Sciences: Insights, Inroads and Intrusions*, Princeton: Princeton University Press.

Rosenbaum, R. and Dyckman, J. (1995) 'Integrating self and system: An empty intersection?', *Family Process* 34, 1: 21–44.

Rosenblatt, P.C. (1994) *Metaphors of Family Systems Theory: Toward New Constructions*, New York and London: Guilford Press.

Rucker, N.G. and Lombardi, K.L. (1998) *Subject Relations: Unconscious Experience and Relational Psychoanalysis*, New York: Routledge.

Rutter, M. (1996) 'Resilience concepts and findings: Implications for family therapy', *Journal of Family Therapy* 21, 2: 119–44.

Sandler, J. (1989) 'The concept of projective identification', in J. Sandler (ed.) *Projection, Identification, Projective Identification*, London: Karnac Books.

Sarbin, T.R. (1986) 'The narrative as a root metaphor for psychology', in T.R. Sarbin (ed.) *Narrative Psychology: The Storied Nature of Human Conduct*, New York: Praeger.

Sass, L.A. (1992) 'The epic of disbelief: The postmodernist turn in contemporary psychoanalysis', in S. Kvale (ed.) *Psychology and Postmodernism*, London: Sage.

Schafer, R. (1983) *The Analytic Attitude*, London: Hogarth Press.

—— (1992) *Retelling a Life: Narration and Dialogue in Psychoanalysis*, New York: Basic Books.

—— (1997) *Tradition and Change in Psychoanalysis*, London: Karnac Books.

Scharff, D.E. and Scharff, J.S. (1991) *Object Relations Family Therapy*, Northvale, NJ: Jason Aronson.

Scharff, J.S. (1989) *Foundations of Object Relations Family Therapy*, Northvale, NJ: Jason Aronson.

Schwaber, E.A. (1996) 'Toward a definition of the term and concept of interaction: Its reflection in analytic listening', *Psychoanalytic Enquiry* 16, 1: 5–24.

Shawver, L. (2001) 'If Wittgenstein and Lyotard could talk with Jack and Jill: Towards postmodern family therapy', *Journal of Family Therapy* 23, 3: 231–52.

Shotter, J. (1993) *Constructing Life Through Language*, London: Sage.

Shotter, J. and Gergen, K.J. (eds) (1989) *Texts of Identity*, London: Sage.

Simon, R. (1985) 'A frog's eye view of the world', *The Family Therapy Networker* 9, 3: 32–5.

Skynner, R. (1976) *One Flesh, Separate Persons: Principles of Marital and Family Psychotherapy*, London: Constable.

—— (1987) *Explorations with Families: Group Analysis and Family Therapy*, edited by J.R. Schlapobersky, London and New York: Tavistock/Routledge.

Slipp, S. (1984) *Object Relations: A Dynamic Bridge between Individual and Family Treatment*, Northvale, NJ: Jason Aronson.

Slipp, S. (1988) *The Technique and Practice of Object Relations Family Therapy*, Northvale, NJ: Jason Aronson.

Sluzki, C.E. (1992) 'Transformations: A blueprint for narrative changes in therapy', *Family Process* 31, 2: 217–30.

—— (1998) 'In search of the lost family: A footnote to Minuchin's essay', *Journal of Marital and Family Therapy* 24, 4: 415–7.

Smith, J., Osman, C. and Goding, M. (1990) 'Reclaiming the emotional aspects of the therapist-family system', *Australian and New Zealand Journal of Family Therapy* 11, 3: 140–6.

Soldz, S. (1996) 'Psychoanalysis and constructivism', in H. Rosen and K.T. Kuehlwein (eds) *Constructing Realities: Meaning-Making Perspectives for Psychotherapists*, San Francisco: Jossey-Bass.

Speed, B. (1991) 'Reality exists O.K.? An argument against constructivism and social constructionism', *Journal of Family Therapy* 13, 4: 395–405.

Spellman, D. and Harper, D.J. (1996) 'Failure, mistakes, regret and other subjugated stories in family therapy', *Journal of Family Therapy* 18, 2: 205–14.

Spence, D.P. (1982) *Narrative Truth and Historical Truth: Meaning and Interpretation in Psychoanalysis*, New York: W.W. Norton.

—— (1987) *The Freudian Metaphor: Toward Paradigm Change in Psychoanalysis*, New York: W.W. Norton.

Spillius, E. (1988) 'Introduction to Part Three: On Thinking', in E.B. Spillius (ed.) *Melanie Klein Today – Volume 1: Mainly Theory*, London: Routledge.

Stagoll, B. (2000) 'Interactions not factions', *Australian and New Zealand Journal of Family Therapy* 21, 3: 124–6.

Stern, D.N. (1988) 'The dialectic between the interpersonal and the intrapsychic: With particular emphasis on the role of memory and representation', *Psychoanalytic Inquiry* 8: 505–12.

—— (1998) *The Motherhood Constellation: A Unified View of Parent-Infant Psychotherapy*, London: Karnac Books.

Stiefel, I., Harris, P. and Rohan, J.A. (1998) 'Object Relations Family Therapy: Articulating the Inchoate', *Australian and New Zealand Journal of Family Therapy* 19, 2: 55–62.

Stolorow, R.D., Atwood, G.E. and Brandchaft, B. (eds) (1994) *The Intersubjective Perspective*, Northvale, NJ: Jason Aronson.

Symington, J. and Symington, N. (1996) *The Clinical Thinking of Wilfred Bion*, London and New York: Routledge.

Symington, N. (1986) 'The analyst's act of freedom as agent of therapeutic change', in G. Kohon (ed.) *The British School of Psychoanalysis: The Independent Tradition*, London: Free Association Books.

Szajnberg, N.M. (1992) 'Psychoanalysis as an extension of the autobiographical genre: Poetry and truth, fiction and reality', *International Review of Psycho-Analysis* 19, 3: 375–87.

Szur, R. and Miller, S. (eds) (1991) *Extending Horizons: Psychoanalytic Psychotherapy with Children, Adolescents and Families*, London: Karnac Books.

Taggart, M. (1985) 'The feminist critique in epistemological perspective: Questions of context in family therapy', *Journal of Marital and Family Therapy* 11, 1: 113–26.

Tansey, M.J. and Burke, W.F. (1989) *Understanding Countertransference: From Projective Identification to Empathy*, Hillsdale, NJ: The Analytic Press.

Tester, K. (1993) *The Life and Times of Post-Modernity*, London: Routledge.

Tomm, K. (1988) 'Interventive interviewing: Part III. Intending to ask lineal, circular, strategic, or reflexive questions?' *Family Process* 27, 1: 1–15.

—— (1993) 'The courage to protest: A commentary on Michael White's work', in S. Gilligan and R. Price (eds) *Therapeutic Conversations*, New York: W.W. Norton.

—— (1998) 'A question of perspective', *Journal of Marital and Family Therapy* 24, 2: 409–13.

Trowell, J. and Bower, M. (eds) (1995) *The Emotional Needs of Young Children and their Families: Using Psychoanalytic Ideas in the Community*, London and New York: Routledge.

Walker, G. and Goldner, V. (1995) 'The wounded prince and the women who love him', in C. Burck and B. Speed (eds) *Gender, Power and Relationships*, London: Routledge.

Walsh, F. (1996) 'The concept of family resilience: Crisis and challenge', *Family Process* 35, 3: 261–81.

—— (ed.) (1999) *Spiritual Resources in Family Therapy*, New York: Guilford.

Watzlawick, P. (1996) 'The construction of clinical realities', in H. Rosen and K.T. Kuehlwein (eds) *Constructing Realities: Meaning-Making Perspectives for Psychotherapists*, San Francisco: Jossey-Bass.

Weingarten, K. (1995) 'Radical listening: Challenging cultural beliefs for and about mothers', *Journal of Feminist Family Therapy* 7, 1–2: 7–22.

—— (1998) 'The small and the ordinary: The daily practice of postmodern narrative therapy', *Family Process* 37, 1: 3–15.

—— (2000) 'Witnessing, wonder and hope', *Family Process* 39, 4: 389–402.

White, M. (1984) 'Pseudo-encopresis: From avalanche to victory, from vicious to virtuous cycles', *Family Systems Medicine* 2, 2: 150–60.

—— (1989) 'The process of questioning: A therapy of literary merit?', in M. White (ed.) *Selected Papers*, Adelaide: Dulwich Centre Publications.

—— (1991) 'Deconstruction and therapy', *Dulwich Centre Newsletter* 3: 21–40.

—— (1993) 'Commentary: Systems of understanding, practices of relationship, and practices of self', in S. Gilligan and R. Price (eds) *Therapeutic Conversations*, New York: W.W. Norton.

White, M. (1995) *Re-Authoring Lives: Interviews and Essays*, Adelaide: Dulwich Centre Publications.

—— (1997) *Narratives of Therapists' Lives*, Adelaide: Dulwich Centre Publications.

White, M. and Epston, D. (1989) *Literate Means to Therapeutic Ends*, Adelaide: Dulwich Centre Publications.

—— (1990) *Narrative Means to Therapeutic Ends*, New York: W.W. Norton.

Wilkinson, M. (1992) 'How do we understand empathy systemically?' *Journal of Family Therapy* 14, 2: 193–206.

Winnicott, D.W. (1971) *Playing and Reality*, London and New York: Routledge.

—— (1986) *Holding and Interpretation: Fragment of an Analysis*, London: Karnac Books and the Institute of Psycho-Analysis.

Wollheim, R. (ed.) (1974) *Freud: A Collection of Critical Essays*, New York: Anchor.

Wollheim, R. and Hopkins J. (eds) (1982) *Philosophical Essays on Freud*, Cambridge: Cambridge University Press.

Wyatt, F. (1986) 'The narrative in psychoanalysis: Psychoanalytic notes on storytelling, listening, and interpreting', in T.R. Sabin (ed.) *Narrative Psychology: The Storied Nature of Human Conduct*, New York: Praeger.

Yeatman, A. (1994) *Postmodern Revisionings of the Political*, Routledge: New York.

Young, R.M. (1989) 'Post-modernism and the subject: Pessimism of the will', *Free Associations* 16: 81–96.

Zimmerman, J.L. and Dickerson, V. (1994) 'Using a narrative metaphor: Implications for theory and clinical practice', *Family Process* 33, 3: 233–45.

Index

abuse 52, 58, 65–6; bearing witness to 59–60, 61; disconnecting effects of 62; emotional 136–7, 148–50; physical 146; sexual 70–1, 81–2, 117–18, 131, 146, *see also* violent relationships

Ackerman Institute, New York 59–60

Adams, Neil 98

Ainsworth, Mary 119–20

Akister, Jane 120

alienation 62

analyst: countertransference 139–40, 147–8, 149–50, 151, 152; projective identification 142, 147, 151, 152; relationality 138; space for thought 164; suspension of memory and desire 164; transference 139, 140, 151, 152; use of self 176, *see also* practice experience; practice reflections; therapist

Anderson, Harlene 32, 33, 35–6, 37–8, 39, 42–3, 45, 46, 49, 62, 84, 86, 87–8, 95, 111, 153–4, 161–2

Anderson, Tom 45, 161

anti-foundationalism 21–2, 24, 29

anti-realism 62, 64–5, 105–7

attachment 13, 96, 115, 117–24, 128–34, 164, 175–6, 178, 180; adults 120; babies/children 119–20; and experience 181; insecure 120; and language 128–30, 131, 132, 133–4, 181;

limits in family therapy 122–3; narratives of 123–4, 127; patterns of 120; practice reflections 117–19, 131–3; as relational process 119–24, 175; transformative possibilities 123; unconscious 127, 128–30

Australia 4, 5, 17, 45, 48, 112

Australian and New Zealand Journal of Family Therapy 97

Balint, Michael 122

Barratt, Barnaby 21

Bateson, Gregory 31–2, 33, 75, 76

'bearing witness' 58–61, 68

behavioural therapies 74

being-in-relationship-with 159

Berg, Insoo 32

Berger, Peter 33

Bertrando, Paolo 143

Best, Steven 18, 19–20

biology, as core metaphor of family therapy 1, 2, 3, 33–4

Bion, Wilfred 13, 115, 122, 126, 154, 161, 163–4, 165, 167, 173, 176, 177, 181

body: finiteness 61, 98; relationality/materiality 56, 94–5

Bollas, Christopher 97, 129

Boscolo, Luigi 32, 143

Boszormenyi-Nagy, Ivan 5, 114

Bowen, Murray 5, 114